DEDICATION

This book is dedicated with deep gratitude to Joy and Molly Jacob,
in whose comfortable home the bulk of this book was written.
But then, they have always given me whatever they have.

First published in Great Britain and the United States in 2003 by Kogan Page Limited

120 Pentonville Road
London N1 9JN
UK
www.kogan-page.co.uk

22883 Quicksilver Drive
Sterling VA 20166-2012
USA

ISBN 0 7494 3582 8

British Library Cataloguing-in-Publication Data

A CIP record for this book is available from the British Library.

Library of Congress Cataloging-in-Publication Data
Jacob, Nina, 1956–
    Intercultural management / Nina Jacob.
        p. cm. – (MBA masterclass series)
Includes bibliographical references and index.
    ISBN 0–7494–3582–8
    1. Management–Social aspects. 2. Intercultural communication. I.
Title. II. Series.
HD31 .J234 2003
658–dc21
                                        2002154765

Typeset by JS Typesetting Ltd, Wellingborough, Northants
Printed and bound in Great Britain by Biddles Limited, Guildford and King's Lynn
www.biddles.co.uk

Contents

Acknowledgements

Special thanks are owed to Dr Emil Kern, founder, owner and CEO of the KS Group, Basle–Zurich–St Gallen, Switzerland, for having arranged access to the companies profiled in this book in the form of opening case studies. The author collected the material for these case studies during the period that she was Visiting Professor with the KS Group. She is extremely grateful to Dr Kern for being instrumental in getting access to global corporations.

Introduction

INTRODUCTION AND OVERVIEW

Intercultural management is an emerging but increasingly vital area of investigation. It is of particular interest to global managers who work for multinational corporations that are located in different countries. It also has something to offer managers who work for diversified enterprises with plants and branches in different locations that are not necessarily in different countries. Essentially, intercultural management concerns itself with the management of workforces functioning in culturally different operating contexts. The cultural differences can be particularly stark when comparison is done across countries. It can be just as much in evidence in companies that have different branches, each branch being imbued with a distinctive cultural heritage.

INTERCULTURAL MANAGEMENT DEFINED

What is being emphasized here is that intercultural management is concerned with the effective functioning of diverse groups of people. Diversity can arise because of variations in ethnicity and nationality. Most of the existing literature deals with getting managers from different countries to work together in cohesive teams.

Ethnicity is not the only source of diversity requiring intercultural management skills. Diversity can also arise because of variations in corporate culture. An organization could have different branches/plants located in the same region of a country, employing personnel with comparable qualifications/competencies, and yet evolving with different cultures.

Diversity can arise because of gender differences. A traditionally male bastion throwing its doors open to women for the first time would need recourse to intercultural management. Similarly, an organization that suddenly increases its intake of personnel at the entry level may find itself dealing with diversity caused by generational differences.

In practice, several of these diverse elements may exist simultaneously in global organizations. In such organizations, intercultural management is a way of life. Much will depend on such organizations' capability to be flexible enough to accommodate diversity. At the same time, these organizations need integrative mechanisms to hold them together. Thus intercultural management is about the management of paradoxes, of ambivalences and ambiguities. It is also about accommodating a range of structural and behavioural dimensions that address different facets of organizational functioning. Intercultural management is expensive, but also yields a high return on investment. Hence it can even be recommended that global organizations retain specialists in the field of intercultural management. Problems that arise on account of intercultural management can then be anticipated and addressed. Otherwise, forces counterproductive to intercultural management can gain ground and become institutionalized.

Intercultural management may be viewed as a subset of international management. It might therefore be relevant to enumerate here those features of international management that are effective. Researchers in the field of intercultural management advocate these features as well. These features are:

▮ fluid structural forms such as organic modes;

▮ teams constituted of internationally representative managers;

▮ leadership encompassing versatile skills appropriate for the global context;

▮ motivation appropriate for diversity;

▮ organizational cultures such as those characterizing learning organizations;

▮ communication methods and systems;

▮ negotiation for the mutual benefit of all the players;

▮ human resource management systems and practices that reflect the dynamics of operating in a global context. These range from managing expatriates, to liaison with foreign consulates, to procuring visas and work permits.

HISTORICAL DEVELOPMENT

Intercultural management is of such recent origins that it assumed an identity of its own, so to speak, only in the middle 1980s. Geert Hofstede's seminal book *Culture's Consequences* (1980) highlighted the fact that multinational corporations had to adopt management styles that were appropriate to the culture of the country they were working in. Thanks to Hofstede, managers of the multinational IBM realized that if they were working in Mexico they would have to adopt a relatively more authoritarian management style, while by contrast, if they were working in Sweden, a more democratic management style would be appropriate. Countries were differentiated by their culture. Hofstede differentiated national culture using four dimensions. He then used these four dimensions to construct a typology for categorizing countries.

Some contemporaries of Hofstede have also categorized countries into matrices defined by different cultural dimensions. They, like Hofstede, emphasized the need for global managers to assess in advance the cultural features of the countries they were to work in. This prior assessment is an important aspect of intercultural management today. In the 1990s, however, the work of Hofstede and others of his genre was criticized for defining national cultures in gross terms. The typologies they had developed were viewed as generalizations. Exceptions to their generalizations were believed to exceed the cases that actually fitted the bill. Additionally, their work encouraged cultural stereotyping and caricaturing.

JC Cheong *et al*'s book *Cultural Competencies: Managing co-operatively across cultures* is one such work that has pointed out the limitations of the intercultural management gurus of the 1980s. It averred that their perspectives were narrow and lacking in comprehensiveness. A range of cultural variations could be discerned within a country. This range for any country comprised a very large number of elements. Some elements could be common for many countries. It is not that the cultural elements of every country are unique.

These common cultural elements form the backdrop against which the global manager has been socialized and conditioned. This commonality of orientation can be discerned, for instance, in the type of motivation that drives the global manager. The global manager's motivation is defined by a high need for achievement. His or her driving force is the desire to show performance. This homogeneity in the character of the global manager has given rise to the global convergence perspective on intercultural management.

According to this perspective, global managers are likely to be similar in motivation, competencies, and exposure. Hence, the way they behave may not vary significantly in many countries. Thus while a worker in Mexico could be different in many ways from a worker in Sweden, a manager in Mexico could be similar in orientation and interests to a manager in Sweden. In fact, the manager for the Unilever group in Mexico might be Swedish, and his counterpart in Sweden could well be Mexican. And managers in both countries may watch CNN and BBC on their Sony television sets, while unwinding with their Heineken beer.

Cray *et al*'s book *Making Sense of Managing Culture* (1998) also contributed to demolishing the utility of the approach adopted by the intercultural management gurus of the 1980s. These authors are sceptical of the extent to which generalizations about national cultures can be extended to predict corporate management behaviour. Additionally, intercultural management gurus of the 1980s designed their research efforts with the expectation of finding cultural differences across countries. Thus, according to Cray *et al*, cultural differences were generated by the research designs used by them. Cray *et al*'s work, important as it is in itself, also paved the way towards the global convergence perspective.

Existing parallel to the global convergence perspective which gained considerable ground during the 1990s is the international diversity perspective. According to this viewpoint, even if managers across the world have similar tastes as consumers, they are still products of different countries, and therefore products of diverse cultural contexts. However similar managers from different nationalities may be, they still have to manage workers who have imbibed the cultural ethos of their countries. According to the international diversity perspective, people take pride in their indigenous cultures, and therefore a culturally borderless world is an unlikely prospect. On the contrary, the sensible approach would be to celebrate diversity. This perspective emphasizes the importance of adaptation to local cultures. It also allows for the incorporation of those features of local cultures that promote efficiency, and are deserving of corporation-wide diffusion.

Both the global convergence perspective and the international diversity perspective can be combined in certain ways. As a combined approach, they suggest that currently, a dialectic exists between divergence and convergence. It is this dialectic that drives intercultural management today. Similarity of social habits, tastes and exposure may be making managers across nations homogeneous, but there are still differences emanating from culture that have to be worked through. To achieve this, special efforts at integration have to be made. Quite a bit of intercultural management today revolves around constructing mechanisms for integration.

This has signalled the need for designing organizations that facilitate intercultural management. Bartlett and Ghoshal's book *Transnational Management* (1999) is one attempt to describe the transnational organization. This longitudinal study chronicles the various strategies adopted by mega organizations operating in a world characterized by varying cultures. Although the focus is on corporate strategy, Bartlett and Ghoshal have discussed substantially such features as integrated networking structure and adaptive coordination mechanisms.

Bartlett and Ghoshal have used the opportunity provided to them by their empirical study to examine management orientations as well. Intercultural management is thus increasingly acquiring a holistic flavour. Strategy, structure and management philosophy have to complement each other before intercultural management can make sense.

The Bartlett/Ghoshal perspective in a sense reflects a change in thinking on intercultural management. The transnational corporation comprises management teams representing diverse perspectives. These management teams appreciate the interdependent nature of managerial capabilities, even if the individuals concerned belong to different nationalities. The diversity has only to be integrated through structural mechanisms. The concept of organizational differentiation followed by integration, first propounded by Lawrence and Lorsch (1967), is a well entrenched notion and operates in large complex organizations everywhere. The Bartlett/ Ghoshal perspective takes this notion further by viewing the challenge of integrating diversity within the context of intercultural management.

Ultimately, successful organizations are fashioned by successful individuals who are professionally competent, able and gifted. The challenge ahead now, as in the past, is to nurture cultures within organizations that promote corporate excellence. Intercultural management today concerns itself with ensuring that mangers are socialized into the appropriate values of the organization. These managers also have to develop an understanding of their consumers and their workforce. This entails understanding the cultural context of, first, the markets they function in, and second, the locations where they have plants and divisions. In essence, the understanding has to be of relevant human behaviour both within organizations and extraorganizationally.

There is an increasing preoccupation today with the leadership and management styles appropriate for intercultural management. Another important issue concerns the repertoire of abilities needed by global managers to feel comfortable in culturally diverse teams. Cultural orientations are learnt behaviours. Therefore, managers can develop the flexibility and openness necessary to transit from one cultural context to another. This is part of the challenge of working for professionally managed and high performance companies.

INTERCULTURAL MANAGEMENT ACTIVITIES

Organizations of some note and repute today need to engage in a fair amount of intercultural management. Only small companies with a single branch or division, making a single or a few products with the same technology, and from the same raw materials, can ignore the aspect of intercultural management altogether. The many decorative-paper making companies of the St Gallen area in Switzerland are of this type. These companies typically employ 20 people or less, and cater exclusively to a local market. These companies need concern themselves with only their internal working culture.

Intercultural management delves quite extensively into the domain of organizational behaviour. Some of the dimensions of intercultural management that have organizational behaviour overtones are enumerated and briefly described below.

Team management

How teams are constituted, and how they can be made to function smoothly, are important aspects of team management. Multicultural teams have members who bring different competencies into organizational decision-making exercises. However, they have to communicate while engaged in decision-making exercises in ways that are acceptable to team members. In any team effort, there are likely to be lacunae in interpersonal skills that could act as a barrier to optimal and synergistic team functioning. One member might put views forth in an aggressive fashion that the others find upsetting. Another might be too passive and unable to influence the group sufficiently. Both members have to learn to be assertive but in wholly different ways. In an intercultural setting, this problem may be compounded because the aggressive individual hails from a context where aggressive behaviour is tolerated. The passive person might originate from a culture where soft-spokenness is valued. Both members thus have to rid themselves of cultural deterrents while learning more team-oriented skills.

Leadership

The Transformational Leader (Tichy and Devanna, 1997) would be appropriate for intercultural managers. A transformational leader motivates personnel to fully realize their potential. He or she enables ordinary individuals to do extraordinary things. However, to be successful in an intercultural sense, a transformational leader must be a team player as well, and be prepared to be influenced by, and learn from, other organizational members.

Corporate strategy

In the context of intercultural management, corporate strategy becomes of the essence in decisions pertaining to entry into new geographical terrain, followed by penetration and consolidation in the markets there. Strategies can also vary depending on the cultural mindset that has formulated them. Some mindsets are more adept at implementing strategies keeping in mind local preferences. The Swiss company Nestlé is particularly dextrous in this regard.

Organizational structure

Peter Senge *et al* (1999) have described a type of organization called the learning organization. The learning organization is well suited in many ways for an intercultural workforce. It has enormous flexibility in its arrangements, which enables it to be global when necessary, and local at other times. It has a network structure superimposed on its learning organization framework. A network structure enables an organization to pursue a global strategy for some products, while simultaneously pursuing local, customized strategies for other products.

Human resource management

Legislation regarding how employees should be treated, and what their rights are, differs depending on a country's cultural bias regarding these matters. Additionally, such traditional human resource management issues as recruitment, selection, training and compensation assume new dimensions in the context of intercultural management. Where recruitment is concerned, for example, companies may like specifically to select individuals with international exposure and adaptable/flexible mindsets.

Knowledge management

This refers primarily to the dissemination of implicit knowledge throughout an organization. Implicit knowledge involves close personal contact among employees. This can be facilitated in several ways. At lower levels, job rotation can be resorted to. At more senior levels, formal mechanisms (such as presentation symposia) can be created.

Core values

There are two important aspects pertaining to the core values of a transnational corporation. The first concerns the process of selection of core values. The second aspect relates to how these core values are disseminated. These values would include respect for all human beings, and a basic people orientation. The overall philosophy would be one of liberalism and a belief that there is always something to be learnt from association with other people.

A range of practices can be used to ensure that appropriate core values are imbibed by all employees and constantly strengthened and reinforced by all managers. An example is selection procedures and systems that ensure that only managers with an intercultural orientation are admitted into the fold. The Anglo-Dutch transnational conglomerate Unilever has a penchant for selecting managers for their operations abroad who have been trained at elitist business schools in the countries where their subsidiaries are located. Thus substantial sources of management recruitment for their Indian subsidiary are the top ten business schools of India, where the students, all in their early twenties, are socialized into management values such as commitment to excellence and flexibility of orientation towards people.

Communications

This implies sensitivity to language differences. Bringing diverse managers together to participate in cross-cultural sensitivity programmes can enhance appreciation of different communication patterns. The under-lying theme here is that cultural differences can exist regarding languages. Thus literal translations from one language to another are not recom-mended. What can be appreciated here is the importance of English as a sort of global lingua franca. Global managers tend to be fluent in English.

Conflict resolution

Conflicts are a part of organizational life, and enlightened organizations prefer differences to be stated and worked through, rather than swept under the carpet. Global companies have to take into account that con-flicts could arise simply because so much diversity exists. Conflict resolution in an intercultural context would require skill in being able to describe conflicts in unambiguous terms. Only then can a diagnosis of the differences causing the conflict be made.

All these dimensions of intercultural management will be examined in detail in ensuing chapters.

INTERCULTURAL MANAGEMENT VERSUS INTERNATIONAL BUSINESS

There are occasions when intercultural management and international business share the same platform. Both share a concern with aligning business practices with cultural norms, with accurately assessing those norms, with adjusting to and influencing those norms, and so on. The two sub-fields of management are however significantly different in many ways. International business views culture from the perspective of an environment that faces an organization. Intercultural management views culture both within the organization and externally impinging on that organization. For international business, culture and its consequences make up only one dimension of the many dimensions that are stressed. The other dimensions international business specifically examines include the external political environment, the external legal environ-ment, the external economic environment, governmental influences, world financial institutions, and the strategic management of various functional systems.

It can be argued that international business employs a compartment-alized approach. The separate strands examined, like the external political environment, or world financial systems, are not always integrated to reflect the reality of organizational life. To be sure, the global manager does require an in-depth understanding of the various strands that constitute international business. This would be a necessary condition for effectiveness. Skills in intercultural management would be the sufficient condition.

Intercultural management, when compared with international business, is integrative in its approach. It also places a strong emphasis on skills development, since intercultural management has borrowed substantially from the behavioural sciences. It is founded on top management commitment, and can have no existence without that commitment. Thus only in companies with a culture that strongly upholds intercultural management can the latter succeed. All employees are thus expected to possess values that are compatible with the tenets of intercultural management.

Knowledge about international business is not tantamount to skill in executing the precepts of intercultural management. Intercultural management is actionable. The actions or behaviour have then to be assessed to ascertain whether they bring people together in compatible associations, or result in conflict. The underlying theme is to find points of commonality that enable people to work together and enjoy those work associations. That is how people work together in most contexts. The same is possible in a multicultural context if people operate with enlightened minds, free of prejudice. The key to success in intercultural management is openness of the mind. Organizations have to discerningly select appropriate employees. They also have to ensure that those employees' skills and abilities are developed with the focus being individual managers, as Bartlett and Ghoshal (1999) have pointed out. Intercultural management requires individual managers to develop and use a 'matrix of flexible perspectives', which is its essence.

This also constitutes a point of departure for intercultural management from international business: that emphasis is placed on the development and enhancement of individual skills and attributes. International business, by contrast, places a lot of emphasis on corporate strategy, and in a sense culture follows strategy here. Intercultural management also formulates strategies that reflect its precepts. However, it does not stop with that. All organizational systems are designed to reflect the precepts of intercultural management.

The cosmopolitan manager that intercultural management is concerned with should not be confused with the culture-shocked expatriate described by Schneider and Barsoux (1997). Culture-shocked expatriates immerse themselves in an 'expatriate bubble', and alienate themselves from other cultures. This is the antithesis of the culturally sensitive and therefore efficient global manager. They become liabilities for their corporation, in more ways than one. In the first instance, as culture-shocked individuals, they are likely to be experiencing considerable stress. They are further hampered by their inability to relate to people outside their 'expatriate bubble', to the detriment of their performance.

Thus a substantial part of intercultural management is about developing what Hall (1995) has described as cultural skills. Some researchers may view these as soft skills, but they are skills that can be learnt. What has to be learnt however is a broad repertoire of skills. A skill-set appropriate in dealing with one cultural context may not be appropriate for another. If ever there was a field for which the contingency approach to management was most appropriate, it is the field of intercultural management. Thus, global managers should not only have at their command a wide array of skills, they should also be able to diagnose a situation and ascertain what behaviour on their part is expected and appropriate. Effective global managers exhibit behavioural responses to situations that are spontaneous and natural. Part of this ability comes from natural propensities that have been further developed and strengthened. These global managers are agile, flexible, and able to learn continuously, as well as being able to 'unlearn' where necessary. This is facilitated when they have a strong sense of self. Intercultural management is not for the faint-hearted.

The following also characterize intercultural management:

- It has an individual focus as much as an organizational one. Additionally, individual skills have to be properly aligned with organizational systems.

- There can be more than one configuration of organizational systems that promotes intercultural management.

- Cultural differences can surface even between managers who appear to have been nurtured by similar cultural influences. For instance, a conservative manager may experience difficulty working with a liberal-thinking manager. These differences can be accentuated when other differences traditionally associated with culture, such as ethnicity, also prevail. On the other hand, ethnic differences may not amount to much when both managers uphold the same values, attitudes and beliefs.

▎ Likewise, cultural differences can surface between divisions of companies that espouse the same organizational mission. The divisions might have evolved in different directions over time.

OBJECTIVES OF INTERCULTURAL MANAGEMENT PERSONNEL

The following is a list of objectives that corporate personnel entrusted with intercultural management may like to keep in mind:

▎ Beginning at the macro level, the culture of the organization should have a learning orientation.

▎ The values embedded in the organization should espouse what has been termed the Protestant work ethic. Thus, managers of such organizations are expected to have a high commitment to excellence, and be capable of demonstrating high performance.

▎ Managers should be socialized so that they share the same values. When those values are the ones mentioned above, then other cultural influences become of secondary consideration.

▎ There are always possibilities for organizations to achieve better performance. Hence a learning organization should be constantly seeking superior modes of management. It should have capabilities for learning from other cultures.

▎ Individual managers should possess personality traits such as cultural empathy and mental flexibility that enable them to be appreciative of diversity.

▎ In manufacturing and marketing merchandise, the preferences of consumers should assume paramount importance. Hence, products should be developed for a particular target group, keeping in mind the cultural preferences of that group.

▎ Internally, organizations should seek homogeneity regarding the values they espouse. Externally, however, they may need to develop an awareness of diverse markets and segment the market along cultural lines.

IMPLEMENTATION ISSUES

This section examines a few issues associated with implementation of the objectives of intercultural management. It is implicitly assumed that culture can be learnt, or culture can be cultivated, as Wilhelm von Humboldt (2000) would aver. Humboldt goes on to observe that among cultivated people, some are more cultivated than others. Likewise we have noted that in modern organizational life, some people are more adept at intercultural management than others.

In this book we are inclined towards the global convergence perspective on intercultural management. Transnational corporations can achieve some measure of global convergence. They must however give attention to the following implementation issues.

Commitment by managers

All perspectives on intercultural management are united in their opinion that organizational culture should support the accommodation of diversity. The norms of organizational culture should include looking for ties that bind people together. The emphasis of these perspectives is on actions, on actual behaviour that is manifested. Often, behavioural change can lead to attitudinal change. (Way back in the 1970s the social psychologist Bem (1970) demonstrated that this could be the case.) Thus in multi-cultural organizations, when new entrants are made to interact with people from different cultures, they learn new attitudes about those cultures.

Ultimately, implementing and supporting the norms of intercultural management is the responsibility of all managers. Georgina Wyman, Managing Director of Bata Shoe Company, is well known for insisting that managers of Bata worldwide function in a way that results in a win-win situation for everyone concerned. Win-win situations for managers in a multicultural context can only be achieved by the concerned managers themselves. Wyman herself believed in communicating and interacting with others so as to widen the scope of mutual opportunities rather than narrow their differences.

Thus implementation of intercultural management is a frame of mind – a frame of mind that is understood and supported by all managers. It can be viewed as being a component of what Scruton (1998) described as 'high culture' attained by effort, study, and application of the mind. It can of course be internalized, so that comfort with diversity becomes akin to a personality trait.

Management styles of working

The styles of working used by managers need to be compatible with the implementation of intercultural management. Generally speaking, the implementation of intercultural management is best achieved through participative styles of management. People are made to feel at ease providing inputs regardless of their position in the hierarchy, or cultural background. They also feel at ease regardless of who their superiors (or colleagues) are; regardless of their superiors' (or colleagues') origins. The hierarchical lines are not viewed as carved in stone. And what matters most of all is displaying a basic respect for people. Without respect, how can managers develop rapport with people from cultures different from their own?

Senior management are expected to act as role models in the appropriate use of management styles. At Royal Dutch/Shell, the senior managers have constituted themselves into a Committee of Managing Directors. These senior managers work collectively. The leadership is distributed and participation is equal. The designated CEO officiates only as a coordinator. The members of this committee represent different geographical locations. The committee engages in intercultural management. Each member appreciates his or her dependence on the other members to achieve his/her own business objectives. Each member also acknowledges that the formulation of a global strategy necessitates decision making by consensus.

Yukl (2001), a researcher on leadership, and participative management, has noted that managers from a wide variety of cultures perceive and report themselves as being participative. The subordinates of those managers, however, did not view their managers as being that participative. There is therefore a widespread need for managers to develop greater dexterity in participative leadership. Otherwise, impediments could arise over the implementation of intercultural management. This lacuna, where it exists, can be overcome with training. The preferred training would be generic rather than concerned with imparting traditional inputs on participative management. This would entail developing a general competence on the job. Individualistic managers need to learn to accommodate others more. Reticent managers need to learn to assert themselves more.

Effective managers operating within an intercultural management context are unique and possess a malleable and open management style. Their skills are valuable, which makes them invaluable. They are therefore well compensated and are found in profitable, high performance companies that can afford them. These managers in turn contribute to the further success of their companies. This would suggest that corporations adept at intercultural management are well resourced companies. They are also especially well resourced in cultural curiosity, which prompts them to look to culture for ways of honing their business skills. They are able to view the world as a global village. They may be contrasted with managers of small, family-owned concerns who are born in the same small town as their great grandfathers, and carry on their grandfathers' businesses. They are more like clan members whose world view cannot transcend tribal traditions.

John Daniels and Lee Radebaugh (1998) have used the term 'geocentrism' to describe hybrid business practices that borrow from several cultures. These practices can even be an amalgam of two ways of conducting business. The best elements of two ways are brought together. Intercultural management resorts to geocentrism quite frequently.

How are hybrid business practices, or for that matter any business practices, disseminated in a transnational corporation? There is an implicit understanding that the unofficial lingua franca holding a transnational corporation together is English. For most intercultural managers, the working language is English, even if it is not their first language. For a large number of intercultural managers regardless of nationality, English is the first language. And of course, all management schools of note and repute use English as the language of instruction.

Participative styles of management are strengthened through human interaction. Hence, the organizational structure and systems need to be designed so as to facilitate the easy flow of communication. Delayering is a mechanism that can be used to dilute hierarchies. Not many managers can embrace and propagate egalitarianism. There are not as many managers adept at intercultural management as there should be. The rarity of intercultural management skills imbues those capable of implementing it with some elitism. Today, Nestlé's managers in India are actively headhunted by other multinationals. The elitism referred to here is not at odds with the spirit of egalitarianism stressed in this section. Intercultural managers are amenable to participative management that makes them effective. Their effectiveness causes others to bestow them with appreciation and treat them as if they belong to an elitist cadre.

Nationalism

An issue that must be addressed here is whether a tension exists between intercultural management and nationalism. Can strong national identities inhibit the application of the global convergence perspective highlighted in this chapter? An optimistic view would be that nationalism serves as a useful stumbling block to thwart the march of cultural imperialism. Cultural imperialism is in many ways the antithesis of intercultural management. It originates from a belief that a particular cultural heritage is superior to all other cultural heritages. Companies that engage in cultural imperialism engage in dumping their products in new markets and muscling out existing and potential competition.

Intercultural management, by contrast, embraces cultural relativism, or a belief that there can be more than one way of getting things done. This catholic cultural sensitivity inherent in intercultural management enables managers operating in that domain 'to recognize that providing consulting services to a pharmaceutical company in Paris will be quite different from doing so to a tire company such as Michelin in Clermont-Ferrand' (Schneider and Barsoux, 1997).

The only scenario in which intercultural management faces a challenge over nationalism is when national governments start interfering in business life. However, in many countries the nature of government–business relations is known, and intercultural managers make adjustments accordingly. For example, in the United States there exists a divide between government and business. In Germany, by contrast, businesses are expected to participate in executing the social obligations of the government. As long as individual governments follow the rule of law, intercultural managers experience no great difficulties. Corporations that have been expelled from countries bring it on themselves in certain ways, by not forging amiable relations with governments.

The last words on the subject of intercultural management cannot be spoken when the first words are still being said. As matters currently stand, intercultural managers do not rush in where nationalist identities are likely to have fundamentalist and jingoist overtones. They leave such islands of closed economies alone. This makes practical business sense. It is also the expedient course of action to pursue.

In general, however, economic operations have become global and the cultures in which multinational managers operate are converging. It is only political systems that remain nationally circumscribed. We thus live in interesting times. And just as Trompenaars (1993) has had his personal life enriched by having parents from different nationalities, intercultural managers enrich their professional competencies by 'belonging to several cultural constituencies'.

Intercultural management – through 21st century communication

The accelerated pace by which intercultural management is being practised worldwide has been greatly facilitated by turn of the century modes of communication. E-mail has enabled employees at all levels of multinational corporations to get connected with each other wherever in the world they might be. A policy formulated at headquarters can be communicated simultaneously to all employees, regardless of whether they are half a world away, or in the same headquarters complex. Intercultural managers are adept at phrasing their communication in ways that are non-threatening to individuals from different cultures. Teleconferencing/videoconferencing allows managers, irrespective of location, to engage in face-to-face discussion. Here too, intercultural managers distinguish themselves by presenting themselves in ways that are universally appealing.

Additionally, international travel is becoming increasingly commonplace. Global companies arrange for their managers from all cultural constituencies to get together at conventions. This ease in bringing together intercultural managers allows them to find commonalities. They can also express their differences and work through them. Thus diverse perspectives can be made congruent. Samsung, Korea's largest corporation, is currently experimenting with this approach in a partial fashion, by sending 400 junior employees abroad every year.

SUMMARY

Intercultural management is an emerging domain of research study. A great deal by way of intercultural management is actually happening in the real world. Effective intercultural management is contributing to high performance in global corporations. Organizations with a learning orientation are able to face the challenge of intercultural management. They can ascend to a world described by the poet Tagore (1997) as one 'which has not been broken up into fragments by narrow domestic walls'. Most truths are surprisingly eternal and, by the same token, universal and for all cultures.

Intercultural management as viewed in this book is inclined towards the global convergence approach. The relevant managerial skills are cultural awareness, cultural sensitivity, and flexibility to accommodate diversity. Within the corporate context intercultural managers, regardless of their cultural background, tend to exhibit homogeneous managerial values and competencies. Their business school training also tends to be comparable. They are driven by professionalism and a desire to show performance. They can learn and unlearn with ease. With respect to management practices, they are able to adopt local methods.

Though intercultural management is concerned with profitability, it recognizes the importance of soft skills in implementing its precepts. Thus, intercultural management has a leaning towards the area of organizational behaviour. However, intercultural management's knowledge base has moved beyond the wisdom contained in organizational behaviour. The contingency approach to management has validity in the field of intercultural management. Intercultural management seeks to ensure that all aspects of its functioning are aligned with each other. The work in intercultural management that has commenced in the real world needs now to be sustained and enhanced by research. There is no turning the clock back now. Corporations who fight shy of intercultural management will be condemned to second-class status.

1

Organizational structure and intercultural management

CASE STUDY: CREDIT SUISSE

In 2001, Singapore was the world's fourth largest financial centre, with the top three being London, New York and Tokyo. (See the following Web sites for more information about Singapore's appeal as a location for banking operations: www.mas.gov.sg; www.Sicc.com.sg; www.gov.sg/sgip/PDA/snapshot.doc; www.tdb.gov.sg/bizspore.sp 1.html; www.singstat.gov.sg.) It was also an offshore financial centre (OFC) designated as belonging to the Group I category by the Financial Stability Forum (FSF) of Basle, Switzerland.

OFCs in Group I have the highest quality legal infrastructure and adherence to internationally accepted standards of supervision, cooperation, and information sharing in the world. OFCs in Group II have the second best infrastructure and internationally accepted standards of supervision and so on. OFCs in Group III reflect the next best international standards after Group II. (Source: Report of the Working Group on Offshore Financial Centres, 5 April 2000.)

It was in Singapore that Credit Suisse Private Banking (CSPB) launched a new first-of-its-kind banking service in 2001. CSPB is part of the Credit Suisse Group, one of the world's leading financial services groups, and the oldest of Switzerland's big banks. CSPB

Table 1.1   *Membership in Group I, Group II and Group III categories of offshore financial centres as endorsed by the FSF, 2000*

Group I	Group II	Group III
Hong Kong	Andorra	Anguilla
Luxembourg	Bahrain	Antigua
Singapore	Barbados	Aruba
Switzerland	Bermuda	Bahamas
	Gibraltar	Belize
	Macau	British Virgin Islands
	Malaysia	Cayman Islands
	Malta	Cook Islands
	Monaco	Costa Rica
		Cyprus
		Lebanon
		Liechtenstein
		Marshall Islands
		Mauritius
		Nauru
		Netherlands
		Niue
		Panama
		St Kitts and Nevis
		St Lucia
		St Vincent & the Grenadines
		Samoa
		Seychelles
		Turks & Caicos
		Vanuatu

came into existence in 1997, when the Credit Suisse Group's private client business was consolidated into a single entity and became one of the four business units of the Credit Suisse Group. Since its emergence, CSPB has been one of the largest private banking institutions in the world, with branches in 43 countries. Its latest reported figure for assets under management (31 December 1999) was 477 billion Swiss francs, while its net profits stood at 911 million Swiss francs, an increase of 14 per cent over the previous year.

CSPB was constituted by the Credit Suisse Group, in response to the volatile changes that have coloured the banking world in the past decade. In recent times, millionaires with new money have shown a proclivity to transfer their assets from one bank to another, if the latter can manage their funds more profitably. The *Economist* (16 June 2001) noted that 'the sleepy Swiss private banks are waking up to the growing threat posed by foreign competitors, especially American ones, which now account for some 25–30 per cent of foreign money managed in Switzerland'. CSPB is the Credit Suisse Group's answer to suggestions that Swiss banks had descended into a state of slothful stupor. The Group recognized that it should adapt its traditional Swiss banking model to the requirements of a more diversified clientele. Globally, there is now greater competition in the area of private banking than ever before, although worldwide still no single private bank has more than a 2–3 per cent market share.

CSPB has experience and expertise in providing both onshore and offshore financial services. As has been the case traditionally with the Credit Suisse Group, CSPB caters to the richest 1 per cent of the world's population. A client with CSPB is expected to deposit assets of at least 1 million Swiss francs. CSPB offers both offshore and onshore services at its branches around the globe, except for those few locations that operate as 100 per cent offshore centres, like the Bahamas. Consequently, its structure has been uniquely designed so as to be global in some respects and local in other ways. As far as the provision of onshore financial services is concerned, a CSPB branch obeys local banking regulations. Thus the CSPB branch in Frankfurt, when providing onshore financial services, caters to German clients, manages assets that are booked in Germany, and operates within a legal framework that is dictated by German law. For many intents and purposes, CSPB Frankfurt is like a German bank. The same strict adherence to Singapore banking laws would hold for CSPB Singapore. In that sense, CSPB Singapore resembles a Singapore bank.

However, CSPB Singapore is structured differently from other financial services institutions in Singapore. One reason for this is that CSPB Singapore is an offshore private banking facility. It is like a Swiss model of a private bank that has been exported to Singapore, with the caveat that it is aligned with Singapore's legal system. CSPB Singapore thus demonstrates a certain duality in its functioning. On the one hand, it is structured to obey all the rules and regulations of Singapore. On the other hand it is part of a bigger organization – CSPB.

CSPB has established brand equity for managing clients' assets efficiently. This work ethic of efficiency and quality service is well embedded in all CSPB subsidiaries. Additionally, being a Swiss bank, it is accustomed to offering confidentiality to its clients. This is after ensuring that there is no money laundering or other illegality involved. Alex W. Widmer, Head of CSPB for Asia-Pacific, Middle East, Egypt, Greece and Turkey, comments:

> To ensure that the integrity of CSPB values are not compromised, the offshore branches are headed by an individual who has been working with CSPB for quite some years. I think it is important that the person understands the way we operate the business, the way we are organized, and to see that the branch meshes in with CSPB, since it has to work well with all units of the organization. All offshore operations are interlinked with the global network in a way that does not apply to onshore banks.

Singapore is currently emerging as a preferred destination for offshore banks. Arguably it is beginning to steal a march over Switzerland, Luxembourg and Hong Kong, the other locations in the FSF Group I Category. Hong Kong is now perceived as being part of China. Switzerland and Luxembourg are currently under pressure from the European Union (EU) to improve transparency and financial supervision. Both countries are being encouraged to adopt measures that will allow for greater information exchange and disclosure, in such areas as tax policy and investment. This will mean that both countries will become less attractive as offshore banking centres.

By contrast, Singapore has a banking law that allows for client confidentiality of the highest order. Hence, to continue as a force to reckon with, CSPB is seeking to strengthen its position in Singapore, the emerging prime offshore banking operation of the world. To this end, it has recently opened the Global Private Banking Centre, Singapore. The services it offers are new and an innovation on the part of CSPB.

The Global Private Banking Centre, Singapore offers its clients global and full access to the entire product range of the Credit Suisse Group, all day (24 hours) every day. Thus, Singapore clients can seamlessly access CSPB services through a number of different channels at any time and from any location. This makes possible a real-time posting of assets and transactions, dispensing with the time zone problems inherent in traditional services. This is enabled by the integration of all channels of access, whether telephone, Internet or personal visits.

This innovative feature is made possible because the Centre has incorporated an e-commerce platform for its operations, the first in the realm of international offshore private banking. Traditionally, clients in a region such as Europe experienced difficulty in assessing banking facilities in Singapore during the latter's office hours, because of the six to eight hour time difference. If a client in Europe wanted to talk on the phone to a manager from a bank in Singapore, he or she had a time window of just two to three hours. To overcome this limitation, in addition to the e-commerce platform, CSPB Singapore has a 24-hour call centre. This feature is supplemented by an all-day videoconferencing facility. A multilingual banking team staffs these communication channels. Hence, a client can access his or her portfolio by communicating in the international language of his or her choice.

Alternatively, clients can pursue the conventional approach of physically visiting the call centre and transacting business on a face-to-face basis with their relationship managers. What clients are looking for is a bank like CSPB, which has an established reputation for giving a high return on investment, and is also conversant with Singaporean banking regulations.

Clients can be assured of efficiency vis-à-vis the management of their portfolios, regardless of whether they are parking their assets as offshore clients with CSPB Zurich, CSPB Bahamas or CSPB Singapore. However, they are likely to prefer banking with CSPB Singapore because it is emerging as the location that can afford the greatest degree of confidentiality and security in the world. CSPB has rushed to make CSPB Singapore the most attractive private bank for offshore clients the world over. This has been CSPB Singapore's response to the fierce competition that exists in the banking sector in Singapore. Singapore has a population of just 3.2 million (1999), but has 661 financial institutions. Of these, 83 are offshore banks. They are all banks of note and repute, but they have been pipped to the post by CSPB.

Side-by-side with this innovation, CSPB Singapore has been concentrating on optimizing its strengths in relationship banking. What CSPB has done is to juxtapose a Swiss banking system, with its 150 year established brand equity for excellence, with a location that is now emerging as the preeminent centre for offshore banking. CSPB has been present in Singapore since 1971. It is therefore fully conversant with Singapore banking regulations. It is in a position to offer premium services at a premium location. In other words, it has married its expertise in private banking with Singapore's capability for providing the best climate for financial operations.

Organizational structure

A CSPB project team is developing the Global Private Banking Centre (GPBC), Singapore. Boris Collardi, a 27-year-old whiz kid, heads the project, identified by the codename Project Copernicus. The project team comprises 130 individuals with 19 to 20 different nationalities. Some of these individuals have been with CSPB for years; others have just joined. The team is remarkable because the organizational structure is what Peters and Waterman (1982) have described as 'loosely coupled'. The team is not hierarchically ordained and all members are on an equal footing. Collardi is a first among equals.

The team members are without exception top-notch professionals. They function as peers with mutual respect. As a result, it is peer pressure that drives performance. This is something of a departure from the traditional mode of CSPB functioning, as exemplified by its headquarters in Zurich. The Zurich headquarters has a well defined, almost bureaucratic structure, in keeping with the nature of its operations.

The Copernicus project team is attempting to deliver and operationalize the GPBC as a world-class system, as quickly as possible. The team does not have a tried and tested blueprint to refer to. Any member of the team can advance solutions to problems. The work thus necessitates that hierarchies and strict reporting lines are dispensed with.

The Copernicus project has gone beyond the 'Swiss efficiency' model mirrored by the CSPB Headquarters, Zurich. These features guarantee that all the organizational members understand their roles, have the competence to discharge their responsibilities well, and therefore do so. The system functions like a well-oiled machine, with every member being like a well-oiled part of that machine. Members have designated roles, but these roles are frequently exchanged, enlarged and shared. This flexibility regarding roles is enabling the project to be creative.

The structure at the Copernicus project has enough flexibility to allow changes in role content. This flexibility also allows the structure to evolve. The Copernicus project thus operates as a learning organization. And as in any organization, interpersonal differences can surface. Collardi observes that 'culture is only one of the factors determining professional behaviour. . . the other factors could be personality, exposure, education, family background, individual attributes, etc'. The non-cultural factors such as education and exposure have ensured that all organizational members share the same work ethic. The learning organization environment encourages members to be tolerant of and learn from other cultures. Comments Collardi:

> The founding principles of working in such an environment are as follows:
>
> 1) lead by example (show/share/teach/etc);
>
> 2) transparent communication;
>
> 3) commitment/motivation (recognition);
>
> 4) ownership and responsibility;
>
> 5) empowerment of the staff.

The CSPB as a global enterprise has an orientation that enables it to be global when necessary, and local at other times. When the GPBC Singapore interacts with other CSPB branches, it does so in the established CSPB Zurich mode, but as a unit it has its own charact-eristics. 'We think global – act local,' explains Collardi.

A noteworthy feature about CSPB as a global concern operating in different cultures has been its ability to appreciate the opportun-ities that other countries can offer. Until now it developed innovative approaches in Switzerland, then exported these approaches to its branches around the world. Now it is developing the GPBC through the Copernicus project out of Singapore. It is accepting that Sing-apore is likely to replace Switzerland (and Luxembourg and Hong Kong) as the preferred place for their clients to bank their assets. Its networked organizational structure is not usually associated with mega banks, but this structure has contributed to CSPB's success in no small measure. Additionally, because of the way CSPB has evolved, every corporate entity has sufficient autonomy to design a structure that fulfils its objectives.

The Copernicus project is divided into several streams. These are the Business Development Stream, IT Stream, E-Commerce Platform Stream, Marketing Stream and Legal Compliance Stream. The Bus-iness Development Stream is responsible for developing a new concept. For instance, it developed the concept of a seamless 24-hour continuous access facility for customers. The concept was then examined by the Legal Compliance Stream to ascertain whether it was in accord with Singapore's banking regulations and laws. The concept was simultaneously examined by the Marketing Stream to ensure that it would find acceptance and favour by clients. It was then handed over to the IT Stream and E-Commerce Platform Stream for operationalization. In reality, the flow is not quite as unidirectional as described above. From initiation to project completion, there is tremendous interface and exchange of ideas between the streams. This is formally facilitated by what Collardi has termed Monday meetings. At these meetings, which can stretch for six hours, the streams report to each other on the progress they have made.

Members of the Copernicus project are encouraged to develop either as managers or leaders. As the terms are used in the Copernicus project, managers are individuals with consummate technical skills. Leaders, by contrast, display such attributes as being able to take the initiative, or coordinate the activities of project members. Ideally, members are encouraged to be both managers and leaders. In practice, the Copernicus project has observed that people have inclinations towards one role or the other. People who do not evolve as either managers or leaders are perceived as misfits, who are then eased out.

This structure has encouraged tremendous creativity and job satisfaction amongst members. Members who make outstanding contributions are suitably rewarded. The reward could be a message of appreciation sent by e-mail by Collardi and project colleagues. It could be applause at Monday meetings. It could also be a financial reward.

Generally, the multicultural mix of the project is not an issue, because all members are professionals who fit into the culture of the project. However, cultural differences are discernible when differences of opinion manifest themselves. For instance, members are expected to be forthright in giving their views on projects and to speak their minds. However, a newly joined IT expert who was Chinese never expressed a candid opinion that a concept was not worth pursuing at Monday meetings, but he would unilaterally decide not to work on a concept if he was convinced that it was not going to work. Initially his behaviour was construed as mystifying, almost rebellious. He was therefore asked why he did not publicly voice his aversions to specific concepts when they came up for discussion. After he explained his rationale, it became apparent that at Monday meetings, his behaviour was influenced by traditional Chinese values. Traditionally, the Chinese do not like to publicly criticize a colleague. They want to ensure that the person being criticized does not lose face.

Collardi therefore worked on the Chinese IT specialist's attitude in this respect, and convinced him that at Project Copernicus he was expected to express his views honestly, and that no one would take offence or lose face. They would in fact feel uncomfortable if they could not fathom his true reactions to a concept. After some counselling, the Chinese IT expert is voicing his opinions at project meetings. That he does so in a tactful and non-threatening fashion is particularly well appreciated. In fact now Collardi believes that project members who aggressively present their viewpoints could learn something from the Chinese IT expert about being diplomatic.

The experience of CS Singapore's Copernicus project suggests that even banks can successfully opt for innovative and organic modes of functioning. The networked structure at CS allows members to access each other's ideas with ease. This structure totally dispenses with the debilitating effects of hierarchies. Members interact with each other laterally. As has already been mentioned, these members are highly qualified and dedicated professionals. They are what Collardi describes as 'best of breed'. They are not only extremely talented, but have potential as either managers or leaders. It is this professionalism that is holding all members together, irrespective of cultural background. They also have sizeable amounts of task-orientation. There is something in their background which has enabled them to emerge as professionals. All these features working in synergy encourage the unleashing of considerable amounts of creativity.

CASE DISCUSSION QUESTIONS

1. What lessons about organizational structure and intercultural management can be derived from the case study?

2. Comment on Boris Collardi's leadership style and skills in intercultural management.

3. What aspects of CSPB Singapore can be replicated to branches of CSPB in other parts of the world, such as CSPB Zurich?

4. Does Boris Collardi have a vision for his intercultural team?

5. Why is there a certain amount of bonding amongst members in his team, despite its intercultural mix?

Inferences

The following may be inferred about organizational structure and intercultural management.

The importance of helping personnel on a case-by-case basis to overcome cultural impediments

There are several reasons why competent and qualified individuals may experience difficulty in getting assimilated into an unconventional organizational structure. One reason could be culture. In this book we are examining only the effect of culture and ignoring other reasons. In what way might culture act as an inhibitor to getting personnel aligned with organizational structure?

An innovative project team, like that for the Copernicus project, comprises members from diverse cultural backgrounds, both ethnic and corporate. When it is observed that the cultural background is at odds with the required work behaviour, it may be necessary to address this issue head-on. As has been detailed, this was done at the Copernicus project with respect to the Chinese IT expert. However, it must be pointed out that individuals need to be assessed to see if culture is an impediment on a strictly case-by-case basis. Thus, what was true of the Chinese expert referred to earlier might not hold for another Chinese IT expert who joins Project Copernicus.

Considerable research in the area of learning organizations suggests that such organizations succeed when the structure is flexible enough to permit continuous assessment. Continuous assessment at the micro level is also what characterizes intercultural management. Hence a cultural impediment that is found to inhibit the work behaviour of a person from one ethnic group need not apply to somebody else from that same ethnic group. A networked structure is compatible with this notion that every project team member must be viewed as having unique attributes. It therefore has to be free of too many standard operating procedures. Excessive standard operating procedures obstruct the creative process, as research has established. A rigid system also reduces individual uniqueness by expecting every-body to fall in line with established norms and codes of conduct.

The Copernicus project has maintained continuous vigilance for signs of strain in interpersonal relations. Right from the time a person joins the team, project members are alert to whether strains could arise because of culture. The following incident illustrates this. In early 2000, a German joined the Copernicus project. He hailed from a typically German corporate culture where there existed consid-erable rules, regulations and standard operating procedures. The structure in that corporation was authoritarian, with a well-defined hierarchy. He was accustomed to being given detailed instructions, and functioning in an unambiguous environment. Collardi and others therefore anticipated that unless he was initiated into the project team culture appropriately, given counselling and mentoring, he would be a cultural misfit. He was coached extensively from the minute he joined the Copernicus project about its norms of work behaviour. After just one month, the German adapted to his new work environment completely and became reasonably comfortable with the prevailing networked structure.

The project team frequently undertake group outings. This enables them to develop a sense of belonging to their team, in which spirit overrides differences of culture, personality type, and so on. On 29 March 2001 all members of the team congregated on a boat, and spent the entire afternoon cruising off the coast of Singapore. On this occasion, André Keel, Head of New Technology, expressed how comfortable he now felt with his associates at Project Copernicus. He admitted that he had made some mistakes initially when he had joined the project group a year earlier, but had learnt to be more sensitive to the sensibilities of people, especially those from cultures different from his own. This learning was possible, Keel averred, because the structure at Project Copernicus was designed to inte-grate people into its cultural melting pot as speedily as possible. In fact, an important criterion in performance appraisal is cultural fit. It is not just a question of whether a person like Keel learnt to fit into Project Copernicus. It is also a question of whether his colleagues and superiors contributed to and facilitated his adjustment.

Keel, a Swiss-German, had worked with Credit Suisse Zurich for a year, before joining the Project Copernicus team in Singapore. Before joining Credit Suisse he had worked with construction comp-anies for many years, first in Uganda and then in Iraq, where the company he worked for built hospitals. While working for these companies, Keel had been accustomed to cracking the whip. He would speak in a rude, almost offensive way to his subordinates, to extract work from them. When Keel came on board Project Copernicus, the Asians working there, particularly the Singapore-Chinese, perceived him as lacking in refinement. The US managers working with Project Copernicus had no difficulty cutting Keel down to size. However, some of the Asians found it difficult to counter his tough posturing with reciprocal toughness. They frequently took recourse to complaining about Keel to Collardi. For some Asians, this is a preferred method of dealing with interpersonal conflict: taking the matter to a higher-up.

Keel was personally mentored and counselled by Collardi. He was even sent to a leadership training course where among other things he was exposed to the rudiments of intercultural competencies. Keel made a conscious effort to align himself with his team members, and over time he succeeded in being not only less offensive, but likeable and popular. Some of the Asians who had been most disconcerted by Keel were encouraged to meet him head on. Thus the Asians were encouraged to assume a more direct role in dealing with difficult colleagues, rather than depend on their boss to intervene on their behalf.

It is said about Asians that they expect authority figures to sort out their on-the-job interpersonal problems. This generalization is something of a caricature. Most of the Asians with Project Copernicus do not conform to this caricature, and the few who did have been weaned away from this tendency. When they conveyed to Collardi that they were not happy with something their boss had done, Collardi would respond, 'Why do you not approach the boss directly?' They would feel awkward about approaching their bosses directly, but they tried out Collardi's suggestion. Meanwhile, Collardi would speak with the bosses so that they could prepare to receive feedback from their subordinates. When the subordinates met their bosses, they would find themselves being received with an open mind, and given a fair hearing. This then encouraged them to sort out matters directly with their bosses, or any other coworkers with whom they had a difference of opinion. Such directness is required for an open environment to thrive. And the open nature of the structure facilitates such face-to-face settling of differences of opinion.

The flexibility inherent in Project Copernicus serves several purposes. Most of all, it enables people to blend into a multicultural team as efficiently as possible. It also places part of the onus of achieving integration into an intercultural environment on the individual managers who have joined Project Copernicus. Considerable effort has been expended in crafting a structure that will facilitate the integration. However, as the maxim states, you can lead a horse to water, but you cannot make it drink. If a manager is essentially lacking in intercultural skills, and more importantly is lacking in the willingness to cultivate those skills, he or she will not become a part of the intercultural mosaic of Project Copernicus. In 2001, a Mauritius-Chinese was recruited. He had 22 years of experience in the banking sector, but he was encouraged to leave Project Copernicus after four months. The reason was that his colleagues rejected him because he had the attitudinal problem of not wanting to learn how to work at the project. The structure requires members to be proactive in achieving a fit with the project culture, as well as in feeling comfortable working with colleagues from other cultures.

Johan, Head of the Call Centre, who was also recruited in 2001, is an example of a person who aligned himself remarkably speedily with the intercultural environment at Project Copernicus. Prior to joining Project Copernicus, Johan had worked for DLG, a US company, which became a Credit Suisse entity in 1999. Johan had imbibed some aspects of the US culture by virtue of having worked for DLG, and also possessed certain typically German attributes, since that was his nationality. The 'Americanness' of Johan's background was reflected in the fact that he was open-minded, prepared to listen, proactive and bottom line-oriented. His German upbringing had given him a structured approach and a capacity for attention to detail. This type of exposure and familiarity with more than one culture is what Collardi seeks when he recruits people. He therefore hunted Johan and spoke with him on the telephone for 10 minutes. By then, Johan had decided that he would like to join Project Copernicus because he was impressed by the structure that was in place there.

ACADEMIC DISCUSSION

The commonly accepted definition of organizational structure is the durable arrangements constructed by a particular organization, to facilitate its processes and help achieve its objectives. However, a more dynamic perspective on organizations places emphasis on such features as working relationships, actual experiences of members, and inter-pretations of occurrences. As opined by Pepper (1995), structure is a form of document, forged, communicated, and responded to over time. There is thus a causal, vibrant connection between the structure and the activities of members. Since interpretation plays a role in how effective a structure is from an intercultural management standpoint, it is desir-able that the structure enables accommodation and cultural integration to take place. Accordingly, the structure suitable for intercultural man-agement is a negotiated one. The greater the scope for widespread participation in the negotiation process, the more representative the structure will be of the diverse constituents of that organization.

A useful analogy is an improvisational jazz concert, or an Indian classical music rendition, which also revolves around improvisation. As Weick (1995) stipulated when he spoke about enacting organizations, 'organizing is a continuous flow of movement that people try to co-ordinate with a continuous flow of input'. Organizational structure attempts to impose form on processes so that there can be order. How-ever, when the processes require a response to unfolding events, having too much order can be counterproductive. And in the case of an organ-ization that is increasing in diversity, the processes themselves are adapting to what is happening. This thus necessitates a structure capable of improvisation. As the case study on Credit Suisse demonstrates, an organizational structure congruent with intercultural management should have sufficient flexibility of form to cope with friction points caused by cultural imperatives.

Common sense suggests that there are a few guiding principles that can be kept in mind when designing structures for intercultural manage-ment. The first is that structure should possess a human touch. The more intercultural the organization becomes, the more preferable it is that people confront each other face to face. Essentially, organizational members should be provided with opportunities to get to know each other. The frequent contact enables people to relate to each other as individuals, and overcome any cultural stereotypes they might have. Sometimes people have reservations about individuals from other cult-ures, because they are ignorant about those cultures. Nothing can educate a person about another culture more than direct contact with people from that culture.

Second, people from different cultural contexts are likely to exhibit different preferences regarding structure, as indicated by the research by Stevens of INSEAD (cited in Hofstede, 1991). MBA students from France, Germany and Great Britain framed markedly different structural solutions when presented with an organizational problem in the form of a caselet. The problem revolved around a conflict between two departmental heads. The French students displayed a preference for referring the problem one level up, to the president of the organization. The German students, for the most part, recommended greater clarity in the description of the structure, with roles, responsibilities, and areas of expertise of the conflicting department heads clearly defined. Most of the British students defined the problem as arising out of lack of proper communication between the department heads, and recommended that they be provided with training in interpersonal skills.

Of course, an organization interested in promoting intercultural harmony and integration would not divide its members along cultural lines. In fact, people with exposure to multiple cultures would protest at being divided into work groups along cultural lines. What is being emphasized here is that a structure should be flexible and esoteric enough to be able to evolve constantly. A structure that attempts to take cognizance of different cultural constituents should be evolving and getting modified. Of course, a structure relevant for a multicultural work force is one that can enable newcomers to align themselves with the organization, not one that tries to please everybody by incorporating everybody's preferences regarding culture. The structure should be designed so that if newcomers do not become aligned, then it is because the problem rests with the individual and not with the organization.

Third, the structure should be capable of modification even on a decision-to-decision basis. It should be remembered that diversity is only one of the variables adding complexity to the functioning of a successful, high-performance global company. The structure of global companies also has to take into account the complexity of the tasks being performed and the heterogeneity of the external environment.

GLOBALIZATION AND ORGANIZATIONAL STRUCTURES

Many companies make their initial foray into the world of intercultural management by exporting their outputs. Such companies are not limited to production companies, but include service organizations as well. The service exported could include advertising expertise, legal expertise, hotel and hospitality expertise, management consulting and training, building construction expertise, or medical expertise. An export department usually manages the export effort. This department comprises home office personnel who are primarily concerned with marketing the exported products in a new location. Once a company finds its products are being sold in an expanding market, it can progress to setting up on-site production facilities.

The setting up of a subsidiary (or subsidiaries) overseas results in an alteration to existing structural arrangements. The general pattern has been for an international operations division at headquarters, to oversee a global corporation's overseas subsidiaries. This international operations division coordinates and supervises overseas activities, and ensures that the objectives of these divisions are in keeping with the overall objectives and mission of the corporation. Over time, local branches may be invested with broad local authority and considerable autonomy. But the system of reporting to an international operations division at headquarters continues, more likely than not.

However, if global corporations want to remain successful, when their scale of operations overseas becomes considerable they typically have to abandon such a simple-minded approach to organization, and adopt more complex modes, as has been argued by Karen Lowry Miller.

Source: based on Lowry Miller (1995).

Transnational corporations have outlived and transcended linear, hierarchical forms of organization. Intercultural management is management in transition; management by continuous learning and adaptation; and management with multidimensional skills. The attendant structures thus have to be flexible and responsive. They have to be fluid, rather than engraved in rock. The latter conjure up images of ossified bureaucracies. The former bring to mind the fabric Lycra, used to make bodysuits for gymnasts and swimmers. Lycra has simultaneous liquid and solid properties. It therefore affords extensive stretch and recovery facilities to users, while retaining its form as a fabric. Such a structure is congruent with systems where roles are constantly being redefined.

This was the case, for example, in the Credit Suisse case study, where the members of Project Copernicus had their roles redefined. Recall the Chinese man who had to learn to express his opinion at Monday meetings, in the interests of being more effective professionally. This entailed having to redefine his view of what he considered acceptable behaviour towards others.

Structures suitable for transnational organizations are thus networked. Although a formal hierarchy exists, often the decision-making respons-ibility is shared by a large number of members, who are more or less on an equal footing. This is most likely to be the case in multinational corporations using cutting edge technology and engaging in software fabrication.

One of the great challenges of organizational structure for inter-cultural management is the relationship between overseas branches and the headquarters. Credit Suisse's Copernicus project may have a 'state of the art' structure consonant with its multicultural workforce and the tasks that are being performed there, but the company's headquarters in Zurich remains the model of a traditional, high-performance bank in Switzerland. When Project Copernicus transacts with headquarters it has to defer to the Credit Suisse mode of functioning, while retaining its uniqueness for all its internal operations. This is the modus operandi evolved by Credit Suisse.

On the other hand, Nestlé's orientation (referred to in two of the opening case studies in this book) is a little different. The basic principles are uniform and are monitored at headquarters. However, within the overall framework, the individual branches are at liberty to make local structural adjustments. Thus there is some divergence in the extent of local decentralization found in Nestlé's various branches.

A very modern type of structure described by McHugh and Wheeler (1995) can, when modified appropriately, be used to facilitate inter-cultural management. McHugh and Wheeler call it the holonic network. They define this as 'a set of companies that acts integratedly and organic-ally; it is constantly re-configured to manage each business opportunity a customer presents. Each company within the network provides a different process capability and is called a holon.'

In this book we view the holonic network slightly differently: as a set of units of a transnational corporation. Being located in different cultures could differentiate the units. Even at different locations, performing different tasks, and therefore having different process capabilities, could differentiate the units. Thus Credit Suisse Private Banking has a unit in Zurich as well as units in Singapore. Project Copernicus is a unit (or holon) separate from the rest of Credit Suisse Private Banking Singapore because it is performing different tasks from the rest. Each holon is capable of being constantly reconfigured, not only to manage new business opportunities, but also to reflect the impact of managers from different cultures, as is the case with Project Copernicus. The units are integrated so that they collectively constitute Credit Suisse Private Banking, and the fact that each unit is free to structure itself as it deems fit does not throw the entire transnational organization out of gear. Although a holon is described as being flexible, it can coexist with units that are not intrinsically flexible. A holon, as we have adopted the definition, is a unit that has been structured with the flexibility required for it to reconfigure itself.

According to McHugh and Wheeler (1995), an organization with a holoniated network has certain properties. In our modified version of the holoniated structure, only a holon has those properties, and not necessarily all units which make up a particular transnational organization. These properties are:

▌ There exists no rigid hierarchy.

▌ There is constant evolution, as a response to both the external environment and the culture of its incumbent managers.

▌ It is a continuously learning entity.

▌ There is easy access to, and exchange of information among, managers.

▌ It manages and regulates itself.

▌ Conditions within the holon are dynamic, without being disruptive.

▌ The holon is connected to other units.

As can be noticed by taking stock of these characteristics, a holon is particularly suited for grappling with the need to accommodate the culture of its managers.

Mention must be made here of Coulson-Thomas (1991), whose writings preceded McHugh and Wheeler. Coulson-Thomas predicted that corporations dealing with diversity and complexity would opt for 'flatter and more fluid organizational structures that (can) develop into networks', as well as have 'greater flexibility and responsiveness to customer needs'. There would also be 'delegation of work to multifunctional, multilocational teams'. All these would be accompanied by 'a management approach which pushes organizational hierarchy to individuals, who require access to expertise and specialists'.

GLOBAL STRUCTURAL INTEGRATION

General Electric is believed to be a model of global structural integration. Through structural integration, it has become globally focused. It also achieved a shift from its previous mode of being widely diversified and dissipated.

In the light of the General Electric experience, Handy's prognosis (1996) is relevant. According to Handy, future concerns about structure should not be viewed in terms of structural integration or decentralization. Instead, organizational design specialists should think more in terms of a structure where 'you can combine small and big, be centralized when it matters, and yet be decentralized and different when it counts'. Bedeian and Zammuto (1991) also articulated this point of view. They aver that the balance between centralization and decentralization shifts continuously. Such shifts occur in response to changes in company size, market opportunities, developments in new technology, the quality of existing decision making, and the expansion of the company into new cultures. As a transnational company from Europe, for instance, moves into emerging markets like China or Eastern Europe, it may choose to decentralize, so that managers at the scene of action can take decisions appropriate to local conditions. After investing in technology that enables all its branches to communicate speedily with each other as well as with headquarters, the same company may prefer to centralize certain facets of decision making.

In many respects, the philosophy embedded in Bedeian and Zammuto, as well as in Handy, was labelled by Peters and Waterman (1982) as the principle of simultaneous loose–tight properties. This principle reconciles the need for overall control with a commitment to autonomy.

Source: based on Dess *et al* (1995).

The appropriate stance to adopt regarding organizational structure may be that of judiciously employing the contingency approach to management. This approach recommends that organizations always keep in mind the context. Thus, an organization should adopt a matrix structure if that is appropriate for the context, or a bureaucratic approach if that is appropriate for the context, and so on. Hence, a global organization may be advised to design different structures for its different branches worldwide, keeping in mind the context of each branch. Among the location-specific considerations that a transnational corporation might like to keep in mind are, as Daniels and Radebaugh (1998) have pointed out, market size, type of competition, nature of the product, labour cost and currency. And of course, the intercultural composition of the workforce should play a part in determining the structure.

Another modern theory appropriate when designing structures in the intercultural context is strategic choice. This theory holds that organizational structure is entirely the outcome of managerial choice and decision making. Hence, it is a matter of managerial choice whether the structure has been made flexible enough to assimilate, adapt, blend and imbibe the influences of many cultures. Strategic choice theory is actually a variation of the contingency approach. Taken together, these two theories imply that a flexible structure capable of constant evolution is appropriate for intercultural management, and designing such a structure is a matter of conscious managerial choice.

CONVENTIONAL ORGANIZATIONAL STRUCTURES OF GLOBAL ORGANIZATIONS

Three varieties of structure are commonly used by global organizations. These are the global product division structure, the global area division structure, and the global functional division structure.

The global product division

When an organization adopts the global product division mode, it manages its product lines from around the world from home-country-based product divisions. Suppose the organization has five products, A, B, C, D and E. It will have a product division to manage the production and sale of A, another product division to manage the production and sale of B, and so on. Product division A will have worldwide responsibility for A. It will also have functional support from the marketing, finance, production and other personnel concerned with product A.

The advantage of the global product division is that it can use to advantage economies of scale. These economies of scale are particularly noticeable in production/manufacturing, where vertically integrated technological and distribution systems are used. Companies that have a diversified portfolio of products opt for this structural mode. The product groups may be so different from each other that they can operate independently of each other. The product division can synergistically use the resources of its operations in various locations. At first glance it might appear as if an organization with a global product division is engaging in avoidable duplication of effort. Its product A division might have its own marketing personnel in Australia, and so might its product B division. However, the companies that opt for a global product division are usually concerned with products that are unique and distinctive, each of which requires its own specialized marketing force. Each specialized marketing force can then sharpen its skills and keep itself up to date. IBM is an example of a company with distinctive product groups, so the functional group attached to one product may lack the specialized expertise to handle other products. However, the more a company requires specialized personnel to handle its products, the more expense it adds to its operations.

Sometimes there is some duplication of effort. Each division might have its own section for liaison with the government, for instance. At the same time, the divisions might operate so independently that there is not much communication between them, and consequently be unable to learn from each other's failures and successes. To quote Daniels and Radebaugh (1998), 'For example, at one time in Westinghouse, one subsidiary was borrowing funds locally at an exorbitant rate, while another in the same country had excess cash.'

The global area division

An organization with a global area division structure divides its operations along geographic lines. Thus it has a division in charge of European operations, a division in charge of Asian operations, and so on.

When an organization opts for a global area division mode, it is attempting to use marketing, distribution, and other such strategies in a locally responsive fashion. At the same time, it is trying to reap the benefits of offering a globally branded product that has considerable brand equity. With this mode, there is no duplication of effort on the part of functional personnel. The local branch is also able to develop itself as a force to reckon with in its terrain. Sometimes the branch can become an entity as large, resource-rich and successful as the headquarters. This type of structural orientation is more in evidence in European-based companies than on other continents. Nestlé, for example, has a geographic area division. It has operations in more than 100 countries, so this structural form makes sense for it, since no one geographic area dominates operations. However, the company has modified the basic framework of the global area division to make it more vibrant, responsive and dynamic.

The global functional division

When an organization has a global functional division mode, operations are arranged so that the production division oversees all its production activities worldwide, the marketing division oversees all its marketing activities worldwide, and so on. Companies with a narrow range of similar products might prefer this type of structure, especially if similar production, marketing and other functional methods are used for the entire product range. This structure is found, for example, in mining and extraction companies such as Royal Dutch/Shell.

As an organization grows, the global functional division structure becomes unwieldy and difficult to maintain efficiently. Sometimes a local branch may start to maintain its own functional staff. For instance, although marketing activities are planned and undertaken globally by a Swiss organization's marketing group, it might still have marketing personnel in Canada who tap the distribution channels of that country in a locally responsive manner. This could lead to a duplication of efforts, or a conflict of interests, if the central marketing group strategizes differently from the Canadian marketing personnel.

This type of a structure is relevant when, for example, an organization is trying to optimize its use of manufacturing technology.

THE INTEGRATED NETWORK CONFIGURATION

Each branch should be viewed by headquarters as a source of ideas, skills, capabilities and knowledge which can be tapped and then placed in a pool for the common use of all members of the global organization.

Efficient local plants may be converted into international production centres; innovative national or regional development labs may be designated the company's 'centre of excellence' for a particular product or process development; and creative subsidiary marketing groups may be given a lead role in developing worldwide marketing strategies for certain products or businesses.

Bartlett and Ghoshal (1999)

The company thus leverages its strengths worldwide and evolves an implementable format for functioning as a single giant company. The capabilities of organizational members are distributed across points on the globe. The capabilities are however interdependent, as all members draw sustenance from the common pool of resources. As ideas are built upon, modified, altered and improved, it is never clear who is necessarily responsible for a widely applied concept, or from which location or culture it has originated. What is of the essence is that the entire global company is reaping the rewards. In this scheme of things, each branch enjoys an equal partnership with all other branches, as well as with headquarters.

Bartlett and Ghoshal's model (see box) is based on the view that the best management practices, concepts, ideas, capabilities and knowledge are transferable. This can be the case with transnational companies employing global managers. Most such managers have roots in more than one culture and have experienced three or four at firsthand. The mind-sets they have developed enable them to learn and accept new ideas. These companies are not likely to exhibit a preference for only a fixed structural form; a preference that is conditioned by their cultural origins. This is counter to the argument of Schneider and Barsoux (1997) that cultural differences can prevent the transfer of best practices.

Thus the corporate culture, core values, and mind-sets of the managers of a global organization all contribute to making it capable of operationalizing Bartlett and Ghoshal's integrated network configuration. To quote David Holt (1998), here, 'as a transnational corporation evolves, [its] diverse systems may blend, each contributing to the new organization until the management process itself no longer reflects any particular cultural perspective, but instead, develops an identity of its own'.

When a network arrangement connects all the branches of a transnational organization, the organization is able to constitute a common pool for its resources. Thus, the design of a transnational organization is all-important and cannot be allowed to evolve by mere chance or accident. It must be carefully and deliberately constructed and dynamically altered on a continuous basis. In an intercultural world, structure does not follow strategy or any other organizational variable. It accompanies all these other variables.

STRUCTURAL MECHANISMS

A transnational organization can employ various types of coordinating mechanism to hold it together as a unified entity. Thus Credit Suisse (see case study) is able to accommodate Project Copernicus within its dist-inctive structure because it is connected to the rest of Credit Suisse by coordinating mechanisms.

Within the Copernicus project, a lot of emphasis is placed on such structural dimensions as the weekly Monday meetings. This brings pro-ject members into contact with each other and obviates the emergence of culturally distinct work groups working apart from each other. Bring-ing together an intercultural work force may involve organizing a large number of trust-building lunches and dinners. Personal contact among members inevitably leads to positive outcomes in the long run.

A problem that can arise in allowing local branches to evolve their own structures is that people might lose sight of the overall objectives of the transnational corporation. The managers interviewed for this book all opine that this problem can be dealt with by insisting on profession-alism everywhere. This involves having clear performance evaluation criteria and standards. Thus, members have individual professional goals to which they can work. They also have to work with their colleagues, some of who may have culturally different backgrounds. The structure should help to bring diverse people together and enable them to connect at the human level.

It is tempting for a global company to try to achieve economies of scale and ease in functioning through standardization. Inappropriate standardization can actually lead to negative synergy. There is a differ-ence between mindless standardization, and drawing from a common pool of resources, practices that can be transferred to another context. Thus, although the Credit Suisse headquarters in Zurich is well aware of the structure at Project Copernicus, and the efficacy of that structure, it is not considering adopting that structure for itself. The reason has nothing to do with intercultural management. The structure of Project Copernicus would not suit the nature of operations at Zurich.

CASE STUDY: RESTRUCTURING AT SHELL

Holt (1998) described how Royal Dutch Shell reached the decision to restructure in 1995. The restructuring was intended to increase efficiency by removing unwanted bureaucracy. Accordingly, the decision was taken to replace the matrix organization by a global team approach, with strategic divisions headed by small groups of senior managers. Ultimately the team concept was to become the

cerned, the US researcher Janis (1982)
group harmony. Such groups could fall
ink. A lot of importance is attached to
eadership in corporate America today.
ng global companies so that all man-
their very best, to articulate visions
d to enable managers to participate in
78). Proponents of transformational
uently present such figures as Thomas
GE, and the late Sam Walton of Wal-
onal leaders.

pposed to shake up established ways
allenge groupthink syndromes, and
hallenge fellow group members may
t is believed to act as a deterrent to

hat they did not find teams to be an
al forms of organizational structure.
replaced by management using peer
red that the latter system could be as
published about the perils of teams
New United Motor in Freemont as
's expectations and under peer pres-
s too hard' (*Economist*, 1995).

of European culture before we return
hell and see how that global corpor-
onal structure changes in Japan, the
management perspective, the form-
as been an interesting development.
EU has undertaken many initiatives
daries. Although the EU has gone a
al regulations and labour laws, there
en countries.

ridge Management College in the
s revealing. This survey took into
anagers in 14 European countries,
l diversity of Europe, that at this
ch is capable of taking into account
lues.' It found huge differences
untries. This conclusion was conducted by the Cranfield School of

norm for every unit of every branch in every country where the
company had operations. This decision was made by the Committee
of Managing Directors, comprising six senior managers who coordinated and oversaw worldwide operations.

Shell organized itself into six major strategic divisions, based on
the global corporation's six main businesses of exploration and
production, refining and marketing oil products, chemicals, gas, coal,
and ancillary polymers. More than 100 worldwide divisions were
created, all of which had to employ the team concept.

By 1997 the restructuring seemed to have paid off. In that two
year period Royal Dutch Shell had overtaken Exxon in terms of sales
and assets. It had become one of the most profitable global corporations in the world. Shell's experience was that the team approach
was taking root and working well in all its units, despite the diverse
nature of its workforce, and the cultural differences between the
worldwide divisions.

The actual reorganizing effort was delegated to the managers at
the local branches. Thus each unit was able to pursue its own agenda
for change. In some places, the change required was marginal. In
others, such as in Argentina, the proposal was to completely replace
the bureaucratic structure by cross-functional management teams. In
some parts of Europe, the reorganization contributed to the rise of
self-managed teams. Various types of team building exercise were
undertaken to encourage camaraderie and an appreciation of team
endeavour. For example, in Belgium managers had to complete
military style obstacle courses as a team.

Many key managers from all cultures learnt to be team players and
take the reorganization in their stride. Others fell by the wayside. These
misfits in the new organizational structure chose to leave or were
forced out by peer pressure. It is more of the essence that because
of the legacy of the previous organizational structure, the changeover to team-based expectations and team incentives generated
different reactions in different units. Company-wide programmes
based on team incentives needed to be introduced in one fashion at
the British/Dutch headquarters, in another fashion in the United
States, and in yet another fashion in Japan. In other words, the
manner in which the new team incentives were introduced at Shell's
units needed to reflect local cultural realities.

Source: condensed from Holt (1998).

CULTURAL ASPECTS OF JAPAN, THE UNITED STATES AND EUROPE

If team incentives are to be implemented successfully in Japan, the United States, and Europe (for example, as in Royal Dutch Shell – see the case study), it is necessary to examine some of the cultural aspects of these three places.

Japanese corporations have attracted a lot of research interest in the last 20 years for their collaborative, team-based cultures. Hofstede (1980) has described the Japanese as having high uncertainty avoidance. At the same time, they attach a lot of importance to saving face and not making a person look bad in public. According to Copeland (1985), the Japanese go to great lengths to give negative feedback in a manner that is palatable to the recipient. People ignorant of the Japanese culture are often taken aback by the 'beating about the bush' that the Japanese resort to in the interests of maintaining harmony.

Katayama (1989) points out that managers in Japan are conversant with English. In many respects the Japanese are quite westernized, and this should not cause astonishment to a foreign visitor. A few practices are quintessentially Japanese. The traditional Japanese flooring, called tatami, is a straw-coloured reed mat laid wall to wall. The Japanese remove their footwear when they enter houses or rooms where tatami is used, and walk around in stockinged feet. Naturally they expect foreigners who come to restaurants or homes that use tatami to remove their footwear first. Managers from other countries who go to Japan should also adopt another Japanese custom immediately, since it means so much to the locals. This pertains to the use of business cards. In Japan, business cards are given and received with both hands. When Japanese people receive a business card, they read it carefully as a mark of courtesy. They also do not feel comfortable with unnecessary physical contact such as backslapping or elbow jostling.

Japanese managers like to organize periodic social events where managers give a performance, usually involving singing, often in the form of karaoke.

However, the Japanese do not necessarily expect managers from other cultures to greet them with a bow from the waist downwards. Japanese managers generally greet managers from other cultures with a handshake, although when they greet each other it may be with a bow. All the managers interviewed for this book agree that greeting with a handshake has become an international practice.

As far as formal groups are con
warned of the perils of excessive
prey to what he termed as groupt
the concept of transformational l
This concept centres on developi
agers are motivated to perform a
that inspire all these managers, an
the leadership process (Burns, 1
leadership in the United States fre
Watson Jr of IBM, Jack Welch of
Mart, as examples of transformati

Transformational leaders are su
of thinking among managers, ch
encourage others to do so too. To
create tension among them, but i
unproductive groupthink.

Many US employees reported
improvement over more hierarchi
Management by bosses was merely
pressure. Many US employees ave
oppressive as the former. An articl
in 1995 quoted an employee of
saying, 'People try to meet the tean
sure they end up pushing themselv

We now examine certain aspects
to the case study of Royal Dutch S
ation was able to effect organizatio
United States, and Europe. From a
ation of the European Union (EU) h
Hendry (1994) has reported that the
to improve mobility within its boun
long way in standardizing commerci
still exist cultural differences betwe

A survey undertaken by the Ash
United Kingdom (Durcan, 1994) i
consideration the views of senior m
and found that 'Such is the cultur
moment there is no single model whi
the complete range of national va
in perspectives among European co
firmed by an independent study cor

norm for every unit of every branch in every country where the company had operations. This decision was made by the Committee of Managing Directors, comprising six senior managers who coordinated and oversaw worldwide operations.

Shell organized itself into six major strategic divisions, based on the global corporation's six main businesses of exploration and production, refining and marketing oil products, chemicals, gas, coal, and ancillary polymers. More than 100 worldwide divisions were created, all of which had to employ the team concept.

By 1997 the restructuring seemed to have paid off. In that two year period Royal Dutch Shell had overtaken Exxon in terms of sales and assets. It had become one of the most profitable global corporations in the world. Shell's experience was that the team approach was taking root and working well in all its units, despite the diverse nature of its workforce, and the cultural differences between the worldwide divisions.

The actual reorganizing effort was delegated to the managers at the local branches. Thus each unit was able to pursue its own agenda for change. In some places, the change required was marginal. In others, such as in Argentina, the proposal was to completely replace the bureaucratic structure by cross-functional management teams. In some parts of Europe, the reorganization contributed to the rise of self-managed teams. Various types of team building exercise were undertaken to encourage camaraderie and an appreciation of team endeavour. For example, in Belgium managers had to complete military style obstacle courses as a team.

Many key managers from all cultures learnt to be team players and take the reorganization in their stride. Others fell by the wayside. These misfits in the new organizational structure chose to leave or were forced out by peer pressure. It is more of the essence that because of the legacy of the previous organizational structure, the changeover to team-based expectations and team incentives generated different reactions in different units. Company-wide programmes based on team incentives needed to be introduced in one fashion at the British/Dutch headquarters, in another fashion in the United States, and in yet another fashion in Japan. In other words, the manner in which the new team incentives were introduced at Shell's units needed to reflect local cultural realities.

Source: condensed from Holt (1998).

CULTURAL ASPECTS OF JAPAN, THE UNITED STATES AND EUROPE

If team incentives are to be implemented successfully in Japan, the United States, and Europe (for example, as in Royal Dutch Shell – see the case study), it is necessary to examine some of the cultural aspects of these three places.

Japanese corporations have attracted a lot of research interest in the last 20 years for their collaborative, team-based cultures. Hofstede (1980) has described the Japanese as having high uncertainty avoidance. At the same time, they attach a lot of importance to saving face and not making a person look bad in public. According to Copeland (1985), the Japanese go to great lengths to give negative feedback in a manner that is palatable to the recipient. People ignorant of the Japanese culture are often taken aback by the 'beating about the bush' that the Japanese resort to in the interests of maintaining harmony.

Katayama (1989) points out that managers in Japan are conversant with English. In many respects the Japanese are quite westernized, and this should not cause astonishment to a foreign visitor. A few practices are quintessentially Japanese. The traditional Japanese flooring, called tatami, is a straw-coloured reed mat laid wall to wall. The Japanese remove their footwear when they enter houses or rooms where tatami is used, and walk around in stockinged feet. Naturally they expect foreigners who come to restaurants or homes that use tatami to remove their footwear first. Managers from other countries who go to Japan should also adopt another Japanese custom immediately, since it means so much to the locals. This pertains to the use of business cards. In Japan, business cards are given and received with both hands. When Japanese people receive a business card, they read it carefully as a mark of courtesy. They also do not feel comfortable with unnecessary physical contact such as backslapping or elbow jostling.

Japanese managers like to organize periodic social events where managers give a performance, usually involving singing, often in the form of karaoke.

However, the Japanese do not necessarily expect managers from other cultures to greet them with a bow from the waist downwards. Japanese managers generally greet managers from other cultures with a handshake, although when they greet each other it may be with a bow. All the managers interviewed for this book agree that greeting with a handshake has become an international practice.

What is most fascinating about the culture surrounding Japanese management is the concept of the Japanese work group. Pascale and Athos (1982) have noted, 'to the Japanese, the birth of a group entails many of the concerns and worries attending the birth of a child'. They realize that mature, cohesive groups that arrive at decisions by consensus are not formed overnight. On the contrary, such groups require continuous attention and monitoring. Japanese managers expect to spend time and effort maintaining group harmony and effectiveness. Hence, Japanese groups tend to encourage participation without conflict or confrontation. Groups strive for qualitatively superior decisions, since it is a group that is rewarded for its performance. Individuals do not aspire for recognition on their own, since there is usually no proviso for this in Japanese companies. Holt opines that when it comes to promotions, preference is given to managers who can contribute to a congenial group atmosphere. When living in Japan, the author of this book noted that the Japanese word 'omayari' was used in conjunction with the managerial effort to enhance group harmony. There is no word in English that corresponds directly to 'omayari'. 'Omayari' is an amalgam of empathy, compassion and concern.

The US management culture has traditionally encouraged and rewarded individual achievement. Individual achievement is so highly valued by American corporations that they place a premium on recruiting managers with a high need for achievement. McClelland (1985) even studied how this trait could be enhanced so that US corporations could benefit.

It has been observed that in US companies the informal group has considerable influence, and may even work against company objectives. Thompson (1983) reported that the group he had observed at a beef-processing plant in the United States 'practically made a game out of doing forbidden things simply to see if they could get away with it'. On the other hand, Krackhardt and Hanson (1993) stipulate that informal networks can yield positive results to a corporation when they are properly understood and handled. These researchers found that three types of informal relationship networks existed in the US banking industry. Their recommendation was that corporations should revamp their formal organization structures to allow these informal relationship networks to thrive. When the informal structure is allowed to complement the formal one, the former can be used to solve problems, improve the quality of work life, and enable the corporation to show superior performance. Among other things, informal relationship networks can cut through reporting procedures in a beneficial way.

As far as formal groups are concerned, the US researcher Janis (1982) warned of the perils of excessive group harmony. Such groups could fall prey to what he termed as groupthink. A lot of importance is attached to the concept of transformational leadership in corporate America today. This concept centres on developing global companies so that all managers are motivated to perform at their very best, to articulate visions that inspire all these managers, and to enable managers to participate in the leadership process (Burns, 1978). Proponents of transformational leadership in the United States frequently present such figures as Thomas Watson Jr of IBM, Jack Welch of GE, and the late Sam Walton of Wal-Mart, as examples of transformational leaders.

Transformational leaders are supposed to shake up established ways of thinking among managers, challenge groupthink syndromes, and encourage others to do so too. To challenge fellow group members may create tension among them, but it is believed to act as a deterrent to unproductive groupthink.

Many US employees reported that they did not find teams to be an improvement over more hierarchical forms of organizational structure. Management by bosses was merely replaced by management using peer pressure. Many US employees averred that the latter system could be as oppressive as the former. An article published about the perils of teams in 1995 quoted an employee of New United Motor in Freemont as saying, 'People try to meet the team's expectations and under peer pressure they end up pushing themselves too hard' (*Economist*, 1995).

We now examine certain aspects of European culture before we return to the case study of Royal Dutch Shell and see how that global corporation was able to effect organizational structure changes in Japan, the United States, and Europe. From a management perspective, the formation of the European Union (EU) has been an interesting development. Hendry (1994) has reported that the EU has undertaken many initiatives to improve mobility within its boundaries. Although the EU has gone a long way in standardizing commercial regulations and labour laws, there still exist cultural differences between countries.

A survey undertaken by the Ashridge Management College in the United Kingdom (Durcan, 1994) is revealing. This survey took into consideration the views of senior managers in 14 European countries, and found that 'Such is the cultural diversity of Europe, that at this moment there is no single model which is capable of taking into account the complete range of national values.' It found huge differences in perspectives among European countries. This conclusion was confirmed by an independent study conducted by the Cranfield School of

Management, which developed profiles of over 2,500 European executives. Nordic countries were seen as preferring teamwork and transparent
communication. However, there was no universal consensus among
Nordic managers about how team processes were to be managed. German-
speaking countries seemed to believe that efficiency was achieved
through hierarchical systems. Those managers who occupied senior
positions owed their position to demonstrated technical competence and
expertise. Managers from Anglo-Saxon countries and those from Southern
Mediterranean ones showed a preference for being led, which implies
they had a preference for companies that are hierarchically structured.
A large proportion of the Spanish managers surveyed wanted to work
for a boss who was benevolently paternalistic. Anglo-Saxon managers
wanted to be led by bosses with superior ability, who could be held
accountable for their professional decisions. French managers preferred
structural arrangements with high power distances between levels and
little opportunity for subordinate participation. There was therefore little
communication between levels.

Although we have drawn attention to the differences in work cultures
within Europe, it must be mentioned that in the last decade several
global companies in Europe have given attention to the concept of high-
performance work teams. These teams are self-managed, self-organized
and self-regulating. They believe in open communications as well as
peer selection and peer review. The University of Strathclyde Graduate
Business School made a recent video documenting a high-performance
work group created by the multinational Digital Corporation at their
plant in Ayr, Scotland, that has attracted some interest in Europe. The
characteristics of the Ayr high-performance work teams are that they
have 'front to back responsibility', targets set by team members, members
who develop themselves laterally so that they have multiple skills,
members who share their knowledge base and skills, a reward system
that is based on skills and how those skills are applied, and are committed to high levels of performance.

High-performance teams in Europe have proved to be a mixed blessing,
despite all the hype accompanying their actual functioning. Comment-
ators have shown themselves unable to decide whether empowerment,
self-determination and team operations are decidedly better than supervision and control, or individual performance. Some of the authority
mandated to high-performance work teams has been retracted. Some
teams have been asked to maintain the levels of performance they
initially displayed, while being given less authority than before. Bergstrom
(1994) reported that he found frustration, disenchantment and distrust in

a premier European corporation that had introduced high-performance work teams.

Keeping in mind some of the cultural features of Japan, the United States, and Europe that have been discussed above, we now examine how the structural changes undertaken by Royal Dutch Shell will impact on its operations in these three cultures.

Japan

It is expected that the team approach will find favour in Japan. Team incentives will also be well received. Group problem solving is well entrenched now in Japanese companies and among Japanese managers. Hence, when Royal Dutch Shell 'initiates' a team approach at its Japanese branch, its Japanese managers will be operating in a fashion that finds ready favour with them. They are likely to adopt an organizational structure that is networked enough to permit the free flow of discussion and cooperation without which true teamwork is problematic.

However, the structure would not be entirely delayered. Japanese managers are accustomed to deferring to their seniors and accommodating some measure of hierarchy. The fascinating feature of Japanese management is that hierarchy coexists with the notion of teams and distributed participation. Teams are constituted so that they comprise managers of the same level. Generally, these teams are self-managed. Nonetheless, Japanese managers feel comfortable communicating their team decisions to senior managers and then receiving affirmation from them. As far as Royal Dutch Shell is concerned, this would suggest that they might have to train Japanese teams to be more self-confident about the quality of their decisions, as well as to accept responsibility for those decisions. Japanese teams have to learn to do without the notion that their decisions are going to be vetted by more experienced people. This slight shortfall is more than offset by the fact that the team approach and team incentives will take root quicker and work much better in Japan than in the United States or Europe.

The United States

The expectation here is that the team approach will meet with resistance initially. US managers are trained, at US business schools and on the job, to be individualistic and achievement oriented. This orientation is further reinforced by the prevailing culture at large. One of the driving forces of US managers is to be rewarded for superior performance. Any attempt to introduce team incentives therefore is likely to be met with stiff opposition. However, US managers have been known to work reasonably well in teams after a corporation has made this structure an explicit policy. Team behaviour is a skill that US managers have to consciously and deliberately learn. Like many management skills it can be learnt, despite the cultural context.

US managers have employed a multi-pronged attack to foster teamwork. First, a significant amount of research in the United States has been devoted to the notion of team building. Not surprisingly, the team building process as recommended by US academicians would appear contrived to managers from cultures like Japan. Second, attention is paid to the development of teams through management training. Third, some companies formally evaluate their managers with regard to team behaviour in performance appraisal systems. This gives US managers a goal to work towards, the goal of being a team player. The individualistic orientation of US managers is usually accompanied by goal-directed behaviour. Corporations have harnessed this very tendency of US managers to work towards goals to encourage them to become team players. The organizational structure that Royal Dutch Shell would need for their branch in the United States would be one that does not accord any special status to a member of a team. This would entail dispensing with hierarchy and one-way communication. Additionally, lateral communication, fewer levels in the branch, and increased transparency will need to be firmly established. Ultimately, team incentives will be accepted provided they are introduced after the managers have been adequately prepared for their new roles.

Europe

In Europe, the team concept is likely to be accepted in principle by Royal Dutch Shell managers. However, it has to be kept in mind that there is variation regarding culture and management practices within Europe. Challenges are most likely to be thrown up when managers from different European countries have to work together as a team.

Scandinavian managers are known to have a penchant for group work and consensual decision making. They have shown this in practice in managerial settings. The British claim to have first propounded the benefits of restructuring work design by focusing on teams. Britain's Tavistock Institute of Human Relations has done pioneering work in this area. The French on the other hand subscribe to the notion of status and differentials. Germans prefer to work in a structure that has its authority unambiguously defined. Hence, the intervention effort to make German or French managers work in teams would have to be designed differently from that for Scandinavians.

The task of inducing team behaviour is complicated when managers of different European nationalities work together. It can be done, however, through training and mentoring. For Royal Dutch Shell the implications for organizational structure are that complete decentralization will be called for. The reporting relationships will have to be to peers rather than superiors. A few levels of authority may have to be removed altogether, so that managers can fall into teams at uniform levels.

SUMMARY

The type of structure assumed by a transnational organization determines the extent to which it can accommodate diversity in its work force. A flexible structure that is networked is more compatible with the systems and processes that permit intercultural management than more traditional modes. Intercultural management necessitates active effort on the part of top managers to ensure that members of all national and ethnic cultures become part of the mosaic within that organization. A flexible, networked organizational structure makes possible such an effort.

The organizational structure appropriate for intercultural management goes beyond being flexible, however. It is also one that is perpetually evolving. Its design is continuously being altered to reflect the cultural backgrounds of its members. As members from a particular cultural background join a transnational organization, they can influence processes provided their influence is positive. The influence that is exerted could well be an outcome of ethnic culture.

2

Communication and intercultural management

CASE STUDY: NESTLÉ

Pierre Listard-Vogt, a former managing director of Nestlé, is quoted by John Daniels and Lee Radebaugh (1998) as having said, 'perhaps we are the only real multinational company existing'. As much as 98 per cent of Nestlé's sales revenue is generated from outside Switzerland, where its headquarters is based. UNCTAD's composite index on transnationality credits Nestlé with being the most international of the world's 100 largest manufacturers. Nestlé prides itself on having an intercultural top management team working at its headquarters. The Swiss are a minority in the top management team. The topmost echelon, called Group Management, has nine members. Of these, two are Austrian, one is Spanish, one is Swiss, one is Mexican, two are from the United States, one is British, and one is Swedish. This Group Management is indeed the apex, and comprises the CEO, the executive vice-president for Europe, the executive vice-president for the Americas, the executive vice-president for Africa/Asia, the executive vice-president marketing, the executive vice-president finance, the executive vice-president HR & corporate, the executive vice-president global programmes, and the executive vice-president, productions.

An important milestone in the global growth and development of the company was the establishment of the Nestlé International Training and Conference Centre near its headquarters in Vevey. This centre was given the responsibility of ensuring that the 'Nestlé spirit', along with Nestlé strategies, and the Nestlé way of doing things, is disseminated throughout the company. The company has, after all, 220,000 people spread over more than 100 countries. With such a wide geographic spread of operations, Nestlé has to ensure that communication is a tie that binds.

In 1997, Nestlé headquarters formulated a paradigm for functioning that had to be communicated to all countries where they had operations. This paradigm was called the Basic Nestlé Management and Leadership Principles, and articulated the 'Nestlé spirit and culture'. The Basic Nestlé Management and Leadership Principles were conceived and formulated by Nestlé's top managers at its headquarters. They carried the stamp of approval of Helmut Maucher, the outgoing CEO, and Peter Brabeck, the incoming CEO. The collaboration of both CEOs in this effort is also a testimonial of the Nestlé spirit. After the Basic Nestlé Management and Leadership Principles were formulated and laid down, they had to be communicated to every employee in every country. The Principles were to be made the credo of every branch, and then applied continuously by all employees. The documents were then despatched to the Nestlé main branch of every country where it had operations. The human resources department (HRD) at the main branch was entrusted with the responsibility of disseminating the Principles to all the Nestlé employees of that country. The HRD in each country had the mandate to decide the manner and method of dissemination. The modus operandi did in fact vary from country to country. Each country adopted a modus operandi that fitted in with the culture of that country.

Headquarters at Vevey however remained connected with all the country branches. It received communication from these branches at specified dates, reporting on the nature and extent of progress. A year after the launch, the head of the International Training Centre, Vevey, was asked to collect material and note the extent of progress achieved. It was observed that a variety of culture-specific methods had been adopted to disseminate the Basic Management and Leadership Principles. Nestlé Italy had prepared an elaborate and riveting educational video to drive home the Principles. Nestlé Switzerland chose first to assess where the branch already stood with regard to the Principles. All the managers then agreed, by consensus, how they would move forward. Nestlé Korea mobilized its entire workforce to attend workshops on how the Principles could be imbibed and fostered.

The successes, failures, and general experiences of the social-
ization programmes in one country were then passed on to others
to facilitate vicarious learning. In fact, the dissemination process that
has been employed in different countries is discussed at all international training programmes conducted on a continuous basis, at
the International Training and Conference Centre. This enables
participants to appreciate how the process of communication can
vary from culture to culture, even when the content remains the same.
Participants can particularly take note of how a company relates to
its internal customers, and how the way it communicates to these
stakeholders will impact on its position in the global market. The
autonomy given to local Nestlé branches to communicate using
processes relevant to local cultures is also aligned with the corporate
philosophy of encouraging adaptation to local conditions and consumer habits.

A senior manager from Nestlé explained:

Although the Training Centre is in charge of the differentiation of the
Nestlé spirit, it is not alone in this task. The dissemination process was
achieved as follows:

1. The document was produced by top management and then des-
    patched to all country branches by Headquarters.

2. Each market (branch) was asked to disseminate the Principles on its
    own.

3. The Training Centre was asked to develop a presentation of the
    Principles. This presentation was made available to the markets that
    wanted it. They were not forced to use this presentation. The Training
    Centre was also asked to make a report after a year on the achievements
    of the markets vis-à-vis the dissemination and institutionalization of
    the Principles. The centre was also detailed to collect and keep the
    markets' documents pertaining to their achievements.

4. The Training Centre also committed itself to discuss the commun-
    ication of the Principles at every course they conduct. During the
    discussion sessions devoted for this purpose, the participants from
    the various markets represented there would explain what they did
    for the success of the communication effort in their terrain. This
    would contribute to what we call a cross-fertilization of ideas.

5. Finally, the Training Centre was charged with the responsibility of
    working with the heads of training worldwide, to integrate the key
    elements of the Principles in each training activity and have the

Principles suffuse these training activities. The general management in the markets continuously constitute study groups to review the application process of the Principles. Both in the markets and at the centre, at each Cadre Meeting, the status regarding the application of specific Principles is always discussed. Thus, at each level, whatever can be done to push the Principles throughout Nestlé is done.

EXTRACTS FROM THE BASIC NESTLÉ MANAGEMENT AND LEADERSHIP PRINCIPLES

1. General principles

- Nestlé is more people and product oriented than systems oriented. Systems are necessary and useful but should never be an end in themselves.
- Nestlé is committed to create value for its shareholders. However, Nestlé does not favour short-term profit and shareholder value maximization at the expense of long-term successful business development. But Nestlé remains conscious of the need to generate a reasonable profit each year.
- Nestlé is as decentralized as possible, within the limits imposed by basic policy and strategy decisions, as well as the group-wide need for coordination and management development.
- Nestlé is committed to the concept of continuous improvement of its activities, thus avoiding more dramatic one-time changes as much as possible.

4. Qualities and characteristics of a Nestlé manager

The higher the level of the position and the responsibility of a Nestlé Manager, the more he/she should be selected on the basis of the following criteria (in addition to professional education, skills and practical experience):

1) courage, solid nerves and composure; capacity to handle stress;

2) ability to learn, open-mindedness and perceptiveness;

3) ability to communicate, to motivate and to develop people;

4) ability to create a climate of innovation;

> 5) thinking in context;
>
> 6) credibility: in other words 'practise what you preach';
>
> 7) willingness to accept change and ability to manage change;
>
> 8) international experience and understanding of other cultures.
>
> In addition: broad interests, a good general education, responsible attitude and behaviour and sound health.

Despite the centralized directives described in the box, Nestlé's country managers and country HRD departments have communicated and institutionalized these Principles using their discretion. In the Philippines, for example, three features of the dissemination process adopted by the local branch reflected the Filipino culture. The first feature is that the Basic Nestlé Management and Leadership Principles were cascaded throughout the organization in top-down fashion. This is in keeping with the Filipino tradition of people wanting to emulate their seniors and superiors. Hence, the uppermost echelon was educated about the Principles first. This effort was made by the President of Nestlé Philippines, JB Santos.

The second feature is that Nestlé Philippines' dissemination process followed the formal organizational structure in managing the downward cascading of the Principles. And finally, the execution of the Principles were integrated into the branch's operational plans. To quote JB Santos, 'the execution of the Principles could then be understood as commitments, and therefore, subject to performance measures'. Further, every manager was assessed to ascertain the extent to which he/she had developed the Principles.

The process by which the Basic Nestlé Management and Leadership Principles were communicated to employees by Nestlé New Zealand was quite different. At this branch an assessment questionnaire was developed, to ascertain the extent to which Nestlé New Zealand managers demonstrated Item Four (qualities and characteristics of a Nestlé manager) of the Principles.

Unlike the case of Nestlé Philippines, however, Nestlé New Zealand's assessment questionnaire was developed entirely as a self-assessment exercise. Managers were requested to assess themselves a priori, just before the intervention to communicate the Basic Nestlé Management and Leadership Principles was undertaken. The Principles were then communicated to branch employees via workshops.

Part II: Assessment of leadership competencies

The organization seeks to develop in each and every member of the management team a set of leadership competencies that would reinforce effective performance on the job. These competencies are aligned with "The Basic Nestlé Management and Leadership Principles", and specific behavioural indicators are listed below.

For each of these competencies, please:

1. Encircle the statements that are deemed relevant to the responsibilities of the jobholder.
2. Check in the appropriate box your best assessment of the jobholder's performance in that area.

	Needs improvement	Proficient
A. Ability to create a climate of innovation. Thinking in context:		
1. Able to generate and encourage creative solutions to work situations. Open to trying different and novel ways to deal with organizational problems and opportunities.		
2. Established goals that are challenging and realistic and applies the appropriate tools to achieve short-term and long-term objectives.		
3. Is able to see the big picture. Takes into account issues that are broader and longer range than those immediately apparent. Considers the impact of one's actions on other parts of the organization.		

Comments _____

	Needs improvement	Proficient
B. Ability to communicate, motivate, and develop people:		
4. Effectively expresses ideas in individual and group situations. Encourages and elicits ideas and suggestions from his people.		
5. Utilizes appropriate interpersonal and leadership styles and methods in guiding others towards goal achievement. Modifies behaviour according to tasks and individuals involved.		
6. Develops people to their full potential by planning effective developmental activities related to current and future jobs. Delegates responsibilities and authority effectively.		

Comments _____

	Needs improvement	Proficient
C. Willingness to accept and ability to manage change:		
7. Remains effective in a changing environment and in different situations and modifies approach and style to achieve goal. Anticipates and accepts changes.		

Comments _____

	Needs improvement	Proficient
D. Courage, solid nerves and composure, capacity to handle stress:		
8. Acts decisively. Displays tenacity in defending and retaining key points. Commits oneself to taking action once a decision has been made.		
9. Takes responsibility and ownership of the problem until it is solved. Makes clear recommendations.		
10. Is confident and emotionally stable. Realistically evaluates own strengths and limitations.		
11. Maintains stable performance under stress and/or opposition. Engenders trust.		

Comments _____

	Needs improvement	Proficient
E. Credibility:		
12. Maintains social, ethical and organizational norms in conducting internal and external business activities. Consistently demonstrates the qualities and competencies of an effective leader, thus setting a good example for emulation.		
13. Maintains and applies technical and professional knowledge and expertise in performing job functions to support business objectives.		
14. Keeps himself abreast with relevant and latest technical and functional developments and trends in his area of expertise. Looks for the opportunity to apply his new knowledge and skills.		

Comments _____

Figure 2.1   *Extract from the internal communication effort of Nestlé Philippines to disseminate the Basic Nestlé Management and Leadership Principles*

Team Nestlé in action!
Is it happening, everywhere, all the time?
Use this sheet to assess the Nestlé Manager who has asked for your feedback. Use a scale of:
1)   Still at the start line;
2)   Has made progress in this area;
3)   Demonstrates this action/attribute more often than not;
4)   Typically demonstrates this action/attribute.
As a Nestlé Manager, this person

Directs:
1 . . . has a clear sense of Nestlé's direction and formulates a carefully calculated position;
2 . . . interprets direction concisely and plans action to achieve budgets and targets;
3 . . . has a strong sense of what can be achieved to meet a goal/task;
4 . . . is highly focused in accordance with economic objectives and targets of the big picture;
5 . . . is a risk taker, a visionary who thinks outside the 9 dots;
6 . . . uses strategic, forward thinking;
7 . . . believes in quality in everything we do.

Involves:
8 . . . seeks ownership by other to ensure quick implementation;
9 . . . encourages cross-fertilization of ideas throughout;
10 . . . shares all relevant information, briefing people fully in plenty of time;
11 . . . establishes a monitored environment of self-control, personal responsibility and frequent feedback;
12 . . . stimulates a great sense of pride, belonging and commitment to the Nestlé team;
13 . . . fosters an open, frank, approachable climate;
14 . . . is positive and supportive of Nestlé and what we stand for;
15 . . . is proud to work for Nestlé.

Communicates:
16 . . . shows openness to others' views, displaying willingness and ability to listen and manage divergent views;
17 . . . listens fully to others' viewpoints, understanding their issues and concerns, yet responding with frank feedback;
18 . . . diffuses anger and tension by listening without interruption;
19 . . . listens openly, participates in all meetings;
20 . . . actively listens, showing supportive gestures during meetings;
21 . . . demonstrates good listening, showing understanding and empathy with team and peers;
22 . . . uses face-to-face direct dealings;
23 . . . communicates through talking, listening, responding and acting.

Leads:
24 . . . identifies performance weaknesses and knows how to close the gap;
25 . . . delegates work and supports self-direction rather than steering;
26 . . . considers him/herself fully accountable for his/her sphere of responsibility;
27 . . . develops people through praise and encourages creativity;
28 . . . recognizes performance and coaches to maximize potential;

29 . . . develops people through effective appraisals and relevant training;
30 . . . demonstrates constructive openness during performance appraisals;
31 . . . acknowledges and praises team members' contributions;
32 . . . encourages dynamic teamwork characterized by mutual respect and empathy;
33 . . . encourages innovation and new ideas;
34 . . . fosters outward looking, to encourage new ideas;
35 . . . has a strong sense of teamwork.

Learns:
36 . . . is always looking for a better way;
37 . . . distils and analyses the relevant information, using own and others' experience or knowledge to make rational decisions;
38 . . . has an ability to analyse data accurately and methodically;
39 . . . has an ability to tune into information that few others notice;
40 . . . is sensitive to cultural differences including politics, customs, habits, etiquette and food preferences;
41 . . . is able to relate to different people and situations from around the world;
42 . . . is able to overcome cultural barriers including language and different thinking patterns.

Changes:
43 . . . is always ready to push the boundaries to test responsiveness to new initiatives (internal or external);
44 . . . is responsive to new ideas and technology;
45 . . . will give something a go . . . a risk taker;
46 . . . has the awareness and knowledge to foresee change;
47 . . . has a balanced view, and drives change positively;
48 . . . is willing and ready to adapt, and has a high tolerance of new ideas.

Knowledge & experience (international & local):
49 . . . has international knowledge and skills providing a broad experience base;
50 . . . has knowledge of reference manuals and guidelines and how these affect the issue under discussion;
51 . . . understands the industry and competitive environments;
52 . . . is fully informed on details and relevant information;
53 . . . has the background, experience, knowledge and skills to make appropriate decisions, and knows when to get help.

Personal strength:
54 . . . uses emotional strength to make sound decisions;
55 . . . has a high level of common sense, respected by others;
56 . . . is quietly confident, being self assured and demonstrating self esteem;
57 . . . has a high degree of personal responsibility that means total dependability;
58 . . . is ethical, fair and trustworthy in all dealings;
59 . . . owns up to mistakes;
60 . . . is intrinsically honest, displaying courage and openness in all interactions, in a way that supports and adds value;
61 . . . sets and maintains high personal standards of quality and reliability;
62 . . . can be described with the word integrity, as a typical way he/she speaks and acts;
63 . . . visibly supports others' viewpoints, or right to express these, maintaining eye contact, and patiently listening;

64 . . . has broad interests and a well-rounded character;
65 . . . uses honesty and openness, leaving no place for hidden agendas; or fears
that threaten the communication and/or flow of information;
66 . . . always talks directly to people, and not about them, to others;
67 . . . is looked to for ideas;
68 . . . stays calm and composed, not overreacting in difficult situations;
69 . . . is fit, healthy and professional in appearance;
70 . . . can be relied upon to carry out decisions made;
71 . . . 'walks the talk' – not paying lipservice;
72 . . . is disciplined, demonstating self-control and restraint;
73 . . . is able to fully accept and support a situation, if required;
74 . . . confidently challenges others' viewpoints or agenda to ensure a balanced,
considered decision;
75 . . . has a sense of style.
Examples:
Can you give some examples?
This is valuable feedback. Especially if you've allocated a 1 or 4 to an attribute or
action, give a 'for instance' that led to your view, using the item numbers.

Figure 2.2   *Extract from the internal communication effort of Nestlé
New Zealand to disseminate the Basic Nestlé Management and Leadership Principles*

These workshops comprised groups of people occupying different
positions in the Nestlé New Zealand hierarchy. Managers used the
self-assessment exercise to determine where they stood as Nestlé
managers. They then used the workshops to gauge how they could
strengthen their competencies, so that they could evolve into the
kind of manager Nestlé (global) hoped they could become.

Only part of the dissemination process adopted by Nestlé New
Zealand reflected the individualistic nature of New Zealand's culture.
The other part took cognizance of the fact that there already existed
a corporate culture at Nestlé New Zealand, and Nestlé New Zealand
managers mostly felt part of this corporate culture. Hence, the
managers assessed immediately before the dissemination intervention knew how they stood collectively. The workshops were then
used to chalk out the direction in which the managers collectively
were to move.

In this part of the case study, we are chronicling in some detail the
dissemination effort of Nestlé New Zealand. While the emphasis of
this case study is on the variety of approaches adopted by Nestlé
branches, we are also reporting more extensively the route followed
by this one branch.

Jot down your thoughts in response to these questions:
1. When you read the Document, what were your immediate thoughts?
2. If you had to choose one of the General Principles as our greatest strength, in New Zealand, which would it be?
3. Which of the Organizational Principles is the greatest challenge, and why?
4. Which of the 'qualities and characterisitics of a Nestlé manager' is most prevalent, and which absent, when considering a typical Nestlé New Zealand Manager?
5. What aspects of the Nestlé Culture, and traditional roots, will come under greatest threat, in the years ahead?

Figure 2.3   *Extract from the internal communication effort of Nestlé New Zealand to disseminate the Basic Nestlé Management and Leadership Principles*

The preliminary workshops conducted at Nestlé New Zealand were intended to communicate the Principles to all employees. First of all the workshops made the employees aware of the Principles. Second, employees had to understand what these Principles signified and represented. All employees had to share a common understanding of the Principles. Further, this understanding had to be an accurate interpretation of what the authors of the Principles had intended.

The next step was to operationalize these Principles at Nestlé New Zealand. There were two facets to this operationalization process. One facet pertained to macro-level reengineering, so that the branch as a collective entity moved in the direction indicated by the Principles. For instance, operationalization of the principles called 'Organizational Principles' stipulated in the Basic Nestlé Management and Leadership Principles called for macro-level reengineering. A sample 'Organizational Principle' reads as follows:

> Nestlé is in favour of flat organizations with few levels of management and broad spans of control, including project team and task forces. Networking and horizontal communication are encouraged without blurring the authority of the managers in the decision-making process. These principles aim to make the organizational structure and working methods more flexible and efficient, without undermining the basic hierarchy (the basic concept being as much hierarchy as necessary, as little as possible).

The other facet of the operationalization process at Nestlé New Zealand referred to micro-level improvement. In other words, changes had to be effected at the level of individual employees. That is why all the employees assessed themselves both before the preliminary workshops and at the conclusion of the workshops. They then had to devise action plans for themselves, so they could become aligned with the style of management outlined in the Principles document.

Employees committed themselves after the preliminary workshops to individual change programmes. To ensure that the change programmes were grounded in reality, emphasis was placed on making them completely actionable. All managers were therefore expected to translate their change programme into practical, everyday actions.

Nestlé New Zealand appointed a project team representative of their managers to consider the practical, real-life application of the Principles document. This project team translated the Principles into 75 everyday actions. All managers had to design a change programme for themselves keeping in mind these 75 actions. These actions were reference points against which they could benchmark themselves. Additionally, they could generate further actions to strive for, which suited their personality and designation, but were also aligned to the Principles.

At the end of the preliminary workshops, the managers of Nestlé New Zealand agreed that the acronym KASH described the components of the change effort. KASH stood for Knowledge, Attitudes, Skills and Habits. They also averred that 'performance is a mixture of skills multiplied by attitude'. Their philosophy about the change effort was based on the premise that skills could be taught and learnt in the short run more efficaciously than attitudes.

Hence the prime initiative for the change effort had to emanate from the individual managers themselves. It was in view of this that managers had to engage in self-assessment. Managers were expected to be so comfortable with the actions they had selected that with time these actions would become habitual.

To ensure that motivation for the change programmes did not wane, arrangements were made to monitor progress. Additionally, it was decided to organize periodic follow-up workshops to support the change efforts made by the managers. The workshops would provide opportunities to the managers to review what they had achieved and commit themselves anew to the change programmes.

Nestlé New Zealand worked at creating an environment conducive to change. Hence, at the preliminary workshops, likely obstacles to managers taking appropriate actions were identified. The workshops also identified what senior managers should do to facilitate their subordinates' change programmes. They were entrusted with the responsibility of setting the example by 'living the principles'.

Linking the micro-level efforts with the macro efforts were team change programmes. Managers were divided into teams of people who actually worked together at Nestlé as teams. The teams also developed strategic plans of action. The objective thus was to achieve a cohesive change effort for the whole of Nestlé New Zealand.

All the dissemination efforts at Nestlé's various locations worldwide have required adaptation to local employee orientation. Nestlé India's first step was to present the Basic Nestlé Management and Leadership Principles to their managers at training programmes. Each of the Principles was supported by illustrations and examples relevant to the local context. This was necessary to strike a responsive chord with the Indian managers from the start. Indian managers are generally sceptical of training programmes where valid principles and tenets are espoused, but the supportive cases and illustrations are western. Thus, Nestlé's country branches have often incorporated features into their dissemination process that have made possible the speedy operationalization of the Principles. Nestlé Nigeria made it a point to present the Principles to workers and other non-management staff at management/union meetings. This reflects the industrial climate of Nigeria. Workers often belong to powerful unions. While they should not kowtow to unreasonable union demands, it is important for workers corporations to ensure that workers do not feel alienated. In the case of Nestlé Brazil, the first step was to have senior managers discuss the Principles, and then prepare a document delineating how the Principles could be enacted in practice. Two groups of senior managers engaged in the discussions in separate workshops. One workshop comprised the 10 members of the topmost echelons. The second workshop involved some 50 managers from the next most senior echelon. The two echelons were separated to ensure that both groups would be highly participative at their workshops, and they were. Otherwise, the managers from the less senior echelon would have felt constrained by the presence of their superiors.

The need for common core values to bind Nestlé together worldwide caused it to articulate its Principles. These Principles then had to be communicated to all its branches. The process of communication has varied from culture to culture. What was actually communicated remained the same. This has helped Nestlé develop its managers regardless of where they are, to espouse a commonly held set of values or beliefs.

Inferences

What can be said about how communication should be facilitated within the context of intercultural management? Based on existing academic research and the actual corporate experience of Nestlé, we would like to suggest the following.

Learning through the cross-fertilization of ideas: the importance of exchanging learning experiences through cross-cultural programmes

Hans Johr, a vice-president at Nestlé, acknowledges that an important aspect of communication across cultures is 'bringing together managers from different markets, and getting them to exchange their professional experiences, and share their success stories'. Nestlé has been doing this continually and consistently at its International Training and Conference Centre. Managers of comparable competencies, but from different cultures, assemble here to learn from each other. It was only natural that the effort of dissemination of the Principles was also used as a source of learning for Nestlé's managers. Here what they learned was how communication can be modified to reflect cultural sensibilities. A Brazilian manager from Nestlé Brazil commented that he had learnt a great deal about communication in different cultures after attending a seminar where the dissemination effort was presented and discussed. To begin with, he learnt that Swiss managers prefer to be addressed by their surname, while US managers expect to be on a first name basis from the moment they are introduced.

In the new world of global corporations, managers are increasingly finding that there is no substitute for the intercultural learning that comes from direct contact with people from different parts of the world. An executive advisor of 3Com notes that in her experience, actual first-hand personal experience accelerates intercultural learning as nothing else can (Solomon, 1998).

Daniels and Radebaugh (1998) have observed, 'People in all cultures have culturally ingrained responses to given situations.' When the cultural indoctrination is very strong, they expect that people from other cultures should communicate in the same fashion as people from their own culture. International experience and exposure moderate such expectations. Such exposure also sensitizes managers to the wide variation in communication processes across cultures. Seasoned global managers have no rigid expectations about how communication should be effected. They appreciate that the purpose of communication is to make a connection between individuals or groups of people.

Like Nestlé, other corporations have constituted programmes to facilitate cross-cultural communication. The US-based Mobil Corporation, for instance, which has operations in more than 140 countries, has a Speed Pass Program, designed to bring together representative managers from all its locations. What Nestlé has always emphasized, however, is the importance of communication in its global programmes. Appropriate communication is the tie that binds. Inadequate attention accorded to the process and content of communication by other global companies has created problems when they constituted global teams.

Another important advantage has accrued to Nestlé from engaging in a cross-fertilization of ideas through its communication experience: the ability to take best practices from one culture, and transplant them to another culture. What is remarkable about the Nestlé effort is that Nestlé headquarters does not impose the dissemination of best practices. Local branches decide for themselves whether they want to adopt a best practice from another branch. The concept of taking best practices and applying them across cultures is considered desirable by Nestlé. However, the company believes that the local market should have a felt need for doing so. Otherwise the best practice will not meet with the local acceptance necessary to ensure its successful execution. The managers of local branches are the best qualified to ascertain whether a practice effective elsewhere would find acceptance within the context of their own culture.

According to the managers interviewed for this book, even if a global company decides that a particular practice developed in one location is so good It merits being made a standard practice at all its locations, it is preferable for local managers to implement it. The method of implementation is also to be left to the local manager's discretion.

Having a lingua franca

Most transnational organizations have a lingua franca that enables all their managers, irrespective of cultural origin, to communicate with each other. More often than not, this lingua franca is English. The largest number of countries use English as a prevalent language. It is a predominant language in 44 countries. It is the unofficial lingua franca of several Asian and African countries, especially the former colonies of the United Kingdom. English is gaining in importance in several emerging-market countries. Vietnam, for instance, has switched to English studies. Newman (1995) observes that globalization is leading to more young people in Europe learning English today than ever in the past.

Sweden is an example of a European country that does not share a common language with other countries. However, Swedes have a very high level of foreign language skills; almost all of them speak English, as Reihlen has noted (2001).

Thus it is that the lingua franca for global management purposes at Nestlé is English. The executive board conducts its business in English. The corporate headquarters management communicates primarily in English, even if such communication is supported by exchanges in French, German or Spanish. The international training programmes are in English. The official document, the Basic Nestlé Management and Leadership Principles, is in English, although it has been translated into the languages of most of the countries where Nestlé has operations. This is despite the fact that Nestlé is a Swiss company and English is not one of the four recognized national languages of Switzerland. However, Nestlé has always managed its headquarters as a centre overseeing international operations, and primed itself accordingly. English is the principal language of communication of all the other companies about which case studies have been written in this book.

That English is the unofficial lingua franca of the corporate world is reflected in the fact that business schools that have an intercultural orientation are offering their programmes in English. Business schools in Europe are increasingly offering MBA and EMBA programmes in English, to supplement the programmes being offered in the local language. The Vlerick Leuven Gent Management School, Belgium, is an example. The executive MBA programmes offered by this business school in English are now oversubscribed, and even have aspiring students on their waiting list. Meanwhile, there are no students shelved to waiting lists for the EMBA programmes offered in Flemish (Anderson, 2001). In spite of the efforts of Belgian business schools like Vlerick Leuven Gent, Belgium's students continue to go overseas to obtain MBA degrees taught in English. Belgium's experience is echoed in several other European countries as well. The Reims Management School, France, is currently offering MBA programmes in both French and English. Didier Develey, the present Dean of the Reims Management School, expects to discontinue its French MBA programme by 2003–4, and be able then to focus entirely on its English MBA, for which the demand is greater. The international ratings of the IESE Business School, Barcelona, Spain, accrue to it partly on account of it offering both an MBA and an EMBA in English.

Having an intercultural workforce of managers who are fluent in English certainly enables a global corporation to get these managers to connect by communicating. However, during face to face communication, managers may find that English is spoken with differing accents, pronunciation, and intonation, which in turn is an outcome of culture.

Communicating common principles to all branches worldwide

Nestlé has found that it is a worthwhile business investment to communicate a set of the Basic Nestlé Management and Leadership Principles to all its branches across the globe. The principles were formulated, and then articulated as a document, as recently as 1997. There were two main reasons the Principles were formulated. First, as operations worldwide increased in scale and volume, 'there was an increasing number of people joining Nestlé and working throughout the globe' (Basic Nestlé Management and Leadership Principles, 1997). Second, Peter Brabeck, an Austrian who had worked for Nestlé in Latin America, was replacing Helmut Maucher, a German, as CEO. The new top management felt it necessary to unite all Nestlé managers with a set of common principles. These principles would then be the superordinate attitudes, approaches, and reference points that guided the professional behaviour of Nestlé managers. The principles were designed to link managers from different cultures. They superseded all other considerations. The corporate culture was expected to have greater paramountcy than other cultures of which a manager may be a part.

What is noteworthy about the Principles is that some of them pertain to attitudes and mind-sets. (See Part 4, of the Principles, Qualities and characteristics of a Nestlé manager, in the box on page 56.) It is obviously a Nestlé belief that these attitudes are not culture-specific. It is noteworthy that one of the qualities and characteristics recommended for a Nestlé manager is 'international experience and understanding of other cultures'. It is the Nestlé credo that intercultural competencies can be learnt.

Appreciating that the process of communication can vary across cultures

Tenets such as the Nestlé Principles can be communicated in more ways than one. Attitudes can be built up and nurtured in diverse manners. The desired attitudes can be fostered more efficiently and speedily, if done in a manner that strikes a responsive chord with the target group. That has been the experience of Nestlé, and that is why the company gave total autonomy to their branches to disseminate the Nestlé Principles using whatever approach they deemed appropriate. More often than not, the approach employed reflected local cultural preferences. Nestlé has comprehensively documented the different processes adopted by all its different branches. It is adding this to its database on intercultural management.

Sometimes, however, the approach used may have reflected the orientations of the particular Nestlé group of managers at the branch. That group of managers may not be representative of the culture of the entire country. After all, not everyone in a country is alike. Additionally, variations within some countries, especially Asian countries, are considerable. Becoming aware of this itself comprises a lesson about intercultural management.

As global managers become more homogeneous, the process of communication may also become more similar. However, allowances and adjustments will still have to be made to accommodate cultural differences. The sheer diversity of the communication processes resorted to by Nestlé branches is testimony to this.

Being cautious about translations

Translations from one language into another may not always convey the intended meaning. Erroneous translations have even resulted in fatalities. As Nicholson observed in the *Financial Times* (1996), faulty translations have led to airplane crashes. This calls for absolute circumspection in the business world, in translations of contracts, advertisements, negotiations and important documents.

As already mentioned, Nestlé had its document containing the Principles translated into several languages. Considerable attention was given to ensuring that the spirit of the document was neither lost nor contaminated by translation.

Communicating continuously

Nestlé encourages a continuous flow of business communication from its branches to headquarters. More importantly, the business

experiences of one country, both successes and failures, are passed
to others almost routinely. Managers from headquarters constantly
visit branches on fact-finding and data collection forays. And people
from branches are posted to headquarters on time-bound assignments. Of course, the international training programmes assemble
together at Vevey large groups of managers from all over the world.
The trainers at these programmes are themselves global Nestlé
managers. In 2000, 1718 participants attended a total of 81 courses
and programmes at Vevey. Dr Huesler, the head till 2001 of International Training for Nestlé, commented, 'these international programs
are an essential contribution to the building and upkeep of a worldwide network of contacts across the whole hierarchy'.

Another application of the notion of continuous communication
as practised at Nestlé is that the Principles are constantly being
reaffirmed and reinforced, so they become part of the ethos and
culture of all branches. In this effort as well, the message remains the
same, but the reinforcement process varies from branch to branch.

CASE DISCUSSION QUESTIONS

1. What lessons can be derived from the case about organiz-
    ational communications and intercultural management?

2. Can organizational core values be considered as being super-
    ordinate to ethnic cultures?

3. Is the approach adopted by Nestlé generalizable? If so, why
    is it so? If not, why not?

4. Why does Nestlé believe that the Basic Nestlé Management
    and Leadership Principles will facilitate intercultural manage-
    ment?

5. What should an intercultural group keep in mind when trying
    to achieve effective communication?

6. What recommendations would you give to Rainer Gut, the
    chairman of Nestlé?

ACADEMIC DISCUSSION

In this millennium, the world has become connected in a way that was envisaged only in science fiction accounts even 50 years back. Instant communication, and travel at twice the speed of sound, are enabling people from all over the world to be in touch continuously. National economies are increasingly becoming part of the globalization process. This phenomenon is carrying in its wake the movement of people, products, and services across the world. Additionally, there is tremendous migration of people especially from the South to the North. Chen and Starosta (1998) report that since 1980, the average age of immigrants has dropped from 46.2 to 28.

All these have resulted in high-performance corporations becoming multicultural in their composition. Consequently, communication within a corporation has to take this into account, and employees need to be encouraged to learn the finer aspects of intercultural communication. The need for skill in intercultural communication is heightened when the corporation is like Nestlé, and has operations in several countries. Understanding the nature of intercultural communication can thus contribute to the creation of mind-sets that are successful in the global business world.

INTERCULTURAL COMMUNICATION

Intercultural communication is quite simply the process of communication between individuals from different cultures. To understand intercultural communication requires an accurate perception of what is conveyed in the verbal mode, as well as what is non-verbal. Beliefs and attitudes about a person from another culture can often be communicated through behaviour, even when nothing has been verbalized. Thus, managers can communicate that they hold a prejudice against a person from a specific culture, even when they have been at great pains to converse courteously.

There are two aspects to communication with global managers. Global managers might share similar values regarding work ethics and professionalism. Hence, communication at the workplace may not pose a problem. On the other hand, the cultural underpinnings of communication may manifest themselves when relationships at the personal level are attempted. And of course, skills in intercultural communication become of the essence when, one, expatriates attempt to integrate into a foreign culture, and two, a corporation has to operate in a foreign culture and market its products there.

That contrasting patterns of communication can exist across different cultures is made manifest in Hall's model (1987) of culturally distinct societies. Hall classified societies into two distinctive groups: high-context societies, and low-context societies. The United States is a typical example of a low-context society, while Japan is an example of a high-context society. According to Hall, low-context societies are characterized by:

▌ heterogeneity;

▌ high social mobility;

▌ high job mobility;

▌ short-term relationships;

▌ insiders and outsiders being not closely distinguished.

High-context societies are characterized by:

▌ homogeneity;

▌ little social mobility;

▌ little job mobility;

▌ long-term relationships;

▌ insiders and outsiders being clearly distinguished.

Hall advises people who live in low-context societies to engage in explicit communication. This is because the nature of those societies precludes the possibility of widely shared meanings. On the other hand, people in high-context societies habitually engage in implicit communication. Homogeneous, almost standardized, patterns of communication exist. Therefore, people from within a high-context society are able to communicate without being misunderstood. By the same token, people from other cultures have to master the communication patterns of a high-context society if they want to be assimilated or accepted there.

Ferraro (2001), while examining the contrasts between low-context and high-context countries, highlights the differences in communication patterns from another angle. Low-context societies are purported to place a lot of emphasis on words. In high-context societies, people are more sensitive to contextual cues, suggestions and nuances.

Quite a lot of research has been devoted to contrasting different patterns of communication based on culture. Most of these studies, like Ferraro's cited above, have concentrated on contrasts. The results make fascinating reading because of the stark nature of the contrast. Edward T. Hall's article 'The silent language in overseas business' (1960) is a case in point. In this piece, Hall notes that American managers will attend to an important and valued client immediately that client comes to their office. In Hispanic countries by contrast, an important client who finds himself waiting outside a manager's office need not take offence: Hispanics are purported to be so people-oriented that they do not cut short a meeting just to ensure that they are able to stick to their appointment schedule. Arabs are purported to be as people-oriented as Hispanics. Thus Hall has presented two starkly contrasting cultures: US people who do not attach deep values to relationships, and therefore make friends and drop friends rapidly and with ease, contrasted with the Arabs and Hispanics, who place a premium on relationships and lifelong friendships. Other aspects of contrast between Americans on the one hand, and Hispanics and Arabs on the other, which are found at different places in Hall's piece, are:

1. US managers appraise the importance of managers by comparing the size of their office to that of other managers in the company. The CEO has the best and biggest office, and so on down the pecking order. In the United States, from middle management levels upwards, people are accustomed to having considerable space around themselves. By contrast, in Arab and Hispanic countries people like to work in close proximity to each other. There is little space around a person. Often, a man might lay his hand on another man, or a woman might lay her hand on another woman.

2. US managers are materialistic and money-minded. People's status is reflected by their material possessions. The loyalty of managers is bought by giving them high salaries. By contrast, Arab managers look not for material possessions, but for family and friendship: relationships. They may possess material wealth, but would not like to be assessed on the basis of material possessions alone. They would like to be known and valued as persons as well.

3. US managers conduct business on the basis of written agreements and contracts. However, they are open to breaking agreements when it suits them, so they take legal recourse more frequently than in

many other cultures. By contrast, for Arabs, keeping a word that has been given is a matter of honour and as binding as a written agreement. When recourse is taken to a written agreement, both Arabs and Hispanics treat the agreement as sacrosanct. Informal agreements are amenable to negotiation a priori.

4. US managers state a deadline against which urgent and important work should be completed. They are prone to feeling insulted if they are made to wait after an appointment has been made. Delay in attending to a business matter is always interpreted as lack of interest. By contrast, in Arab and Hispanic countries, relationships determine how time should be spent. More important people get their work done first, as do people with whom the manager has a valued, close relationship. Attempts to impose deadlines are viewed as being overly demanding and pushy.

Managers interviewed for this book have mixed reactions to studies that present communication patterns in terms of starkly contrasted cultural clusters. Most believe that such clusters tend to be exaggerated caricatures which can be misleading if taken as the truth. For example, an Arab taxi driver's notion of what constitutes an agreement between himself and a passenger cannot be extrapolated to predict the likely behaviour of an Arab working for a global corporation. In fact, many have found that senior Arab managers follow the US notion of time in their professional lives. Likewise, in the United States as in Arab and Hispanic countries, there are managers who perceive relationships as important. After all, it is in the United States that the typology that characterizes managers as either task-oriented or relationship-oriented was developed. And global managers interviewed for this book testify that there are US managers who like to cultivate and nurture relationships.

Different cultures may be distinguished by different communication patterns to greater or lesser degrees. There is an ideal type to which a global manager can aspire. According to this type, intercultural communication ensues between two individuals based on a mutual understanding of cultural similarities and differences.

Another example of a factor that can lead to contrast in communication patterns across cultures is language. Although English is often perceived as the international language in the world of business, proficiency in that language varies significantly across countries. Additionally, even if global managers are conversant with English, expatriates residing in continental Europe need to know the local language, to have a life outside the workplace. Schneider and Barsoux (1997) observe how a Franco-Swedish team working together decided to adopt English as the working language. However, the French managers' fluency with English was considerably less than the Swedes'. Hence the French were ill at ease when communicating with the Swedes, and their relationship with them was hampered by the language factor.

The following are aids that facilitate the process of intercultural communication.

Intercultural training

In layman's parlance, intercultural training involves a person being educated about the rules that govern communication, interaction and behaviour in another culture. The awareness and insights are then compared against the rules that govern the person's own communication, interaction and behaviour. The similarities and differences are noted and appreciated.

Through intercultural training, managers can learn the basic communication rules of a foreign culture, such as when to speak and to whom, and how others may be addressed. At the same time, they can learn when not to speak and what sort of mannerisms would be inappropriate. In many Asian countries, Korea being a typical example, people are careful not to disagree openly with a person much older in age. So a global manager in Korea would have to be extremely diplomatic in dealing with older Koreans.

Research shows that many employees of multinational companies would like to see changes in the management styles of expatriates, especially in the areas of leadership, decision making, communication and group work. It is possible that lack of awareness about effective management styles in other cultures causes expatriates to commit errors of omission and commission. Even within Europe, a continent that exhibits more internal homogeneity than Asia for instance, considerable disparity exists in management styles. Reihlen (2001) has opined that the following European countries are distinguished by the extra emphasis that they place on certain management practices. France is characterized by a propensity for engaging in a bureaucratic form of management. In Great Britain, considerable importance is attached to managers exhibiting social skills, such as politeness and good manners. German management is purported to be differentiated by a high degree of professionalism, requiring considerable self-discipline and self-programming. Italian managers often use the metaphor of the family to describe their company.

Thus in Italy, personal contacts are important for building a familial network of work relations. In Sweden, the management style is tilted towards being democratic and consensus-oriented.

We recommend as particularly useful by way of intercultural training the attempt to get managers to see themselves as individuals from various other cultures see them. In this type of workshop, participants are assigned various tasks and then people from different cultures observe their behaviour. These participants comprise managers from different cultures, who have to interact with each other to complete their tasks. The observation can be done through one-way glass to reduce self-consciousness among participants. Feedback is then given to the participants by the observers in turn. Thus, an aspiring global manager can get feedback from an Arab as to the quirks in his behaviour which would not find favour with Arabs, feedback from a Swiss as to what aspects of his behaviour might annoy a Swiss, and so on. To be palatable the feedback must include positive aspects as well. The intention of the feedback, both positive and negative, is to heighten the cultural sensitivity of participants and provide them with opportunities to both learn and unlearn. Various levels of feedback can be given. For instance, managers who have little exposure to other cultures would be given the preliminary level of feedback.

Even primitive attempts at imparting cultural sensitivity to trans national managers have proved fruitful. A Japanese company that had bought out an Australian firm recently undertook a rudimentary cultural sensitization effort directed at both its Japanese and Australian managers, as follows. A consultant took a group of Japanese and Australian managers to the Queensland rainforest for four days. The managers had to jointly master an obstacle course. They performed tasks that might have been straight out of the Tarzan School of Management or the Spiderman School of Management. Inter alia, the managers had to walk across swaying rope bridges 40 feet above the ground. They also had to help one another climb down those bridges using ropes. The nights were spent with the Australians talking about the Australian way of doing business. The Japanese felt that this programme, even though it was essentially Outward Bound in nature, prepared them a little for their work life ahead. And the channels of communication between the two groups of managers opened.

Intercultural training for managers should also include education about what constitutes effective management in other cultures. A manager may learn about another country's customs and heritage, and therefore might be able to function as an individual there without too much difficulty. It must be emphasized that intercultural training does not end with an initial orientation. On the contrary, it is an ongoing, continuous effort that can never end.

Often, there may be a need to demonstrate performance in a foreign culture. The global managers interviewed for this book revealed that they were usually under pressure to show that they were being productive. Since they were foreigners, their work behaviour was constantly under close scrutiny. There is no research yet about how managers should present themselves when trying to obtain acceptance for their professionalism in a new culture. However, insights may be obtained by delving into work done in the area of newcomers and women trying to make an impact in their work environment. Based on the work of Haslett, Geis and Carter (1992), and extending their conclusions to managers operating in a new culture, it is recommended that instead of letting work speak for itself, managers should draw co-workers' attention to their achievements in non-threatening ways.

Language training

The possibilities for communication and interactions are considerably enhanced if managers are proficient in the language of the culture in which they operate. An effective global manager is well versed in at least two languages, if not three. It may be true that English is a widely spoken language in the business world. However, it is also true that it is spoken by only a small percentage of the world's population. Paul Orleman records that the global training and development team at Rhöne-Poulene Rorer, a French-US joint venture in pharmaceuticals, explicitly takes into account that all team members may not be equally proficient in English. One of the rules established is that team members have to speak slowly. Additionally, if individuals become too frustrated trying to make a point in English, they are welcome to revert to their preferred language. Translation is then arranged.

Knowledge of, and some fluency in, a local language enable a manager to understand communication patterns as they exist in the new culture. Some people have argued that it is not really necessary for expatriates to learn the language of the country they are assigned to, since they will not be residing there for long. However, language proficiency is a long-term asset, since expatriates will find opportunities to use their language skills professionally, even after returning to their own country. After all, the world is getting smaller on a continuous basis, especially in the world of multinational corporations. When Jaguar introduced an in-company German language training facility for its employees, its sales in West Germany the following year jumped a dramatic 60 per cent (as reported by the *Economist*), despite stiff competition from rivals Mercedes and BMW. An Asian global manager interviewed for this book recalls how he had been unable to live a full life in Germany because of his inability to speak German. However, he started taking lessons immediately on arrival, and after a year could speak a little German. His experience was that after learning to speak a little German, he felt as if he had been handed the keys to that country. He could now chat a little to people in bars and in shops, and began to feel much more at home than would otherwise have been the case.

Other things being equal, clients opt for doing business with the company that has managers conversant with the language spoken in the clients' country. For this reason, a few global companies are considering making mastery of an international language other than English a mandatory requirement for promotion to senior levels. And before they send a group of managers to a new country, they want at least half those managers to have a working knowledge of the language spoken in that country.

Culture-specificity versus pan-culturalism

Global managers interviewed for this book are united in their opinion that the communication mode that works for them is neither culture-specific nor pan-cultural. In other words, they do not believe that a single, universal approach to communication, irrespective of culture, is appropriate. On the other hand, they do not believe it is necessary to go completely native, and adopt the entire gamut of communication mannerisms of another culture. What is recommended is an appropriate blend of both approaches. In some situations, it may be necessary to adopt the host culture's norms of communication more vigorously than in others, especially when interacting with persons typical of that culture. For instance, adopting local ways of communicating in public places may be required in Arab countries, especially in the case of different gender interactions.

At the same time, the communication patterns of other people are not set against the scale of a global manager's own cultural background. This type of an approach has been termed ethnorelativism by Buoyant (1991). Ethnorelativism maintains that 'cultures can only be understood relative to one another; there is no absolute standard of rightness or goodness that can be applied to cultural behaviour; cultural difference is neither good or bad; it is just different'.

Additionally, global managers may like to become attuned to experiencing more than one culture simultaneously. This is possible because in any country there can be more than one ethnic group. Also, even in a foreign country, a multinational corporation may have expatriate groups from third and fourth countries. In any event, a global manager assigned to a new country would have to adjust to a new corporate culture, as well as to life in a new national culture. Thus, global managers need to be sensitive and pick up cues suggesting cultural differences, be they ethnic, corporate or functional.

Communication infrastructure

A considerable amount of the communication engaged in by global managers involves the use of modern technological systems. Hence, corporations interested in transnational operations invest heavily in the physical infrastructure necessary for global communication. Modern communication systems range from e-mail to videoconferencing. High-performance companies who have invested in modern methods of communication also have managers who have mastered the skills required to be on top of global communication. 3Com's managers have learnt how to make their transnational teleconferencing more efficient and successful through the following means: speaking louder, more clearly and slowly; using extensions of phone speakers so that everybody participating can hear equally loudly; being proficient at describing materials, situations, events and people; and involving people by soliciting their opinions. Sophisticated teleconferencing and videoconferencing facilities allow many managers from anywhere in the world to enter a discussion in a very natural way. Managers can even listen to minutes of what has transpired, if they enter a discussion late.

One system used by some global companies for this purpose is called Meeting Place. A practical problem faced by companies when teleconferencing and videoconferencing is timing. A conference scheduled for the morning in one part of the world will take place in the afternoon in another part, evening in a third part, and an inconvenient time of the night in yet another part. Many global companies have addressed this problem by rotating the timing, so the inconvenient timings are shared among their various locations. A further ingredient for the effective use of communication technology by global companies, suggested by O'Hara-Devereaux and Johansen (1994), is that managers at all locations have equal access to the modes of communication used by that global company.

INTERCULTURAL RELATIONSHIPS

Intercultural communication is enhanced when individuals actually have opportunities to relate to people from other cultures not merely as work associates, but as friends as well. The global managers surveyed for this book mentioned that those individuals who succeeded in building relationships with people from other cultures became more adept intuitively in the art of intercultural communication. However, intercultural relationship building is facilitated when both the individuals involved are culturally sensitive. Thus in the interests of congeniality, a manager is advised to select polycentric people from other cultures as friends. The mutual desire to respect each other's cultural heritage, and to seek common human grounds for relating to each other, ensures that the relationship develops in a positive fashion. It also ensures that feedback is given and received in an atmosphere of comfort, and the giving and receiving of feedback is an important aspect of any communication.

Cultural friction arises when either or both individuals trying to relate to each other repeatedly make the same cultural gaffe. Urech (1998) writes that Australians like to be addressed by their first names, while Belgians prefer to be addressed by their surnames. An Australian manager who spent an entire evening with a Belgian was disconcerted when the latter said on parting company, 'Yes, we will meet again tomorrow at 6.00 pm, Mr Wilson.' The Australian immediately said, 'I would really be happy if you call me Alan. After all, we are friends, are we not?' And the Belgian immediately replied, 'Yes, of course Alan, if you say so.' Thus that day the Belgian learnt that Australians like to be addressed by their first name, and the Australian learnt that Belgians are not on a first-name basis unless they invite a person to use their first name.

Intercultural relationships are built on the premise of mutual give and take. This give and take has, however, to be preceded by some awareness of the areas for likely differences of approach. It is said that Italians like to spend a great deal of time with people they befriend. The Finns, on the other hand, can be good friends without feeling the need to hang around with their friends continuously. For an intercultural relationship to develop between a typical Italian and a typical Finn, both would have to be aware of how each person defines a friendship in terms of time spent together. Both would have to be prepared to deviate from the path they normally take, to accommodate the other's preferences. And most importantly, both would have to communicate to each other their preferences regarding how they should relate as friends. It is communication that enables people to realize in what ways their cultural underpinnings might impact on their friendship. Savvy managers enter an intercultural relationship prepared for give and take; for being educated about how the other views relationships, and educating the other in turn. Intercultural relationships require an investment of effort that is rewarded by the fact that they contribute to enriching life's experiences with variety and depth. Managers who opt for intercultural relationships do so because they like it. The investment of effort therefore comes naturally and effortlessly.

In his book, which is much referred by preachers, gurus and aficionados in the field of intercultural management, Trompenaars (1993) has quoted Clifford Geertz thus: 'Culture is the means by which people communicate, perpetuate, and develop their knowledge about attitudes to life.' Trompenaars then goes on to opine, 'Culture is not a thing, a substance with a physical reality of its own. Rather, it is made by people interacting, at the same time determining further interaction.' At this point we diverge from Trompenaars and would like to develop a different line of argument pertaining to culture and communication. If culture is made by people interacting, which premise we accept, then it follows that intercultural relationships can cause culture to be redefined, as both parties to the relationship influence and are influenced by each other's culture. Global managers who have related at fairly deep levels to managers from other cultures, and/or have lived for substantial periods of time (at least three or four years) in other cultures and imbibed aspects of those cultures, would have redefined their own cultural contexts many times over.

EFFECTIVE CORPORATE COMMUNICATION

Global managers should feel secure that there exists a common set of core values in the corporation they are working for. Thus, the core values of the company are the same regardless of whether it is a branch in South America, Africa, North America or the Asia-Pacific region. As recorded in the case study given at the beginning of this chapter, that has been the steadfast philosophy of Nestlé.

NANCY ADLER'S MODEL OF CULTURAL SYNERGY

Define the problem from both points of view

Consider the case of a Latin American employee who takes an entire day off every time he takes his wife to see a doctor. His wife can drive and has her own car. This employee's US boss is not amused.

The first step is to examine the perspective of both men. How does each person view the situation? The boss thinks the employee is malingering, and is upset that his services are not available when he needs them. He may even deem the employee to be irresponsible. The employee, on the other hand, perceives his boss as being without human compassion.

Uncover the cultural interpretations

Each man is interpreting the other's actions from his own cultural premise. Suppose instead the boss were to view the situation from the employee's standpoint, and the boss examine the situation based on his employee's cultural programming. The boss might then see that in the context of the employee's culture, his position as head of the family required him to accompany his wife to the doctor, even if the visit was a routine one. The employee was thus fulfilling his familial obligations in a responsible manner.

If the employee were to consider matters from the standpoint of his boss's cultural heritage, he would realize that his boss believes that work responsibilities should take precedence over everything else. In the boss's scheme of things, family members should look after themselves in non-emergency situations. The issue now is, how can this situation be resolved?

Create cultural synergy

Once both men have perceived the situation from the other's point of view, they could try to find a feasible compromise. For instance, the solution could be that the employee uses the days off he is legitimately entitled to for domestic activities like accompanying his wife to the doctor. Alternatively he might not take the entire day off when he takes his wife to the doctor. What is of the essence is that both men try to understand the other's cultural programming, and accept that such cultural conditioning is going to influence work-life decisions.

Source: Adler (2001).

ELIZABETH URECH'S COUNTRY-BY-COUNTRY ACCOUNT OF NON-VERBAL COMMUNICATION PATTERNS

Argentina: People who have an informal manner are appreciated. Eye contact is direct.

Belgium: People who have a formal manner are well received.

Canada: Canadians like people who have an open and friendly manner. Eye contact is direct. Avoid pointing or using any grand gestures.

China: Chinese like people who are respectful. Once the Chinese get to know you, they can be 'touchy-feely', but it is best if you are very polite until you know them. Eye contact is direct. Never put your feet on the table, do not raise your 'pinkie finger'. Avoid any aggressive gesture. Do not laugh loudly.

Finland: Eye contact is direct, but keep some distance. Avoid broad gestures.

Germany: Germans like people who have a formal manner.

Hungary: Hungarians like people who are straightforward and natural. Eye contact is direct.

Italy: Italians like people who have an informal manner. Eye contact is direct.

Korea: Koreans like people who are respectful. Eye contact is indirect. Instead of looking in someone's eyes, one should look just under their eyes, at their cheeks. Avoid pointing and any broad gestures.

Malaysia: Malays like people who have a respectful and quiet manner. Eye contact is indirect. Avoid crossing your legs or showing the soles of your shoes. Standing with arms on your hips is considered aggressive.

The Netherlands: The Dutch like people who have an informal and forthright manner. Eye contact is direct.

Norway: Norwegians like people who have an informal manner. Eye contact is direct. Norwegians like their space.

Poland: Poles like people who have an outgoing, easy manner. Even if they appear formal, they will warm up after the initial contact. Direct eye contact is essential. Otherwise, you will be thought to be hiding something.

Russia: Russians like people who have an informal manner. Eye contact is direct. Avoid pointing at your temple, that means 'you are an idiot'.

Singapore: Singaporeans like people who are respectful and polite. Eye contact is indirect. Gestures to avoid include pointing or standing with your arms crossed in front of you.

Sweden: Swedes like people who are open-minded. Eye contact is direct. Swedes feel more comfortable with some distance between them and you.

Thailand: Thais like people who have a respectful manner. Avoid speaking loudly. Eye contact is indirect. Avoid pointing a finger, crossing your legs or using your foot to point out something.

United States: Americans like people who have an outgoing and direct manner. Eye contact is direct. The gesture forming a circle with thumb and index finger means 'OK'.

Source: Urech (1998).

SUMMARY

Communication is an important mechanism for holding an organization together, especially when it is a global organization with branches all over the world. Many global companies like Nestlé believe that it is the core values of a company that enable it to grow as a vital, successful, humane organization. These core values have to be communicated to all its branches worldwide. This entails communication across a wide variety of cultures. Increasingly it is found that the content of what multicultural organizations communicate to all their branches is the same regardless of culture. What is varied depending on local culture is the process of communication. The process is aligned to local culture to ensure acceptance of the content.

Communication from headquarters in one culture to a branch in another culture, or from a branch in one culture to a branch in a different culture, is one facet of intercultural communications in a management context. The other facet pertains to expatriates learning how to communicate in cultures other than one's own. Intercultural communication possesses both pan-cultural properties and culture-specific properties. Expatriates need to cultivate sensitivity to the culture-specific properties. Knowledge of the local language is one of the many factors that enable an expatriate to communicate better with local national employees.

3

Core values and intercultural management

CASE STUDY: NESTLÉ

In 2001, Nestlé was the largest and most diversified food company in the world, with nearly 500 factories in more than 100 countries. In fact, over the period 1867–2000 it surpassed other food manufacturers and purchasers of agricultural raw materials in scale of operations. Over 230,000 people worldwide work in Nestlé's factories, research laboratories and offices. In 1999 Nestlé generated a total income of 4,007 million Swiss francs.

This case study is based on a series of interviews with prominent Nestlé managers engaged in strengthening Nestlé's core values. Niels Christiansen, Vice President, Public Affairs of Nestlé SA, explains that even though 98 per cent of Nestlé operations are outside Switzerland, the company still originated in Switzerland. The corporate headquarters is located in Switzerland. Hence some Swiss cultural values are an integral part of Nestlé core values. Many Swiss values are embedded in the Nestlé General Management and Leadership Principles and the Nestlé Corporate Business Principles. These Principles reflect not only Nestlé's basic corporate values, but some of the 'Swissness' of the company as well. What has been described as the Swissness of the company refers to the pragmatic and results-oriented nature of the Principles. The Nestlé General Management and Leadership Principles are presented in our case study on communications and intercultural management (see Chapter 2). The box on page 87 reproduces the Nestlé Corporate Business Principles.

NESTLÉ CORPORATE BUSINESS PRINCIPLES

Nestlé is committed to the following business principles in all countries taking into account local legislation, culture and religious practice:

■ Nestlé's business objective, and that of management and employees at all levels, is to manufacture and market the company's products in such a way as to create value that can be sustained over the long term for customers, shareholders, employees, business partners and the large number of national economies in which Nestlé operates.

■ Nestlé does not favour short-term profit at the expense of successful long-term business development, but recognizes the need to generate profit each year in order to maintain the support of the financial markets, and to finance investments.

■ Nestlé believes that, as a general rule, legislation is the most effective safeguard of ethical conduct, although in certain areas, additional guidance to management and employees, in the form of voluntary business principles, is beneficial in order to ensure that the highest standards are met throughout the organization.

■ Nestlé is conscious of the fact that the success of a corporation is a reflection of the professionalism, conduct and ethical values of its management and employees, therefore recruitment of the right people and ongoing training and development are crucial.

■ Nestlé recognizes that consumers have a legitimate interest in the company behind the Nestlé brands, and the way in which the Nestlé company operates.

Although core values can be propagated across a multicultural corporation in a variety of ways, Nestlé adopts certain approaches that are characteristic of it. These approaches have been used consistently and for a considerable length of time, even though the company's various Principles have been written down only recently. One important approach is careful and meticulous selection of personnel. This approach has been enshrined in the Nestlé Corporate Business Principles. Potential employees are assessed as to whether they possess the attributes that would enable them to fit into the Nestlé way of life. An assessment is also made of whether they can achieve complete integration into Nestlé culture over time. Nestlé's selection process has been so effective that most of its employees have pursued a lifetime career, spanning at least 30 years with the company. This lifetime association with Nestlé enables employees to completely imbibe and operationalize the Nestlé core values. Additionally, new recruits are given extensive coaching as well as training, to ensure that they fully understand Nestlé's core values. Both the Nestlé Management and Leadership Principles document and the Nestlé Corporate Business Principles document contain personal messages from the CEO. The CEO, as well as all senior managers, make it clear that they expect all employees to subscribe to and implement the company core values. Of course, members of the top management echelon also live the core values themselves so that they serve as role models.

Nestlé uses extensively another means to propagate its core values: its international management cadre. Members of this cadre go from country to country working as managers in different Nestlé branches. These international management cadre managers ensure that the Nestlé core values are institutionalized at all Nestlé locations. They occupy a significant proportion of the key positions at all Nestlé branches, and can therefore exert a tremendous amount of influence. All managers of Nestlé, irrespective of ethnic origin or geographic location, are part of the Nestlé culture and share the same core values. Additionally, by rotation, they spend some time at the Nestlé headquarters in Vevey, Switzerland. During the initial stages of their career, Nestlé employees (from all over the world) attend residential training programmes at Vevey, which are of approximately one month's duration. These programmes reinforce the core values which Nestlé employees have already assimilated. They also make Nestlé employees realize that regardless of where they are from, they all share these core values.

Although Nestlé's core values are the glue that holds together all its managers distributed across more than 100 countries, the company is also sensitive to local cultures. Brabeck, CEO of Nestlé, has remarked, 'Since Nestlé's activities in Switzerland, its country of origin, account for less than 2 per cent of its global turnover, Nestlé learned very early to respect the social, political and cultural traditions of all countries in which the products are produced and sold, and to be a highly decentralized people and products oriented company rather than a systems oriented company.' The interesting question that presents itself is, how does Nestlé manage the dialectic between having well-entrenched core values, and respecting national cultures?

Vietnam is a country in which Nestlé has established a branch only recently (in 1996). It is a challenging country in which to start operations. In the first instance, it is a communist country with a state controlled market. Additionally, the cultural ethos and ambience of Vietnam are quite unique. When Nestlé started its branch in Vietnam, it had to embed and institutionalize its core values there from scratch.

Nestlé's initial step was to translate the two documents, Nestlé Management and Leadership Principles, and Nestlé Corporate Business Principles, into Vietnamese. During translation, it was found that some concepts could not be translated literally. Literal translations would lead to some loss of intended meaning. Hence, some of the concepts were elucidated using Vietnamese metaphors and symbols. For example, recourse was made to the metaphor of the family. The sort of relationship that Nestlé expects from employees was compared to the sort of relationship that exists between family members. The importance of teamwork and team spirit was likewise advocated by reference to family values. Thus, a document was created especially for Nestlé Vietnam that encapsulated the Nestlé core values in the local idiom. This document is given to every employee who joins the branch.

Before employees can join Nestlé Vietnam, they have to satisfy the recruitment criteria. This includes whether the prospective employees can understand and appreciate the core values of Nestlé, and align themselves with these core values. Individuals who will be unable to operationalize Nestlé core values, because of either their background or their personality, are screened out. The background of a prospective employee is thoroughly checked. This is to ascertain what kinds of influence have conditioned him or her. At Nestlé branches that have been in existence for some time, considerable autonomy is given to line managers in the matter of recruitment. In start-up branches like Nestlé Vietnam, however, the HR department and top management are very closely involved in the recruitment process. They admit into their fold only those individuals who can subscribe to Nestlé core values. Nestlé believes that if employees are deficient in technical skills, but have the appropriate attitudes and values, they can be trained and learn those skills. On the other hand, values are more difficult to change. If prospective employees have attitudes incompatible with Nestlé's core values, then no amount of

coaching can successfully bring them in line with Nestlé's expectations.

One of the core values of Nestlé is that its employees should have
intercultural competencies and be able to interact effectively with
people from all over the world. Hence, as part of the recruitment
process at Nestlé Vietnam, prospective employees' attitudes to
foreigners are assessed. Also assessed is how they view people from
other parts of Vietnam. Preference is given to prospective employees
who are tolerant and liberal thinking, and have experience of associ-
ating with people from diverse backgrounds.

Sometimes it transpires that prospective employees would not like
to work with foreigners from other parts of Asia, such as Malaysians,
Japanese or Taiwanese. They do not mind working with Europeans,
however. In such cases, Nestlé Vietnam tries to ascertain whether
the prejudice emanates from ignorance or from a deep-rooted
emotion. If it is the former, training and coaching can eradicate the
prejudice, as can first-hand experience of working with Malaysian,
Japanese or Taiwanese managers. This is particularly true of young
recruits who are perceived as being malleable. They are very receptive to being guided by a coach or mentor, much more so than in
the case of their European counterparts. Thien Luong Van My,
currently Issues Manager – Public Affairs at Nestlé headquarters in
Vevey, Switzerland, and Country Head of Nestlé Vietnam for the
period 1996–2000, comments:

> They really enjoy this coaching like from an elder brother to a younger
> brother or sister. They really like to be guided not only about how they
> should work, but about how they should behave as well. And we pay
> a lot of importance to our newly joined recruits' patterns of inter-
> action. We observe them closely. And the elder brother recommends
> to his younger sibling how he can improve himself. This system appears
> to be working for us. We started in 1996 with three employees. I had
> a driver and a secretary. Today, there are 300 employees with Nestlé
> Vietnam, all of whom are committed to Nestlé's core values.

The core value of team spirit had to be nurtured with special effort
at Nestlé Vietnam in its early years. It is the experience of Nestlé
Vietnam that the Vietnamese are a fairly individualistic people. They
may be loyal to a small group of people who are usually family
members. Nestlé Vietnam was in its crucial initial six years when
headed by Thien, who is Vietnamese and grew up there. He therefore positioned himself as the patriarch of the company, somebody

who could be considered an uncle or elder brother. He then capital-
ized on his position to encourage team spirit. He also ensured that
team spirit was propagated in a manner appropriate to the Vietnamese culture. For instance, a practice integral to Vietnamese
culture is showing respect and deference to elders. At Nestlé Vietnam, a few units are headed by individuals who are younger than a
few of their subordinates. A careful watch is kept on these individuals, to ascertain whether they treat those subordinates who are
older than them with respect and regard.

Nestlé Vietnam has tried to design approaches for institutionalizing the Principles that comprise the Nestlé core values. For example,
consider the Nestlé Corporate Business Principle regarding protection of the environment:

▌ Nestlé integrates environmental policies, programs, and practices
  into each business as an element of management in all its functions,

▌ develops, designs and operates facilities and conducts its activities
  taking into consideration the efficient use of energy and materials,
  the sustainable use of renewable resources, the minimization of
  adverse environmental impact and waste generation, and the safe
  and responsible disposal of residual wastes,

▌ applies Nestlé internal standards suitable to local conditions in
  those regions where specific environmental legislation is not yet in
  place,

▌ improves environmental protection relevant to its activities on a
  continuous basis,

▌ provides appropriate information, communication and training to
  build internal and external understanding about its environmental
  commitment and action.

Nestlé Vietnam has had to work very hard to inculcate the value of
conducting business in an environmentally sound manner amongst
its employees. Many of the non-management staff come from rustic
backgrounds with no higher education. Hence, courses are organized regularly so that these staff members can be educated on how
to conduct themselves in an environmentally friendly fashion. When
any staff members deviate from the Nestlé standards for hygiene and
environmental protection, their lapse is pointed out to them. Newly
joined staff members have to be told that trash should not be littered
anywhere, but should be put into garbage bins.

On one occasion, a newly joined member of the cleaning staff was asked to clean the warehouse adjacent to a Nestlé factory. He was asked to do this on a Sunday when there were no senior managers at the factory site. While cleaning, he threw some discarded paints and oil into the drainage system. It was entirely a spontaneous act. Fortunately, a manager came to know about this occurrence the following day, and the drainage system was stopped before it discharged its contents into a river flowing nearby. If the paints and oil had found their way into the river, a major catastrophe would have resulted. After this incident, Nestlé Vietnam provided even more stringent instructions about hygiene and environment protection to its entire staff.

Another core value that had to be addressed explicitly by Nestlé Vietnam was one termed 'Conflict of Interest' in the Nestlé Corporate Business Principles document. This core value stated that Nestlé requires its management and employees to avoid personal activities and financial interests that could conflict, or appear to conflict, with their jobs. In Vietnam, it is customary for people to hold more than one job. They might work for half a day at a primary job, and then be employed elsewhere, in a job that is in some way competitive with the primary job. Nestlé Vietnam has had to adopt a firm stance here.

Thien and the other expatriate Nestlé employees who set up Nestlé Vietnam were succeeded by Vietnamese managers in early 2001. This has contributed to institutionalizing the Nestlé core values at the branch. It also signifies that the branch has assimilated the Nestlé core values. In fact, the job success of Thien and his expatriate colleagues is being evaluated in terms of the performance of their successors.

Inferences

Fostering of uniform core values in a global corporation is a key to successful intercultural management

The challenge of intercultural management for organizations lies in the appropriate juxtaposition of corporate culture and ethnic cultures. This is the challenge that Nestlé, with its many, many branches located all around the globe, had to grapple with constantly. Ultimately, however, corporate culture transcends ethnic culture. In other words, corporate culture, which is governed by the organization's core values, is superordinate to other cultures such as ethnic culture. This has been the mode of functioning of all the organizations profiled in this book: Nestlé, Credit Suisse, BMW, International Committee of the Red Cross, IBM, ICAS and so on. These companies have not specifically articulated that this is their mode of functioning. It may not even be recognized as a conscious strategy by the top management echelons. Certainly, the key players in the individual companies are not aware that this is a mode of functioning shared by high-performance transnational organizations. Nonetheless, we record in this book that this is the case.

The core values of an organization determine the nature of its corporate culture. The corporate culture can influence the mind-sets of its employees, which in turn will have been shaped by a wide variety of factors. For individual employees, one of these factors is definitely their ethnic culture. When an organization has branches in different locations and cultures, it is inevitable that those branches are affected by local cultures in more ways than one. In the first instance, the products and services offered by the organization must find a resonance in the local culture. Otherwise there would be no market for those products and services. Thus, Nestlé offers many food products that are culture-specific in that they reflect the food preferences of the local consumers. One of Nestlé's food products is Maggi instant noodles. These noodles are available in a wide variety of cultures, and offer a feature that is appreciated in all these cultures – they can be prepared in a matter of minutes. However, the noodles are concocted differently in different cultures. In Switzerland, for instance, the noodles are sold with a cheese garnish. In India, Maggi masala noodles are a runaway success. Maggi masala noodles have a pungent, spicy flavour, which might not find favour in Switzerland. Likewise, Maggi noodles as sold in Switzerland would be too bland for the average Indian.

Local cultures can impact on organizations in more complex ways, however. They can influence (though not determine) corporate culture. This happens when a significant number of employees of an organization hail from a specific ethnic culture. The corporate culture of Nestlé has a certain 'Swissness' about it, as observed by Hans Jöhr, Assistant Vice-President at Nestlé headquarters. This is to be expected, since Nestlé originated in Switzerland, and is headquartered in that country. However, the fact that Vietnamese personnel staff Nestlé Vietnam signifies that elements of Vietnamese culture that are venerable are incorporated into Nestlé Vietnam. This enables the Vietnamese workforce to be productive and happy. For instance, the notion of projecting the CEO of Nestlé Vietnam as a father figure, who can then engage in team building by encouraging employees to think of each other as siblings, was an approach that reflected Vietnamese culture. This is a case where the dialectic between corporate culture and ethnic culture has been managed successfully. This in fact is an objective of intercultural management: to harmonize the juxtaposition of corporate cultures and ethnic cultures.

However, there may be individual employees whose cultural backgrounds give rise to values that conflict with the core values of an organization. The resulting dissonance can be resolved satisfactorily by the employees either leaving the organization, or modifying their values. In other words, the core values of an organization are superordinate. The International Committee of the Red Cross faces the dilemma of dealing continuously with conflicts between corporate culture and ethnic culture. For example, in Afghanistan they are determined not to uphold conventional local attitudes to the treatment of women. If this entails having to enact a more diminished role in Afghanistan, then so be it.

The dialectic between corporate culture and ethnic culture has been described by Nestlé as follows: 'The Company's business practices are designed to promote a sense of identification among all employees all over the world, and apply a number of common rules, while at the same time adapting the expression of these rules to local customs and traditions' (Nestlé Corporate Business Principles). This of course is easier said than done. However, it must be emphasized that high-performance companies have strong cultures with well-defined core values. These core values are capable of adaptation to local customs, traditions and cultures. They cannot be supplanted by the values of other cultures.

CASE DISCUSSION QUESTIONS

1. Why is Nestlé successful in inculcating its core values in its branches around the world?

2. What is the dialectic between corporate core values and ethnic culture? How does this impact on the performance of cross-cultural managers?

3. What would be the differences in the dissemination process of Nestlé core values in Vietnam and in Germany?

4. Do core values play a special role for a transnational corporation?

5. Should Nestlé rest content with its core values? What likely modifications could Nestlé make in the next decade?

6. Why is it not incongruous for a transnational corporation like Nestlé to have some core values that originate in Switzerland?

ACADEMIC DISCUSSION

Organizational core values play the pivotal role of tying employees together, irrespective of cultural background. They imbue the employees of a global organization, distributed all over the world, with a sense of commonality of purpose. There is an emotional component to the sense of identification with these core values.

Core values of organizations tend to be durable. A core value of an organization could be that it is a learning organization. The organization would then be open to learning from other cultures and incorporating within its own systems practices that have worked well elsewhere. Credit Suisse is to some extent a learning organization, and is therefore prepared to learn from other cultures where it has operations. Nonetheless, even with Credit Suisse the corporate culture remains superordinate. This ensures that conflicting cultures do not clash and undermine performance. Thus, practices from a different culture that a transnational organization incorporates into its functioning are generally compatible with its core values. Effective global companies have at their command a portfolio of eclectic management practices.

An organization desirous of functioning successfully in diverse cultures must therefore select its core values appropriately. One of Nestlé's core values has been termed by them as 'Respect of other cultures and traditions'. The description of this core value is, 'Nestlé accepts cultural and social diversity' (Basic Nestlé Management and Leadership Principles). A Nestlé manager is expected to have 'international experience and understanding of other cultures'. Credit Suisse expects its international managers to develop cultural sensitivity. BMW insists that its managers have international exposure and acquit themselves well in culturally different scenarios before they find a place in the topmost echelons of management. All the organizations profiled here have as one of their core values 'respect of other cultures and traditions', although only Nestlé has articulated it and recorded this in document form.

SKILLS IN INTERCULTURAL MANAGEMENT: A CORE VALUE

The American Michael Todd, a former MBA student of mine at the IESE Business School (in 2001, while I was a visiting professor there), told in a student submission for a course on intercultural management of his failed attempts to procure a job in another culture. In May 2001 he tried for a summer internship in a multinational company, but his approaches to well-known multinationals operating in America such as Clorox, Nestlé and Del Monte proved unsuccessful. This was because recession was setting into the United States, and the major multinationals were hiring only one intern from every 50 who applied.

Todd expanded his search from well-established multinationals to less-known companies, and came to know about a vacancy with Target Japan, the Tokyo-based subsidiary of US multinational Boston Scientific, a medical device manufacturer. Their vacancy was in marketing management. The job required a comparative analysis of the existing distribution system and alternative systems. Todd felt that working in Japan, a country he had never visited, would be an interesting experience. He was quite hopeful about his prospects when he e-mailed his CV to the Vice-President, Marketing of Target Japan. He did not know Japanese, but the company had said it did not require a Japanese-speaking intern. He was also buoyed up by the fact that the Vice-President, Marketing was a Haas Business School alumnus.

A few days later Todd received a reply that the Vice-President, Marketing and a colleague were coming to Boston Scientific within the week, and wanted to interview him. The Vice-President, Marketing said he was impressed by Todd's background, especially his prior experience as a consultant. He also suggested that there might be a good fit between his company's requirements, and Todd's background and potential.

Todd spent time before his interview becoming familiar with both Boston Scientific and Target Japan. He learnt about the multinational's prime product, a coil used to prevent brain aneurisms from rupturing. He tried to think of arguments to offset the fact that he did not have a background in the medical devices industry. He even tried to anticipate questions he would be asked at the interview, and prepared appropriate responses.

On the day of the interview, Todd drove to the Boston Scientific office in Freemont feeling quietly confident. Within minutes of arrival he was ushered into the interview room and met the Vice-President, Marketing and his colleague. After they had introduced themselves to each other and exchanging formal greetings and handshakes, Todd was astonished to find the men facing him continued to stand. The vice-president then took out a business card, held it with both hands, and presented it to Todd with the print side facing him. Todd said 'thank you', and put the card in his pocket. The vice-president's colleague then presented his business card in the same way. Todd thanked this man as well, and put his card too in his pocket.

All three then sat, and the interview commenced. At the conclusion, Todd was quite pleased with his performance, and returned to Haas Business School confident that he would be going to Tokyo that summer. He went over the interview with a friend who had worked for some time in Tokyo. The friend opined that Todd had spoilt his chances by putting the business cards in his pocket in an offhand way.

In the Japanese culture business cards are accepted ceremoniously, especially if they are presented by someone senior. A card is received with both hands. The recipient examines it and makes a comment on its information: for example, on the person's title. What Todd had done was cavalier.

Target Japan did not hire Todd, who now says, 'in performing due diligence for this particular opportunity, I would have been well served to have researched the culture as well as the company'.

Target Japan values employees who display intercultural skills. High-performance multinational corporations expect their managers to have intercultural management competencies, and state this as a company core value, as has been done by Nestlé. Such companies prefer to hire expatriates who demonstrate not only professional competence, but intercultural management skills as well. For such companies, professional competence is a necessary but not a sufficient condition for being considered for a managerial position.

When the Target Japan senior managers presented their business cards to Todd, they were gauging whether he was aware how the Japanese handle them. Had he taken the trouble of finding out anything at all about Japan? Global companies that espouse as a core value the possession and development of intercultural skills do not want to hire foreigners who would behave like nerds sitting behind a desk crunching numbers. They are looking for people who will visit local museums in their spare time and acquaint themselves with local dance forms, music forms and so on. The question such global companies ask is whether the manager they are hiring will want to become accepted by local managers, by attempting to integrate into their way of life. Is it a meaningful value for that manager to learn about other cultures? Is it a meaningful value for that manager to imbibe aspects of another culture while living and working there?

A manager has to be adept at working with and through other people, and managers who detach themselves from their colleagues because of cultural differences will be unproductive. A cultural value is relatively durable in an adult, and difficult to modify in the short run. Hence, a sensitive multicultural corporation would prefer to hire a manager who already has some intercultural capabilities and can demonstrate evidence of this at an interview. Given globalization patterns, large numbers of managers are interested in knowing more about other cultures and becoming assimilated in those cultures when working there. Hence global companies are not finding it difficult to obtain managers with some measure of intercultural management skills, as Todd discovered. All the global managers interviewed for this book averred that transnational corporations should state as a core value that managers possess intercultural management skills.

CORE VALUES AS TIES THAT BIND ACROSS CULTURES

In their article about the Moscow McDonald's management education system, Vikhanski and Puffer (1993) have described how McDonald's success in Russia is attributable to the emphasis it placed on the dissemination of core values. The core values it disseminated in Moscow were the same as those disseminated in McDonald's America, or anywhere else in the world. These made the Russian employees of McDonald's feel part of the worldwide family of McDonald's. In fact, it is a core value of McDonald's that 'McDonald's is one big family and McDonald's cares about its workers' lives at work and outside work'. To operationalize this core value, Moscow McDonald's organized monthly social events for its employees. These included boat cruises along the Moscow River, sports meets, cultural programmes and other leisure time occupations, all paid for by Moscow McDonald's.

The employees of Moscow McDonald's were collectively called the crew of the restaurant. This is the term used at all McDonald's restaurants. McDonald's believes in using the same terms at all its restaurants worldwide to increase the sense of belonging to a single family. As an extension of this concept, Moscow McDonald's celebrated Hallowe'en, which is not normally celebrated in Russia. The Canadian staff at the restaurant initially took the lead in introducing the festival to their Russian co-workers. The celebration of Hallowe'en soon became an enjoyable and entertaining intercultural event. The crew found it fun to decorate their restaurant, wear Hallowe'en costumes, and have a party. They also liked the idea that they were engaging in an activity that their counterparts in many parts of the world participated in.

Professional events are also organized to strengthen the sense of family at Moscow McDonald's. These events, conducted as part of the chain of events engaged in by McDonald's restaurants worldwide, exert a strong motivational influence on the crew. One such professional event is the crew meeting, staged every three months. Another is the recognition of specific achievements of crew members, such as the attainment of certain milestones or excellence in performance.

Vikhanski and Puffer (1993) opine that because Moscow McDonald's employees feel special they had no difficulty adopting the work practices of McDonald's. 'They like the fact that, regardless of their position, they all call each other by their first name. They like to wear their nametag on their chest. They like to talk to customers with a smile, as if playing a theatrical role.' They were also proud to declare that they were part of the McDonald's family and were happy to wear the McDonald's uniform. There was nothing comparable to this core value of McDonald's – of all employees being part of a global family – in Russian corporations at that time. Consequently Moscow McDonald's employees had a sense of being unique, and wanted to demonstrate that they were worthy of their special status through exceptional performance.

There are two facets to a global corporation's successful operationalization of a core value. First, the core value should be worthy of being accorded core value status. It should have an inspirational component, and give the workforce a sense of direction. Second, the corporation should have the expertise to disseminate it across diverse cultures. Once this is achieved, a powerful unifying force holds the global corporation together. According to Wilmott (1993), the possibility of employees espousing heretical views leading to conflict situations is severely limited if the core values are strongly embedded. The strong core values held by McDonald's restaurants worldwide have enabled the corporation to be a high-performance company, free of debilitating conflict.

The success of Moscow McDonald's is reflected in the fact that it was the McDonald's restaurant worldwide that catered to the largest number of customers in the 1990s. In the first year of its operations it served 45,000 customers a day. The Russian customers were prepared to wait in line for 30 minutes to 1 hour to be served. Meanwhile, the motivated internal customers of Moscow McDonald's, the crew, provided speedy and quality service with a smile, in less than a minute.

At Moscow McDonald's, the employees did not feel schizophrenic about being part of the McDonald's family worldwide, while still being recognized as Russians. The strong work ethic that was communicated to them only served to imbue them with a sense of pride in their work. This made them admired by their compatriots. The crew were willing to reinforce the strong work ethic expected of them, by subscribing to it in fact. In the early 1990s there was never any evidence of discontent on the part of the Moscow McDonald's crew: so much so that Ivan, a maintenance person interviewed by Vikhanski and Puffer (1993), opined that he thought Russians were just like Canadians.

Moscow McDonald's did many things to ensure that their core value of a strong work ethic could take root in Russia. To begin with, it hired Moscow teenagers rather than adults as its crew. This was because Moscow McDonald's wanted employees without any work experience. That ensured that the core value of a strong work ethic could be engrained in employees who were unsullied by poor work habits. A few other companies have pursued this method of recruiting people with no prior work experience. Stephen Robbins (1990) has described how Sony Corporation recruited primarily school leavers who did not have any manufacturing experience for its branch in California. Since the new employees had no rigid views about their work life, they were easily inducted into the 'Sony family'. The employees at Sony California today feel proud to be part of the Sony family worldwide.

In the Russian culture, teenagers generally do not work, and labour laws exist to ensure that their academic pursuits do not suffer. Companies have to give time off for teenagers to take examinations. Since Moscow McDonald's felt that it would be difficult for teenagers to study and work for McDonald's with commitment to the company's core values, it decided to hire youngsters between the ages of 18 and 25, and not teenagers per se. In spite of this, it managed to attract droves of applicants with no prior work experience willing to be trained. This is aligned to McDonald's North America's policy of investing in the socializing of new employees so that they learn the company's core values. New employees of McDonald's in North America attend Hamburger University and are given inputs on how to behave.

Moscow McDonald's devised its own hiring procedures adapted to the Russian context, to ensure that its core values could take root among its employees. This was a departure from the route normally followed by transnational corporations operating in Moscow at that time. Transnational corporations in Russia usually took employees recommended by their joint venture partner. The joint venture partner recommended candidates it wished to patronize. Such employees did not have an appropriate work ethic and were therefore not of the same calibre as the transnational corporation's employees in other parts of the world. Such employees could not become part of that global corporation's family of employees.

Moscow McDonald's instead placed an advertisement in the Moscow newspapers inviting applications. The restaurant received 27,000 applications. This gave the company a huge pool of candidates from which to select those who could imbibe the company's core values. Additionally, it conducted a recruitment competition to shortlist candidates. The competition served to eliminate unsuitable candidates. It also invested the selected candidates with a sense of achievement, and motivated them to put their best foot forward.

Moscow McDonald's used the standard McDonald's training techniques. This strengthened its employees' sense that they were a part of the McDonald's family worldwide. In the United States, many employers are happy to take on former McDonald's crew members because of their good work ethic. This testifies to McDonald's capability for getting its employees to internalize company core values.

This is the case with Moscow McDonald's as well. New recruits are taught what work ethics and attitudes are expected of them. They learn to be responsible and disciplined, and adhere to high standards of quality and customer service. When crew members fall short of the mark in their work behaviour, they are given remedial instruction and training. A crew member is generally not fired for unsatisfactory performance. This helps employees feel that they are part of the McDonald's family.

Four Russians were selected to be managers at Moscow McDonald's when the restaurant first started operations. They received the same training as all other McDonald's managers. Thus the same management techniques were employed at Moscow McDonald's as are used in the other 10,500 McDonald's restaurants around the world. To ensure this, the managers were first sent to McDonald's Institute of Hamburgerology in Toronto for five months. The management programme included video-based education, lectures and on the job training. The four managers were then sent to McDonald's Hamburger University in the United States. This University was established in 1961 by McDonald's as a full-time international training centre. It gives its graduates a degree in hamburgerology.

There, the four Moscow McDonald's managers found that they were among McDonald's managers from all over the world; 235 on that occasion. They truly felt part of McDonald's global family. They also attended a course about advanced restaurant operations where they further imbibed McDonald's work ethics.

The way McDonald's successfully disseminated its core values at its Russian restaurant may be sharply contrasted with the inability of Canadian aerospace giant IMP Group Limited to embed its core values in the joint venture it started in Russia. IMP entered into a joint venture with Russia's national airline Aeroflot to start a hotel, the Moscow Aerostar.

Reference to the Moscow Aerostar experience will illustrate that the achievements of McDonald's were well earned, as they do not happen without thought and effort.

While McDonald's concentrated on youngsters who could be socialized into a given set of core values, Moscow Aerostar targeted 'the pick of the litter' who responded to their advertisements. These candidates were qualified professionals like medical doctors, psychology professors, engineers and lawyers. They were grossly over-qualified for many of the jobs they accepted such as receptionist, but at the same time had no experience of the hotel industry and had to be trained from scratch and treated like novices. The security supervisor had a 'degree from the Highest School of the Militia and a 5-year Law Degree' while the Bellman Supervisor had a 'degree from the Institute of Geological Prospecting'.

Given this information, it is not difficult to conclude that the employees of Moscow Aerostar did not experience a sense of pride in their work. Shea (1994) notes that when the Russian employees at Moscow Aerostar were quizzed about how they felt about the rewards they received, typical responses were as follows: 'The salary is not good but management treats me well', 'The hotel is not doing enough for me, I expected more', 'In general, I am pleased with what I am earning, but with respect to the West, it's nothing', and 'The bonus is not very useful, things are quite expensive at the hard currency shops.' By way of another example regarding the lack of satisfaction amongst the Moscow Aerostar employees, consider the following:

> On the first anniversary of the opening of the hotel, a banner was displayed thanking employees for their hard work and each one was personally handed a food basket containing a bottle of French red wine, a kilo of French cheese and a pineapple. Only one employee said thank you. In

fact, one employee said that he did not like red wine and asked for a bottle
of white.

(Shea, 1994)

The Russian employees at Moscow Aerostar were paid an average salary
of US$25 per month. This salary was double the state average. The
employees were also paid a performance-based bonus that for the better
performing could be as much as US$140 per month. IMP felt that they
were being generous to their Russian employees because they were
being paid more than Russian companies were paying their employees.
The Russian employees at Moscow Aerostar however could not resist
comparing themselves with what the Canadian expatriates were receiving.

IMP had originally envisaged that it would halve the number of
expatriates at the end of one year. Instead, at the end of one year the
number of expatriates increased. Considering the blatant disparity
between the Russian employees' income and the Canadian expatriates'
income, the Russians can hardly have been expected to feel part of a
family. Additionally, employees who feel that they are being treated as
second-class citizens in comparison with employees from another culture are not going to be mentally receptive to corporate core values.
Moscow McDonald's, by contrast, pulled out all its expatriates within a
year and a half of starting operations, and replaced them with Russian
managers.

Major impediments to developing Russian managers and communicating Moscow Aerostar's core values to them were IMP's defective
orientation and training programmes. In the first instance, all training
was done in Moscow. One reason the Russians were not given training
in Canada was because it was feared they would not return, but would
find ways of staying on in Canada. After all, they were engineers,
doctors, scientists, computer specialists and so on, who might attempt to
locate jobs in Canada where they could use their professional expertise.
Additionally, and more to the point, it was more economical to conduct
the training in Moscow. By contrast, Moscow McDonald's ensured that
all its managers were trained in Canada. The top managers were further
trained, as has already been mentioned, at the McDonald's international
training centre in America. Naturally, far from feeling discriminated
against, the Moscow McDonald's managers felt integrated into the
McDonald's worldwide family. Consequently, they felt motivated to do
their best for the company.

Far from having a clue why she was having no success in transmitting
IMP's core values to the managers of Moscow Aerostar, Laurie Sagle,

the Canadian Director for Training and Personnel, surmised that the fault must rest entirely with the Russians. In fact, most of the fault lay with her and the fact that she had imposed a quasi-Canadian system of training on the Russians. One day of the training was devoted to teaching employees how to smile. This was done using role plays and evaluations. After the employees had mastered the art of smiling, they learnt how to listen. Those who had to handle telephones were then given input on telephone manners. This was followed by a day devoted to teaching female employees how to use make-up. On this occasion, Laurie Sagle went to great lengths to demonstrate that 'the woman who rated highest on productivity and efficiency was the one with an appropriate amount of make-up on, because she looked like she was ready for business'. After the employees had learnt how to smile, listen and speak on the telephone, they were subjected to a written test.

A transnational orientation programme is an important vehicle for transmitting a company's core values to their employees. If the wrong values are communicated at this point, the damage done is almost irreversible. At the Moscow Aerostar orientation, what message were the highly educated Russian employees likely to pick up? One possibility is that they are being trained to 'act out' a role, and in the process make inroads into the wallets of their customers.

Meanwhile, the employees could observe that Moscow Aerostar was making a great deal of money. The Canadian newspaper *Globe and Mail* (9 February 1993) reported that a single-occupancy room with breakfast at the Moscow Aerostar cost US~$205 per night. A suite for triple occupancy cost US~$395 per night. Moscow Aerostar's restaurants charged prices comparable to similar restaurants in Canada. The main restaurant offered the full buffet meals that the restaurants of international four-star hotels normally offer. Lobster dinners were available three nights a week. Moscow Aerostar also had a steak and seafood restaurant. Thus the Russian employees of Moscow Aerostar who were not entitled to a bonus earned less in one year than the hotel charged per night for a triple occupancy suite.

Under these circumstances, the Russian employees of Moscow Aerostar had no reason to believe that they were part of a family of global employees. They would not perceive the company as possessing any core values worth mentioning. On the contrary, it is likely that they saw themselves as being exploited. First, their compensation was not commensurate with the profits generated by Moscow Aerostar. Second, their expatriate colleagues were paid substantially higher salaries. And third, they were expected to act out in an artificial and contrived fashion in front of their patrons with the sole intention of getting these patrons to spend money.

At McDonald's, by contrast, the employees perceived that they were being paid equitably. They were provided with perquisites that were eminently suitable for them. Perquisites as a form of compensation offered by a global company will be appreciated more fully if they are relevant for a specific culture. At Moscow McDonald's the perquisites included free healthcare facilities at premium hospitals and clinics, free meals on the job and free vacations. Moscow McDonald's employees were also able to order groceries from the restaurants' suppliers at wholesale cost. This provision was to help employees offset problems of unreliable supplies of groceries that they otherwise had to contend with in Moscow.

Any effort at talking in terms of core values by Moscow Aerostar is likely to be viewed with scepticism by their Russian employees. After all, they believe that they are not being treated fairly. To add insult to injury, IMP made a bonus system a part of the compensation scheme. The Russians probably perceived this system as a mechanism by which IMP could 'play with them'. Laurie Sagle had intended that the bonus system should act as a motivational tool. However, the Canadian system of trying to build up star performers was not going to work at Moscow Aerostar, where the employees had been accustomed to a collectivist regime. That is not to say that a bonus system cannot be introduced for a Russian workforce. However, under conditions where the employing multinational company is viewed as lacking in core values, any attempt to use systems different from what the local nationals have been accustomed to would be resented. The Canadian senior management was astonished whenever they were faced with such situations as supervisors wanting to know why non-supervisors were excluded from attending the special functions that were organized for the supervisors alone. The situation that seems to have emerged is one of the Canadians and Russians being so culturally different that they were unable to share the same core values, which need not have been the case at all.

At Moscow McDonald's by contrast, attempts were made to tap productively the collectivist mentality that may have existed among the Russian employees. Contests were periodically held to get teams of employees to compete against each other. The restaurant managed to organize these events in a spirit of fun, and these efforts were not resented. The multinational company was assessed as having deeply held core values that they adhered to in practice. This enabled the Russian employees to accept any practices the company introduced in Russia in good faith.

At Moscow Aerostar, Laurie Sagle believed that the training programme she had implemented was the cornerstone of her effort to build an effective workforce. Unfortunately, she missed a golden opportunity to win the loyalty of Russian employees. Unfortunately she saw the training programme only as a mechanism for 'elevating' the Russian employees up to international standards. She did not see that there was also a requirement on IMP's part to use this as an occasion to try to bond with its employees. The relationship between employing corporation and employed personnel has to be viewed as a mutually symbiotic relationship. In the case of Moscow Aerostar, the Russian employees were viewed from a condescending angle and not as equal partners.

During the training programme, an entire session was devoted to teaching the Russian employees how to communicate better. A game used at the session was the 'broken telephone line game'. For this game the participants sit in a row. The participant at one end whispers a message into the ear of the next person, who in turn whispers what he or she hears into the ear of the next person, and so on down the line. The last person in the line says out loud what he or she has heard. This, more often than not, is a garbled version of the original message. The object is to demonstrate that communication can get distorted if a message is not conveyed properly, and that as the communication is relayed to more and more people who engage in distortion, the message can get completely twisted out of shape.

Although the game is amusing and can serve as an icebreaker, the learning derived from it is quite trivial. It is rather outdated as a training technique. The highly qualified Russians who attended the communications sessions must have found it farcical. Inadvertently, IMP was presenting itself as a multinational that over-valued itself. Was this the best training session in communications that IMP could conceive of for its Russian hotel?

As has already been stated, it is the core values of a transnational corporation that hold it together. To ensure that these core values can be disseminated effectively, a transnational corporation must first of all have core values that are worthy of dissemination. Second, it should begin the process of inculcating these values to a branch in a new culture from the beginning. Many successful transnational corporations begin the process of dissemination at the initial orientation and training programmes. Third, the senior management functioning in the new culture, especially the senior management from the home country, should be seen as operationalizing those core values in their own work lives.

NATIONAL CULTURES AND CORPORATE CORE VALUES

A classic view about the linkage between national cultures and corporate core values is reflected in the work of Hofstede (2001), a highly respected scholar. However, the view we espouse in this book diverges from the traditional perspective, and will be discussed in this section.

The classical view avers that attempts by a multinational corporation to establish a common culture in all its branches across the globe will be offset by the influences of national cultures. We suggest that especially since different cultures exist, it is important to hold a transnational organization together with core values. Core values are not synonymous with culture. Core values are certain beliefs about what the organization stands for; how it values its customers, both internal and external; the direction in which the organization should move; and the nature of its work ethics. For a transnational corporation to be effective in intercultural management, not only should it have meaningful core values that must be effectively disseminated across all cultures, but also the employees must hold these core values as superordinate to all other beliefs, whether individual, societal, or national. Thus, if a multinational corporation operates in Russia and has as a core value 'respect for time', it should find ways of ensuring that its workforce is punctual and delivers services on time. This can be done, as McDonald's proved. To say that the national culture of Russia precludes the possibility of a Russian workforce respecting time is to err on the side of using cultural stereotypes. In every culture there are people who have received quality professional education, and can work according to internationally acceptable standards. If the skills of the local workforce require upgrading, training should be provided. The training methodology can reflect local culture. The core values, however, need not be modified, as was described in the opening case of this chapter.

The locally hired employees of transnational companies often talk about how they conform to high standards of work ethics at their place of work, and then adjust to different attitudes to work elsewhere. But they do it.

Returning here to the traditional view of national cultures and corporate core values, let us examine the traditional view and juxtapose that view with a modern counterpoint. Fombrun (1984) saw corporate culture as being conditioned by societal forces. That may be true up to a point, and hence it may be useful to examine a commonly cited definition of corporate culture:

> Corporate culture is the pattern of basic assumptions that a given group has invented, discovered or developed in learning to cope with its problems of external adaptation and internal integration. These have worked well enough to be considered valid, and are therefore taught to new members as the correct way to perceive, think and feel in relation to those problems. (Schein, 1984)

This definition indicates that to some extent, culture follows an evolutionary path. Culture must adapt, alter, enlarge and discard in order to be relevant and functional. A definition of corporate culture normally subsumes some aspects of core values as well. However, core values once articulated have a durable quality, and normally are invariant over time. The core values of a corporation are akin to the constitution of a nation-state. They are amended only occasionally, and after considerable reflection and cogitation. Hence, the core values of a transnational corporation need not change just because the corporation is located in different cultures. Other aspects of culture must be altered suitably as the corporation discovers its own way of achieving external adaptation and internal integration in a new culture.

Laurent (1989) also upholds the traditional view regarding national cultures and corporate core values. Laurent saw national cultures as being more powerful and stable than those of individual companies. National cultures do tend to be powerful. Hence, successful transnational corporations do not seek to influence national cultures. They only try to select managers from other cultures who can accept their core values.

Hofstede (2001) made the most important contribution to the classic view on culture. He looked at the employees of IBM in different cultures to ascertain their similarities and differences. He looked at operations in 50 countries, zeroed in on the differences between employees, and established a means of defining those differences in terms of culture. He identified five dimensions, of which four are classical and the fifth has only recently been added. Hofstede called the four classical dimensions power distance, uncertainty avoidance, individualism–collectivism, and masculinity–femininity. (The fifth dimension is short term versus long term.) Employees of IBM were rated on a scale on each dimension, and the employees of each country were then constituted into a cluster. Ultimately what emerged was a typology vis-à-vis the dimensions for each of the 40 countries in which IBM employees were working. The effects of individual and organizational variables were controlled so that what emerged, Hofstede attributed to the effect of culture. We place here definitions of the four dimensions as presented by Buchanan and Huczynski (1997):

Power distance is the extent to which members of society accept an unequal distribution of power. Uncertainty avoidance is how much members of a society are threatened by uncertain and ambiguous situations. Individualism–collectivism is the tendency to take care of oneself and one's family versus the tendency to work together for the common good. Masculinity–feminity is the extent to which highly assertive masculine values predominate (acquisition of money at the expense of others) versus showing sensitivity and concern for others' welfare.

It is not abundantly clear why Hofstede selected these dimensions as a way of differentiating national cultures. The dimensions also do not reflect the range of cultural variation within a single nation. Generally, competent managers from most countries belong to a subculture that may not be described by Hofstede's categories. The impact of national cultures can be mitigated somewhat, by companies doing what Nestlé does: selecting the right people and then reinforcing company core values through ongoing training and development.

Since Hofstede's work has received much notice, and many transnational corporations educate their managers about Hofstede's dimensions, it is desirable that we devote some attention to his four dimensions.

From a management perspective, the power distance dimension assesses the extent to which a culture accommodates the use of power by a boss figure. Nations that rank high on the power distance dimension expect bosses to behave in a directive manner, while the bosses themselves tend to be autocratic. Low trust prevails between bosses and subordinates, so the subordinates prefer to have the bosses take decisions as well as the responsibility for those decisions. Generally, subordinates avoid arguing with their bosses. In nations that register a low score on the power distance dimension, a more collegial relationship exists between bosses and subordinates. Decision making is more participative and there exists a greater degree of mutual trust.

The uncertainty avoidance dimension indicates the extent to which the culture of a nation encourages or inhibits risk taking. According to Hofstede, the people of different cultures vary in their capacity to take risks as well as tolerate ambiguity. Nations that rate high on uncertainty avoidance have employees who prefer jobs for life. These employees work hard to counteract the stress that arises from uncertainty on the job. They expect their co-workers to follow established norms and rules. People from cultures that rate low on uncertainty avoidance take risks, and do not feel uncomfortable when faced with ambiguity. They are not very particular that rules should be followed.

The individualism–collectivism dimension gauges the extent to which a culture emphasizes individual requirements as opposed to group concerns. In cultures where individualism is high, emphasis is placed on individuals achieving their goals and objectives, and rewards being accorded to individual performance. Individuals are concerned primarily with themselves and their immediate families. In collectivist cultures, people are also concerned about their extended family, as well as their community. Employees in companies give their loyalty, in return for which they receive support and protection.

The masculinity–femininity dimension reflects the kind of achievements that are appreciated by a culture. Masculine cultures place an emphasis on the acquisition of material possessions, being ambitious, and on a distinct differentiation between male and female roles. Hofstede averred that masculine cultures value people for their material possessions. In feminine countries, the divide between male and female roles is not rigid, and men and women view each other from the standpoint of equality. Also, considerable importance is accorded to the environment, quality of life, and to caring.

Using his four dimensions, Hofstede constructed a cultural map of the world, and positioned the forty countries he had investigated in this cultural map. This cultural map is depicted in Table 3.1.

Each of the four dimensions is measured by a continuum. Hence, a country can be positioned anywhere on a continuum and not merely at either end. For example, Hofstede has assessed Japan as having a culture that allows the moderate exercise of power by bosses. It also accommodates moderate individualism, and by the same token, moderate collectivism.

Hofstede placed the 40 countries he had studied into eight categories. He employed the statistical tool of cluster analysis to arrive at the classification. Each culture cluster comprises countries that are homogeneous with respect to their positioning in Hofstede's typology. Each cluster is also significantly different from the other clusters. The scores for the answers given to questions posed to the IBM managers of a country were arrived at separately for that country. The final score for each culture was the average value of that culture.

Since the scores are averages they have limited predictive value. Most of the managers interviewed for this book found that the managers from other cultures they interacted with did not necessarily behave as suggested by Hofstede's cultural map. When multinational corporations like Nestlé stress that sensitivity to intercultural management should be a core value, they are approaching the phenomenon from a different angle

Table 3.1 *Hofstede's cultural map: national cultures classified by the four dimensions*

1. More developed Latin	2. Less developed Latin	
high power distance	*high power distance*	
high uncertainty avoidance	*high uncertainty avoidance*	
high individualism	*high individualism*	
medium masculinity	*whole range of masculinity*	
Belgium	Colombia	Portugal
France	Mexico	Yugoslavia
Argentina	Venezuela	
Brazil	Chile	
Spain	Peru	

3. More developed Asian	4. Less developed Asian	
medium power distance	*high power distance*	
high uncertainty avoidance	*low uncertainty avoidance*	
medium individualism	*low individualism*	
high masculinity	*medium masculinity*	
Japan	Pakistan	India
	Taiwan	Philippines
	Thailand	Singapore
	Hong Kong	

5. Near Eastern	6. Germanic	
high power distance	*low power distance*	
high uncertainty avoidance	*high uncertainty avoidance*	
low individualism	*medium individualism*	
medium masculinity	*high masculinity*	
Greece	Austria	Switzerland
Iran	Israel	South Africa
Turkey	Germany	Italy

7. Anglo	8. Nordic
low power distance	*low power distance*
low to medium uncertainty avoidance	*low to medium uncertainty avoidance*
high individualism	*medium individualism*
high masculinity	*low masculinity*
Australia	Denmark
Canada	Finland
Britain	The Netherlands
Ireland	Norway
New Zealand	Sweden
USA	

Source: Open University (1985) *International Perspectives, Managing in Organizations*, T244, Unit 16, Block V (Wider Perspectives), p 60.

from Hofstede. Instead of using models to predict uniform behaviour for an entire nation, they prefer that their employees view all the managers they interact with from the standpoint that they are unique, and that culture is too complex to be pinned down to four dimensions.

Generally in every national culture, there are a large number of sub-cultures at variance with each other, and with the overall national culture. This makes it all the more vital that transnational corporations articulate and implement core values that enable their employees to have a clear organizational identity. A Nestlé manager working in France, for instance, would answer the question 'Who am I?' by emphatically stating, 'In my professional life, I am a Nestlé manager. I therefore have to learn how to function as a team player and assume a collegial relationship with my boss and subordinates, even if I belong to a culture that rates high on the power distance index.'

Fons Trompenaars (1993) is another luminary in the field of inter-cultural management who has developed a typology for assessing the national cultures of countries. Since Trompenaars' typology has generated a fair amount of interest, we will take a look at it.

Just as Hofstede constructed a model on the basis of his four dimensions, Trompenaars advanced four types of corporate cultures, on the basis of which he constructed a typology. According to Trompenaars, 'differences between national cultures help determine the type of corporate culture chosen' in different countries. In our book, we argue that the branches of an international company do not undergo the kind and extent of differentiation suggested by Trompenaars. Differences in national cultures may lead to some differentiation in the various branches of a transnational corporation. This only serves to highlight the requirement for appropriate core values to hold a transnational corporation together.

Trompenaars has labelled the four types of culture he has described as the family, the Eiffel Tower, the guided missile and the incubator.

▎ **The family:** Trompenaars uses the metaphor of the family to describe a type of corporate culture where relationships between managers are personal. There exists a well-defined hierarchy.

▎ **The Eiffel Tower:** Trompenaars chooses the metaphor of the Eiffel Tower to symbolize a corporate culture that is bureaucratic. There exists a clear division of labour, with various roles and functions coordinated by the top management.

▎ **The guided missile:** The guided missile corporate culture resembles that of project teams used by the National Aeronautics and Space

Organization (NASA) to fabricate guided missiles. Organizations that adopt the guided missile culture are egalitarian. When an organization with the guided missile type of culture is superimposed on one with an Eiffel Tower type, the result is a matrix organization.

▌ **The incubator:** This type of a corporate culture strives to make organizations serve as incubators where managers can achieve self-expression and self-fulfilment. Relationships amongst managers are both personal and egalitarian.

Table 3.2 *Trompenaars' cultural map: national patterns of corporate culture*

Family	Eiffel Tower	Guided missile	Incubator
France	Denmark	USA	Sweden
Belgium	Netherlands	Canada	
India	Germany	UK	
Spain			
Japan			

Countries that belong to a cluster are differentiated from each other in the extent to which they are formal or informal, and centralized or decentralized.

Multicultural action points

Neale and Mindel (1992) have described how the British Petroleum office in Brussels developed some core values specifically for enhancing intercultural skills, which they called 'multi-cultural action points'. The office had employees from 40 countries. These multicultural action points include, 'Do not judge people, functions or cultures; Create a climate where people are not embarrassed to ask; Give time to express yourself; You are talking to a person not a country; Give and ask for feedback; Accept the differences; Avoid clique building; Try to eliminate stereotyping.'

According to Neale and Mindel, it takes much more time and effort to get a multicultural team to coalesce than it does for a monoculture. However, it is worth the time and effort involved, because a cohesive multicultural team is capable of exceptional performance. It has to be kept in mind that the team-building effort for a multicultural team requires great planning and skill. Neale and Mindel's specific advice is that multicultural teams have to tolerate and accept a diversity of approaches, while preventing the formation of cliques.

The important learning point is that when accepting of a diversity of approaches is made a core value, the team-building effort in a multi-cultural corporation becomes that much more simple.

We would like to draw special attention to two of British Petroleum's 'multi-cultural action points' as reported by Neale and Mindel: 'You are talking to a person not a country' and 'Do not prejudge people, functions or cultures.' Intercultural managers are advised against deciding in advance how to interact with a manager from, say, Australia. They might take some pointers from Hofstede's cultural map and decide in robotic fashion to assume a particular style. They might then be tempted to alter their style, again taking pointers from Hofstede's cultural map, when they have to interact next with a manager from Austria.

Neale and Mindel reported that until a multicultural team was established around the multicultural action points, the employees behaved in ways that confirmed cultural stereotypes. The British managers when working late viewed such behaviour as an indication of loyalty and work dedication. The Scandinavian managers felt that by working late, they were displaying their inefficiency and incapacity to complete work on time. The French liked to shake hands every day as an indication of friendliness. The American managers tended to eschew the daily shaking of hands, deeming the gesture to be unnecessarily formal.

We would like to posit here the hypothesis that when a multicultural group of managers is formed from groups of monocultural managers, the managers tend to form subcultures along national lines. Each then tends to exaggerate its national characteristics as a mode of coming to terms with the new environment. This then underscores the need for core values to bring all the subcultures together.

CORE VALUES AND THE INTEGRATIONIST/ DIFFERENTIATION PERSPECTIVE ON CULTURE

The differentiation perspective on culture focuses on diversity, and has been advanced most appealingly by Martin (1992). When the different-iation perspective on culture is applied to transnational corporations, these are seen as made up of subcultures that are 'sometimes in harmony, sometimes in conflict, and sometimes in indifference to one another' (Martin, 1992).

The differentiation perspective on culture is an extreme description of culture, like the other two perspectives put forward by Martin, the integration perspective and fragmentation perspective. Of the three perspectives, the integration and differentiation perspectives are most germane to our discussion here. Since they are extreme descriptions, not everything posited in the integration and differentiation perspectives is referred to. However, the perspectives, being modern, are deserving of mention.

Although differentiationists are interested in emphasizing subcultures, they do accept that certain features of a dominant culture exist in all organizations. They acknowledge the existence of unifying forces in much the same way that integrationists do. Where they diverge from integrationists is in insisting that subcultures within a transnational corporation are hierarchically arranged, and power struggles exist between various subcultures. We accept the existence of differing subcultures in transnational corporations, these subcultures being defined by national or ethnic cultures. However, based on the interviews conducted for this book, we would like to suggest that subcultures need not be hierarchically arranged or habitually in a state of opposition.

At this juncture, we would like to draw inspiration from the integrationist perspective. This perspective holds that the culture of a corporation is enshrined in its core values. This acts as an integrative mechanism or organizational glue holding together the diverse groups within that organization. There are two aspects to the integrationist perspective that we consider important. These are the existence of an organization-wide consensus among members regarding the core values that hold them together, and clarity regarding what these core values mean in differing cultures. As per the integrationist perspective, uncertainty and ambiguity regarding roles and identities are dispensed with when resort is made to the unifying effect of core values. Cultures, or core values, as we have defined them, are 'existing to alleviate anxiety, to control the uncontrollable, to bring predictability to the uncertain, and to clarify the ambiguous' (Martin, 1992).

Integrationists like to focus on those organizational manifestations that contribute to consistency and ignore inconsistencies. We beg to differ. Core values contribute to a global organization having some consistency regarding orientation. Meanwhile, the inconsistencies are not ignored. Successful global organizations find mechanisms for dealing with the inconsistencies induced by culture. They also devise methods for detecting inconsistencies before these inconsistencies become deeply entrenched.

Integrationists have emphasized that consistency is achieved via three facets: action consistency, symbolic consistency and content consistency.

Action consistency refers to the congruence of managerial behaviour with an articulated core value. For a global company, this implies that an articulated core value is operationalized at all its locations. Thus the Nestlé managers of Vietnam are expected by the company to enact the core values of Nestlé with as much commitment as their counterparts in Switzerland.

Symbolic consistency occurs when the rites, rituals and customs of a global company are aligned to its core values. When Moscow McDonald's gives the same training to its Russian managers in Moscow as it does to its Canadian managers in Toronto, it is underscoring the McDonald's core value that all employees belong to a single global family. Content consistency ensues when all the core values of a global corporation are in synchrony with each other. Thus, Nestlé stresses long-term viable goals that are consistent with its core value of respecting customers.

Some well-known researchers in the field of organizational behaviour, especially with reference to the study of culture, are integrationists. These include Schein (1986), and Ouchi (1981). Most of the managers interviewed for this book concur that the integrationist perspective makes sense. The appeal of this perspective lies in the fact that it partially explains the experience of high-performance transnational corporations. Since it posits core values as entirely within the gift of a corporation to define, the integrationist approach offers scope for managerial control on outcomes.

SUMMARY

It is core values that hold a transnational organization together and constitute the common thread that binds its employees hailing from a myriad of cultures. High-performance organizations tend to have well-defined, strong core values that have been internalized by their entire workforce worldwide. The core values impact on all other aspects of organizational functioning such as structure, strategy, conflict resolution, communication and human resources management. Successful transnational organizations include the value of 'respect for diversity and proficiency in intercultural management skills' as part of their core values. The process of embedding core values is a continuous one and requires constant monitoring, evaluation and reevaluation.

When there is a conflict between core values and corporate culture on the one hand, and the cultural heritage of individual employees on the other, it is core values that ought to be paramount. Thus, transnational organizations go to great lengths to recruit managers who can align themselves with their core values. They also spend considerable resources to ensure that the managers they have inducted are able to internalize organizational core values and successfully apply these values in their work life.

4

Strategy and intercultural management

BMW AND 'GLOCALIZATION': CASE STUDY IN INTERCULTURAL MANAGEMENT

BMW is a European company of note that is making concerted efforts to address the issue of intercultural management. Its efforts have resulted from its multinational operations. This company has managed to carve out an enviable niche market for itself in the premium segment of the automobile industry through technological innovation. Through its R & D efforts, it has always striven to be at the cutting edge. In July 2001, it became the first automobile company to unveil a prototype version of a 7-Series saloon car with a hydrogen-powered engine. That BMW has done so is not at all surprising, given that the prestige of this company relies on the engine-making ability of its brilliant engineers. The demand for hydrogen-powered cars that can replace petroleum-based fuel vehicles is a real one, given the capacity for these cars to emit fewer toxins.

The company has had to manage a companion challenge to its success in the market. This challenge is that of evolving and applying a corporate strategy that facilitates its advancement as a global corporation. BMW has evolved a corporate strategy that reflects its global interests. This global strategy BMW has described as 'glocalization', 'where the aim is to find the right combination of global networking and local policy'.

BMW has developed a unique training system designed to take cognizance of 'glocalization'. At the apex of this system is the International Management Training Group. This Group first convened in 1990. The group, with a different membership every year, comprises 16 top managers from different countries who are candidates for promotion within the BMW Group. The objective of the International Management Training disseminated to each group annually is to ensure that BMW can, first, think and act globally but also, second, work within the framework of different cultures.

Intercultural management orientation for top managers

We looked recently at the International Management Training Group (IMTG) for 1997. This Group comprised seven senior managers from Germany, four from the United Kingdom, and one each from the United States, the Caribbean, Austria, Australia and Switzerland. These managers were formally presented with an opportunity to form a network, which has since stood them in good stead, as they have been able to draw on each other's resources. They also collectively analysed a live BMW case requiring intercultural management expertise to resolve successfully. This case centred on the consolidation and enlargement of BMW operations in Thailand. A member of this IMTG, Jesus Cordoba from BMW (Caribbean), was CEO-designate for BMW Thailand.

To better understand the situation on the ground, the IMTG went to Thailand for a week.

Actual problem-solving
Every morning, the group discussed and debated various issues pertaining to BMW operations in Thailand and formulated recommendations, which Cordoba subsequently adopted. BMW was at that time buying back the local licence to market its automobiles from a leading Thai-Chinese business family. IMTG 1997 thus obtained insights into managing intercultural problems in Thailand, a territory hitherto unknown to most of them. They were also members of a culturally diverse group, which in itself was a learning experience.

A year after IMTG 1997 had assembled in Bangkok the group convened again, this time in Geneva.

Information sharing by competitors

One of the highlights for the IMTG 1997 in 1998 was attending the Geneva Road Show. All non-Swiss members were astonished by the extent of information sharing among rival automobile companies in Switzerland. Data on orders received and sales achieved were in the public domain. By contrast, the German members of the group admitted that they would never be given comparable data by say Mercedes-Benz in Germany.

Open-mindedness

The rationale behind the International Management Training as imparted to IMTG 1997 is to foster open-mindedness among its global managers. Observations made at the Geneva Road Show reinforced their awareness that ways of transacting business can differ across cultures. Hence BMW managers did not commence their factory operations on the supposition that German management practices were the best in the world and should be imposed on the Thai.

What IMTG 1997 found out, according to one senior member of the group, was how difficult it is for a European to pursue entrepreneurial activities in Thailand. The local people tend to be extremely reserved, with the result that outsiders cannot fully gauge the reactions and responses of their Thai counterparts.

BMW adopted a three-step procedure for Thailand. This procedure was developed by IMTG 1997 after having examined the functioning of other German companies like Siemens in Thailand. The first step was to induct Thais into key positions in BMW. These were second-line management jobs reporting directly to the CEO. The Thai senior managers acted as gatekeepers, communicating to BMW what various Thai groups (employees, customers, government) really wanted and expected.

The second step was to inculcate and disseminate BMW values among these newly appointed Thai managers – a good example of 'glocalization' in action. These individuals had been recruited meticulously and felt proud to work for an internationally reputed and top-rated corporation like BMW. They were keen to imbibe BMW values. It then became their responsibility to exert influence over the remainder of the Thai workforce, and bring them in line with BMW's organizational objectives. As Thais, they naturally understood the Thai mind-set as no expatriate could. A member of the IMTG 1997 observed that Thais just smile politely even when they disagree. This could cause a serious problem for non-Thai managers unacquainted with this trait.

The third step was for BMW to consolidate itself in Thailand, as a company that respects and values Thai culture. The commercial rationale is compelling. If BMW was viewed as a 'killer' company, it would be forever alienated from the local population. One example of this was to adopt the same environmental protection standards as in Germany, even though the legislation is not as stringent in Thailand. This sort of policy perhaps explains why BMW has topped the Dow Jones Sustainability Index.

Once the company becomes well established, it is expected that a Thai CEO will be appointed. This is already the practice of the company in countries where there is a large and well-grounded operation: Italy, France and Switzerland for example.

'Glocalization' is the key concept driving BMW's intercultural orientation. The company is operationalizing this concept in its own way. It has been pursuing a global approach to corporate strategy, which is then implemented in each country after being adapted to that country's cultural heritage. The managerial challenge lies in resolving the apparent contradictions involved. BMW prefers to develop and depend on the expertise of managers from the countries in which it has operations, rather than extensively use expatriates. Its management practices are also sufficiently permeable to allow the adoption of culture-specific approaches. Some of these approaches, when found successful and inherently sound, are then recommended for use worldwide.

Inferences

The following tentative inferences may be drawn from the BMW case:

▮ Global companies require managers possessing intercultural management skills. These skills can be learnt, just like other behavioural science skills like leadership or team spirit.

▮ BMW believes in fostering intercultural management expertise through education. The International Management Training Groups are part of this educational effort.

■ Members of International Management Training Groups develop sensitivity to local cultures, and thereby formulate country-specific policies that reflect cultural tones and flavours.

■ Divisions may be differentiated by the need to take cognizance of local cultures, but they are integrated by a common set of values, orientation and global strategy.

■ Cultures however are not static. This truism applies with equal force to ethnic cultures and corporate cultures. Corporate cultures functioning in an intercultural context must be permeable enough to imbibe what is useful from ethnic cultures. They must also be sensitive enough to assess trends and changes in ethnic cultures. Ethnic cultures of emerging economies are more susceptible to change than those of mature economies.

■ In the BMW case, intercultural management is characterized by the fact that operational decision making has been delegated to its various country divisions.

■ Local talent who have internalized BMW values and then transferred these values to the local context manage these local divisions.

■ BMW stresses learning about cultures through first-hand exposure. Issues about the management of country divisions are discussed by International Management Training Groups. These groups comprise top BMW managers from different countries. The groups often discuss and analyse issues pertaining to a country of which they have no first-hand knowledge. In order to make worthwhile recommendations, the group travels to the country in question for a short sojourn, to learn about it.

The company is now poised for further growth. Its plans for the future are based on assessments made at its various country divisions. In the United Kingdom, it has divested itself of both the Rover and Land Rover brands of automobile, having sold the former to Phoenix Corporation and the latter to General Motors. In Thailand, on the other hand, it acquired its operations in 1997, at a time when the baht had fallen to an all-time low and purchasing power was also low. The Thai economy has since recovered fairly well. BMW has panache for financial prowess combined with skills in intercultural management.

CASE STUDY DISCUSSION QUESTIONS

1. What are the elements of BMW's corporate strategy that have contributed to its success as a global corporation?

2. How did BMW enact its corporate strategy in Thailand keeping in mind the local culture?

3. In what ways would BMW enact its strategy differently for its operations in the United Kingdom?

4. Why does BMW encourage its top management echelon to be in a continuous learning mode vis-à-vis national culture?

5. How can BMW further refine its intercultural approach to strategy formulation and implementation?

6. Does BMW believe that formulating strategy that can adapt to local culture is an evolutionary process?

ACADEMIC DISCUSSION

This chapter examines the dynamics involved in the formulation and implementation of strategy by global companies. As already mentioned in the case study presented above, the challenge of corporate strategy in an intercultural management context is finding a balance between global policy and local approach. The balance in reality is in a state of flux.

Transnational aspects of corporate strategy

Certain tools and techniques of corporate strategy contribute to the effectiveness of organizational functioning, irrespective of culture. Practically all the global managers interviewed for this book concur that the following techniques of corporate strategy can be adopted in any culture.

Action planning
This ensures that the various strategies formulated by a transnational corporation are implemented in every culture, and the appropriate managers are held accountable for their responsibilities.

Action planning is particularly efficacious if it is formulated in a clear fashion. This reduces misinterpretations arising out of cultural differences. Generally, the first step in action planning is conceptualizing how the project should be executed from beginning to end. This is followed by a description of how each project task is to be performed. The description contains the names of managers who will perform the tasks, as well as those who will provide support functions. Care should be taken to ensure that all the necessary tasks have been included.

At this stage, the MASTERS criteria referred to by Cushway and Lodge (1999) can be used. The acronym MASTERS stands for measurable, achievable, specific, time related, encompassing, realistic, and stretching. These criteria are used to assess whether the task descriptions have been formulated properly.

The next step is to ensure that everybody's assumptions about the business programme being operationalized are congruent. The tasks then have to be arranged in a proper sequence, with the tasks that have to be completed before subsequent tasks can be started being performed first. Tasks that can be performed parallel to other tasks should be identified as well. The time required for the execution of each task also has to be gauged and recorded. The date on which each task has to be initiated and completed has to be noted. The managers and other resources required for task completion have then to be deployed. Finally, the managers have to decide on a reasonable time frame for reviewing the action steps.

The balanced scorecard

This is a corporate strategy tool that has been developed by Kaplan and Norton (1996) so that global companies can be more competitive in modern times. This tool enables global companies to optimize the use of their intangible assets. The balanced scorecard also places a lot of emphasis on the key drivers of a company's performance. This enables planners to focus their efforts instead of spreading themselves thin by trying to fulfil too many objectives.

Kaplan and Norton recommend four key measures. These are the customer perspective, the internal perspective, the innovation and learning perspective, and the financial perspective. The customer perspective is concerned with how the global company is perceived by its customers in all the cultures in which it has operations. The internal perspective examines the extent to which the global company is leveraging its core competencies. The innovation and learning perspective is concerned with continuous improvement. The financial perspective investigates whether the financial performance of the company is aligned to shareholder expectations.

Kaplan and Norton assert that the balanced scorecard is being used with telling effect. It enables global corporations to update strategies, communicate strategies effectively to all their branches in different cultures, align the goals of branches in different cultures to the corporate strategy, align strategies with long-term goals, conduct periodic reviews and take remedial action if necessary.

Kaplan and Norton have also argued that the balanced scorecard can be used for developing a global corporation's long-term strategy. Usually, there are four stages involved: one, translating the vision; two, communicating and linking; three, business planning; and four, feedback and learning. Translating the vision involves obtaining the necessary commitment to accomplish the strategy from branches in all cultures. It also entails getting managers from various branches to agree what the corporate strategy should be. Communicating and linking refers to communicating the strategy to all employees worldwide, and tying up rewards with performance measures. Business planning entails the establishment of appropriate milestones to gauge progress, as well as the setting of achievable targets. Feedback and learning is achieved through strategic feedback and strategic learning.

CORPORATE STRATEGY AND INTERCULTURAL MANAGEMENT

In essence, corporate strategy is the setting of organizational objectives followed by the establishment of a comprehensive course of action for realizing those objectives. De Wit and Meyer (1998) have averred that corporate strategy is best understood when viewed from the three dimensions of strategy process, strategy content and strategy context.

The three dimensions of strategy, taken together, are concerned with the efficient use of resources, as well as the mobilization of those resources. Accordingly, a concern of corporate strategy is the pursuit of markets with high growth potential.

According to Walker (1980), companies engaged in strategic decision making adopt the following five steps:

1. Definition of corporate philosophy and the development of a mission statement.

2. Scanning of environmental conditions.

3. Evaluation of the organization's strengths and weaknesses.

4.   Development of objectives and goals.

5.   Development of action plans.

Global companies need to go beyond corporate strategy. They have to proceed to the realm of industry-level strategic design and implementation. This involves gauging trends in a company's industry, and then planning its competitive position in that industry. For instance, when BMW engages in industry-level strategizing, it analyses global trends in the automobile industry and then positions itself in relation to its competition.

After strategizing at the industry level, a global company progresses to the stage of formulating and implementing strategies at the international level. At this level, global companies evolve approaches pertaining to international trade and negotiations. The main players here are governments of countries in which they have operations.

When a global corporation operates in other countries, it often engages in country-specific corporate strategizing. This means using Walker's five-step strategic planning approach. BMW could use the Walker approach for its operations in Thailand. It would also apply the Walker approach for its operations in Switzerland. The Walker approach, or a variation of that approach, would be used at all its locations. These independent corporate strategies then need to be tied into BMW's industry-level strategizing. They also need to be aligned with BMW's international strategy formulation and implementation scheme. Additionally, many global companies including BMW have a corporate-level master strategy. A focal issue of corporate strategy within an intercultural management context is how the local and global strategies are to be reconciled.

Thus for a global corporation, there exists a dialectic between the external application and adaptation of strategy, and the internal integration of that strategy at the corporate level. The dialectic also exists in terms of all members of a global corporation worldwide first subscribing to the corporate strategy, and second, realizing that strategy through location-specific approaches. The location-specific approaches have to reflect cultural realities.

This dialectic corresponds partially to what Chakravarthy and Perlmuter (1985) term 'geocentrism'. The phrase 'think globally, but act locally' epitomizes geocentrism. An emphasis on corporate strategy formulation enables a company to have a global competitive advantage. At the same time, since a geocentric company spans the world, its success depends on its ability to respond to local cultures and markets. It may draw global managers from all over the world; but it grooms local managers to deliver at the local level.

Holt (1998) has described this dialectic. He spoke of companies simultaneously pursuing the 'national responsiveness strategy' and the 'global integration strategy'. The national responsiveness strategy focuses on local markets and competitors, while the global integration strategy focuses on broad-based markets with global competitors. Prahalad and Doz (1987) also viewed this dialectic as the need to simultaneously ensure 'global strategic co-ordination' with 'local responsiveness'. 'Strategic coordination refers to the central management of resource commitments across national boundaries in the pursuit of a strategy. Local responsiveness refers to resource commitment decisions taken autonomously by a subsidiary in response to primarily local competitive or customer demands.'

Global strategic co-ordination is facilitated through sophisticated multinational customers, the presence of multinational competitors, investment intensity, technology intensity, pressure for cost reduction, universal needs, and access to raw materials and energy. Meanwhile, pressures for local responsiveness arise from differences in customer needs, differences in distribution channels, the availability of substitutes and the need to adapt, market structure, and host government demands.

Cultural realities also play a role when a global corporation anticipates the moves of its partners and competitors around the world.

For a global corporation to strategize effectively, it should have a central core set of objectives. Achieving these objectives is then the corporate strategy for the entire global organization. This central core set of objectives should be sufficiently flexible to allow local adaptation.

Schneider and Barsoux (1997) argue that managers from different cultures articulate strategy differently. According to these researchers, individuals trained in the US tradition tend to view strategy formulation and implementation as a rational and analytic process viewed similarly by all intelligent managers. Muslim managers accord importance to emotions and sentiment in addition to logic and rationality. Traditional Japanese managers maintain a long-term perspective in their strategic thinking, which could be as much as 250 years. The long-term perspective is then divided into manageable segments of a few years. Latin European managers tend to collect strategic information through personal contacts and from the grapevine. This makes the database by which they strategize subjective and open to interpretation. Nordic managers tend to view strategizing as the purview of top management. After top management has formulated corporate strategy, it is expected to state this corporate strategy clearly to the rest of the organization. In Germany, banks exert considerable influence over corporate strategy. In France, it is the government that is supposed to wield comparable influence.

Thus, ethnic culture plays a role in the definition and formulation of strategy for a company. The industry culture also exerts an influence. So does corporate culture. Corporate strategy, like other dimensions of organizational behaviour, juxtaposes corporate culture and ethnic culture. The trick is to ensure that the juxtaposition is of corporate culture with ethnic culture, rather than corporate culture against ethnic culture. To avoid a conflict of interests, corporate culture must be superordinate. Corporate strategy must be guided primarily by corporate culture and only secondarily by ethnic culture.

At the international level, strategizing becomes complicated when two or more organizations transact business with each other. There may not be a common corporate culture that influences joint strategizing. Likewise, complications arise when companies engage in transnational mergers and acquisitions. An ever-present issue is how different approaches to strategizing can be brought together.

Prima facie it appears that cultural similarity between collaborative organizations would lead to a common or similar approach to strategizing. However, there is no empirical evidence in support of this. Cartwright and Cooper (2000) suggest various ways by which organizations can achieve transnational collaboration. One is that the partners achieve a workable integration of their separate strategic approaches. A second is that the strategic approach of the dominant partner is adopted for the collaboration. The success of this type of collaboration hinges on the extent to which the dependent partner accepts and adopts the strategies of the dominant partner. There must thus exist a recognizable difference in the power balance between the partners.

A third possibility is that the dominant partner allows its dependent partner to pursue its own strategies, provided it also achieves the dominant partner's objectives. As long as the secondary partner achieves the objectives according to predetermined criteria, they can both live with differences in their strategizing approaches.

A final possibility is that the partners have a long-term relationship based on equality. Both partners perceive the collaboration as mutually beneficial. They view their different strategic approaches as complementary. This permits them to integrate their separate strategic approaches. The partners create a 'best of both worlds' strategic approach for their collaborative endeavour. They learn from each other. Their success in integrating their strategic approaches hinges on the managerial capabilities of their senior managers.

Two factors determine the extent to which the secondary partner can adopt the dominant partner's approach painlessly. The first factor is the extent to which the subordinate partner views the dominant partner's culture and strategic orientation as attractive. The second factor is the extent to which the subordinate partner is dissatisfied with its own culture and strategy. When both factors are conducive, cultural and strategic assimilation can occur. Such assimilation is encouraged when the culture of the dominant partner favours participation and employee satisfaction.

According to Cartwright and Cooper (2000), for the British, US managers are the most compatible strategic partner; for the French, US managers are the most compatible strategic partner; for the Germans, US managers are the most compatible strategic partner; for US managers, the British are the most compatible strategic partner; for the Dutch, the Germans are the most compatible strategic partner; for the Swedish, the Germans are the most compatible strategic partner; and for the Danish, the British are the most compatible strategic partner. Cartwright and Cooper further aver that the least preferred collaboration partners are the Japanese, the Italians and the Spaniards. This suggests that collaborative partners need to understand the cultural underpinnings of the other's strategic orientation before actually entering into a collaborative arrangement.

TRANSNATIONAL COLLABORATIVE ARRANGEMENTS

In practice, corporations do not enter into collaborative ventures in one go. They generally proceed from low levels of transnational collaboration to increasingly higher levels. Initially they may prefer collaborations where the responsibility for success in a new culture rests with the local collaboration partner. In the BMW case, initially in Thailand responsibility for its operations rested with the local collaboration partner. Subsequently, as BMW's confidence grew it graduated from licensing to wholly owning and managing local facilities. The shift was deemed worthwhile by BMW, even though it sustained hefty termination fees. A corporation progresses from exerting least control to most control by going through the following activities: exporting/importing, licensing, franchising, contracting, going in for a joint venture, and having a wholly owned subsidiary.

Companies need collaborative arrangements when they engage in indirect exporting. Indirect exporting requires companies to market through expert intermediaries.

Franchising is also a term that requires a little explaining. It is a special form of contracting. The franchiser allows a franchisee to have rights over a complete business. In return, the franchiser receives fees and royalty payments. The franchiser usually provides patent or trademark rights, as well as equipment and materials. Examples of international franchisers are US fast food companies like McDonald's and Kentucky Fried Chicken.

A global company can have different collaborative arrangements for different products. It can also have different collaborative arrangements for different markets. Multinational companies function in constantly changing contexts. It is advantageous for them to assess constantly whether their collaborative arrangements are achieving their objectives. In other words, they have to review whether their collaborative arrangements are aligned with their overall corporate strategy.

Multinational corporations need to formulate, implement and review strategy at various levels. Strategy could be for a collaborative arrangement, a local subsidiary, an industry, or for external associates. Ultimately all strategies have to be configured with the overall corporate strategy.

The strategy to be adopted by collaborating partners can be negotiated a priori. If a partner is extremely powerful and dominant, it can negotiate all agreements to its advantage. Where that is not the case, prearrangements are often drawn up to protect the interests of both parties. This is increasingly becoming the case where a transfer of technology is involved. The partner transferring state of the art technology may fear that its buyer will use that technology without paying. The buyer in turn may hesitate to pay in advance for a technology it could find not relevant.

Today, collaborative arrangements are increasingly made within the framework of contracts. Some partners have detailed contracts that cover every possible contingency.

PEPSI'S GLOBAL STRATEGIZING FOLLOWING THE COLA WARS

As recently as 1990, Pepsi had a proprietary contract with the Indian government, which allowed it to be a cola provider in India without competition from Coca-Cola. Since then a paradigm shift has occurred in the Indian government's policies, with domestic protectionism being replaced by global market competition. The proprietary contract with Pepsi was relinquished and Coca-Cola was allowed to market its product in India.

Pepsi's experience in other parts of the world parallels its Indian experience. It was accustomed to enjoying a monopolistic position in Eastern Europe and Latin America as well. Now, Coca-Cola is selling its product in these areas and giving Pepsi a run for its money. These global developments necessitated Pepsi's rethinking its strategic orientation.

The rethinking in practice proved to be very expensive. The strategy developed was to capture a larger share of the global market through an international expansion programme. In 1994, Pepsi launched a major offensive in Brazil with a plan to sell more than 250 million cases a year. In 1996, the company was nearly disgraced in Brazil, when its bottling company faced insolvency. Meanwhile Pepsi's Venezuelan experience was also painful, with its bottling company defecting to Coca-Cola around the same time. In Mexico as well around this time, the company's main bottler was sustaining heavy operating losses. And in Eastern Europe, it was unable to make much headway because during the Communist era, it had enjoyed the patronage of Communist leaders. In the post-Communist era, it had to find its way in foreign cultures entirely on its own. The same was the case in Latin America. As the region started moving towards market competition, Pepsi lost its competitive advantage, and had to find its way almost like a new entrant.

Industry analysts have been highly critical of the strategy Pepsi devised and operationalized at this time. Its focus was on achieving a boost in sales in the short run, instead of emphasizing a build-up of brand loyalty. Its strategy was characterized by an 'all or nothing' or 'go for broke' approach. It also employed marketing tactics which may have served it well in the United States, but which were out of synchrony with cultures of other countries.

Between 1990 and 1995, Pepsi managed to double its international sales. This however does not detract from the fact that its strategy was not the best it could have been. In Brazil during this time, it launched three glitzy marketing campaigns that it subsequently had to jettison. Its main problem was its inability to develop a network of bottling partners. The key to marketing success in a country like Brazil, or India, is not publicity through circus-style advertising gimmicks, but point of purchase appeal. And the latter requires mastery over a local distribution system.

Despite all this, Pepsi remains a major player on the global scene. Its product quality is unchallengeable and it employs talented personnel. However, industry analysts do believe that major problems exist in Pepsi's strategic positioning, and its configuration of various corporate plans. Underlying all this is a lack of honing of intercultural understanding.

O'Hara-Devereaux and Johansen (1994) recommend that global companies entering into intercultural strategic engagements be prepared to find 'third ways' of developing vision plans and strategies. This 'third way' emphasizes the creation of a space where all partners have equal importance and are prepared to devise new ways of working together. O'Hara-Devereaux and Johansen term this the 'collaborative space'. These researchers suggest the following pointers for the creation of a collaborative space:

▮ The process of creating visions is as important as the vision itself. It enables managers to bond together, and to understand how the other thinks and functions.

▮ The common strategy developed should be a living tool, capable of constant adaptation as new realities present themselves.

▮ Top management should be actively involved with the strategizing process, and set the example in being committed to the creation of a collaborative space.

▮ There should be some ground rules for the conducting of strategy meetings between the top management teams of all partners. The existence of some structure for the meetings enables people from all cultures to conduct themselves appropriately.

▮ There should be database systems for storing information about strategy formulation and implementation that all partners can access with ease. Sharing of information is a key to making collaborative spaces viable. Putting all relevant information on the table allows players to accept or modify strategic plans in an open environment.

Alterman (2000) has recommended that the feelings of the people concerned be kept in mind when a decision is taken about the management practices to be used by a strategic collaboration straddling several cultures. A collaborative arrangement may find it has two billing systems, for instance. It then has to choose. This might result in employees from one culture having to use a system that was developed in another culture. They could take the position that 'our system is better than yours'. Or they could transcend such narrow perspectives.

Lerpold (2000) recommends the creation of a separate identity for the collaborative arrangement, even if the arrangement is a temporary one, to solve this problem. This offsets the complications that arise when several ethnic cultures and at least two corporate cultures are juxtaposed. Unfortunately, according to Lerpold, global corporations entering into collaborative arrangements tend to neglect the people aspect. Instead financial matters are meticulously examined and their implications anticipated. This was the case with the BP–Statoil strategic venture. The differences between ethnic and corporate cultures turned out to be greater than anticipated, but initially they were ignored.

BP is a British corporation, Statoil a Norwegian one. The British perceived the Norwegians as being passive; the Norwegians felt the British were aggressive. With the passage of time and the non-resolution of differences, it became necessary to engage in damage control efforts. These included team-building exercises and cultural sensitivity training. Simultaneously, an identity was established for the collaborative arrangement. As the identity took hold, differences started to become less significant. And managers reported that they felt the work was fulfilling and the intercultural factor was exciting and invigorating.

PROBLEMS WITH GLOBAL STRATEGY

Many warning signals can alert a multinational corporation to the fact that its global strategy is being resisted by local branches. For instance, there could be a rise in customer complaints and a sudden downturn in sales. Or there could be increasing militancy on the part of a local trade union. Employee enthusiasm for company activities might be waning, registered in significantly decreased participation in those activities, especially if they are social events. There could be poor registration for employee development programmes, with little respect for the company's capacity to help people actualize themselves. There could be a considerable increase in the incidence of sickness or accidents. Or there could be increasing incidences of personality clashes between managers as well as dysfunctional interdepartmental rivalry. There might be difficulty in attracting personnel to the company where no difficulty existed in the past. Perhaps a sudden inability to meet deadlines has cropped up.

A single factor cannot be connected to corporate strategy. However, several factors arising simultaneously would suggest that the particular local company is having problems. This would be particularly disturbing if they surfaced suddenly or abruptly. Have they arisen after a new global strategy was initiated?

The problem could have arisen because of a hiatus between strategy formulation and implementation. A global strategy when formulated may be convincing, especially when the objectives have been projected as attainable. However, problems can arise at the local implementation stage, if the local culture has not been taken into account. This is exemplified by Pepsi's experience (see page 130). Problems can also arise when various local strategies have not been configured into the overall corporate plan in an appropriate fashion. When an attempt to configure is made, strategists can assess whether or not the local corporate plan is synchronized with the global plan. A local corporate plan that is developed keeping in mind local culture, and considered as a stand-alone feature, may be feasible. But a global strategy that just cannot strike a responsive chord at the local level can cause problems. When this happens, strategists should ask why this is happening. Is it that the global strategy has not found acceptance at the local level? Cultural mores regarding adaptation are particularly relevant to strategy, as strategy is about managing the organization–environment interface. Japan is a country that has understood the implications of adaptation:

> The Japanese don't use the term 'strategy' to describe a crisp business definition or competitive master plan. They think more in terms of 'strategic accommodation' or 'adaptive persistence', underscoring their belief that corporate direction evolves from an incremental adjustment to unfolding events. Rarely, in their view, does a leader (or a strategic planning group) produce a bold strategy that guides a firm unerringly. Far more frequently, the input is from below. It is this ability of an organization to move information and ideas from the bottom to the top and back again in continuous dialogue that the Japanese value above all things.
>
> (Pascale and Athos, 1981)

Other researchers support Pascale and Athos's contention that the Japanese are prepared to adapt aspects of their strategies when exigencies demand this. Burgelman (1988) describes Japanese strategy as evolutionary. Top management sets an open-minded vision and vaguely delineated fields of strategic action. He is of the opinion that innovation evolves from the tension created by 'setting ambiguous directions together with very challenging parameters which serve as criteria for supporting emerging projects'. Nonaka (1988) explains that the role of middle management is to take the abstract strategies of top management and match them to the practical experience of the front lines. Strategies evolve and re-evolve. He argues that:

> The centrepiece of the Japanese approach is the recognition that creating new knowledge is not simply a matter of 'processing' objective inform-ation. Rather it depends on tapping the tacit and often highly subjective insights, intuitions, and hunches of individual employees and making those insights available to testing and use by the company as a whole.

Thus, Japanese organizations function as learning organizations even where strategy formulation and implementation are concerned.

As already stated, global strategizing rests on the ability to create a common overall global strategy which is also capable of cultural adjustment. Ghoshal and Nohria (1993) suggest a few industries where a global company can formulate a global strategy, which can then be more or less uniformly applied to a wide variety of cultures. The products of such industries include construction and mining machinery, nonferrous metals, industrial chemicals, scientific measuring instruments and engines. Ghoshal and Nohria also suggest companies whose strategies should be devised for near-complete local responsiveness. The products of such companies include beverages, food, rubber, household appliances and tobacco. Most products do not fall into these extreme categories. What is of the essence is the ability not merely to strategize, but to continuously remodel strategies, adding, replacing and/or removing variables in response to shifting realities. Craig and Grant (1993) suggest that high-performance global corporations worldwide are moving in that direction. They aver that once centralized Japanese companies are moving away from their orientation, while once decentralized European companies are likewise shifting away from their orientation.

Related to the notion of corporate strategy is business strategy. Business strategy is concerned with matters of competitive advantage over rivals. The internationalization of markets affects even companies that function exclusively within a domestic market and are not multinational. These companies are constrained to operate in an international business environment whether they like it or not. For instance, they may be forced to compete against global corporations who erode their customer base. As a response to such competition, domestic companies adopt the management practices of global companies. They start strategizing in some ways like their multinational competitors. When multinational corporations enter a domestic market, seller concentration in that market falls. The number and diversity of companies offering products or services in a particular market increases. This further alters the characteristics of the business market as far as a domestic company is concerned. And finally, non-government barriers to entry are reduced. Thus in particular markets, the methodologies employed to develop appropriate business strategies may be similar for both domestic and transnational corporations.

Michael Porter (1998) has argued that nations possess specific advantages. When domestic companies exploit their nations' advantages, these companies begin to enjoy an international competitive advantage. Porter has identified four factors that influence national competitiveness. These factors are: resources, related and supporting industries, demanding home customers, and domestic rivalry.

Resources

These are the resources found in relatively abundant supply within a nation. These could comprise not merely natural resources, but distinctive features associated with that country's education, culture, infrastructure and workforce capability. For instance, Craig and Grant (1993) suggest that the distinctive resources of Switzerland are a well-educated and well-trained population, many of whom have mechanical engineering skills. Additionally, this population possesses a conservative and punctual national temperament and is affluent. It has enjoyed 600 years of political neutrality and stability. All this has enabled the country to develop a competitive advantage in banking and finance. Its cultural heritage of political stability has given it a strategic and competitive advantage. Its banks have optimally used this competitive advantage. Swiss banks enjoy a global reputation for security.

Related and supporting services

This is the extent to which a market can attract world-class companies as suppliers to, customers of or partners of domestic companies.

Demanding home customers

If customers in a home market are educated, sophisticated, discerning and demanding, they exert pressure on companies for high-quality products and services. Thus, the Germans' love of high-performance cars has driven up the quality of cars in Germany and made those cars some of the best in the world. The cultural heritage of a nation influences the type of industry that will enjoy a competitive advantage. This in turn influences the type of corporate and business strategies those companies foster.

Domestic rivalry

When a domestic market has a large number of rival companies, each trying to develop a best in class product, such rivalry is likely to push up the quality of that product.

According to Porter's model, a key aspect of international competition within an industry is whether companies hail from nations with the required competitive advantage for success in those industries or not. Shifts in a nation's competitive advantage can occur. New natural resources may be uncovered or existing reserves may get depleted. A nation's workforce may develop certain expertise through changes in the educational system. Companies with natural resources may develop a strategic link with those emphasizing education. According to Porter (1990), Holland is the world export leader in flowers because of the synergistic nexus between flower producers and top research institutes. France has placed a great deal of emphasis on engineering and administration in its educational system. This has enabled French companies to invent the TGV high-speed train and the Ariane rocket.

The foregoing discussion may suggest that companies are limited by the cultural heritage of the countries they hail from, and strategizing cannot transcend this. There is no evidence in support of this contention, however. Porter himself has not implied this. What can be suggested is that companies can make it part of their corporate strategy to develop the natural resource of people in the countries they hail from.

GLOBAL STRATEGY AND LOCAL ADAPTATION

Transnational corporations need to formulate global strategies that lend themselves to local adaptation. Schulling (2000) described how this has been done at Procter and Gamble (P & G). The following have been useful for P & G.

Market sensing capabilities

It is useful if transnational corporations have excellent market sensing capabilities. All their branches around the world should have this. Schulling points out that at P & G, brand managers at every branch undertake monthly analysis of Nielson data. This enables the company to keep abreast of developments in the market, particularly with regard to what customers want and what competitors are doing.

P & G managers keep in touch regularly with the stores that sell their products. This is done in every branch irrespective of culture. P & G managers also keep a tab on customer preferences. Gurcharan Das, long-time CEO of P & G India, was known for spending hours with house-wives at stores obtaining feedback from them about the detergent Ariel. This brand today has a faithful following among the upwardly mobile in India.

P & G managers all over the world periodically undertake qualitative consumer surveys, such as those done by Das in India. They also conduct periodic assessments of new product launches. The reactions P & G gleans from customers could vary from culture to culture. Hence the way it responds to market sensing would also vary from culture to culture.

Customer-driven culture

A global strategy of P & G is of being customer-driven. Branches are given discretion in this. However, the organizational system used is the same at all branches. P & G has called this the brand manager system. This system requires that every branch has brand teams. If a particular P & G branch is marketing three brands, a brand team is assigned to each one. Each brand team then has to gauge customer wishes and satisfy them. The brand teams are multidisciplinary and have representatives from the fields of marketing, R & D, manufacturing, logistics, finance and accounting.

Fact-based decisions

At every P & G branch, stress is placed on making decisions that are logically thought out and based on facts. Several management tools and techniques are used, such as PERT, technical tests, force field analysis, concept and use tests, optimization tests, and blind tests. Periodic formal reports are written about the management process of each brand. These reports are then shared with the rest of the global corporation. Branches are free to adopt approaches found successful in other cultures. However, before an approach is fully adopted, it is test-piloted in the new culture.

The three features of P & G's global strategy described above are without pitfalls as far as intercultural management is concerned. Where their views on corporate strategy can be questioned is with regard to global brand positioning. During the 1990s, P & G created centralized global category teams to manage their 11 product categories. According to Schuller (2000), these centralized global teams are too removed from local markets and local customer tastes to be able to reflect local cultural imperatives. There are short-run monetary advantages in trying to standardize a brand globally and not engage in local adaptations. However, it is local adaptations that reflect a global corporation's intercultural management skills. All the companies profiled in this book uphold the perspective that a transnational corporation requires overall global strategies to bind the corporation together, but that these strategies should be capable of reflecting the local culture when implemented. Shell (referred to in Chapter 1) is a global company that has linked its ideas on appropriate structure with its thoughts on strategic thinking. It made the corporation more decentralized so it could reflect local culture when implementing its strategy. This is true of BMW as well. A transnational corporation's global strategy has to be complemented by an appropriate organizational structure as well as core values if it is to be effective in intercultural management.

The current strategy of transnational corporations is to be market-driven. This entails being sensitive to different local markets, each coloured by a different set of cultural factors. Each local market has to be understood thoroughly, and the preferences of the customer base taken into account. At the same time, the same levels of quality have to be maintained worldwide. The demands made on transnational corporations are thus extraordinary.

STRATEGIC COLLABORATIONS IN THE AIRLINE INDUSTRY

Swissair, the once respected airline, shocked the world when it grounded all its aircraft in early October 2001, without giving prior warning to passengers. It subsequently went bankrupt. It was however a national icon till October 2001. An article entitled 'Squeezing the gnomes' published in the *Economist* (2002) states: 'For a small country, Switzerland has produced more than its share of distinctive national brands. Swiss cheese, the Swiss army knife, Swissair and, of course, the Swiss numbered bank account. Swissair alas is no more.'

Among the many reasons cited for Swissair's unfortunate demise, one could be that it did not pay heed to the cross-cultural aspects of corporate strategy.

Swissair made it its corporate strategy to become a heavyweight in the airline industry by establishing linkages with other reputed airlines. By a reciprocal arrangement with the American airline Delta Airways, the two companies own a stake in each other. Swissair and Singapore Airlines also own stakes in each other. Swissair also secured an interest in Austrian Airlines. In 1995, Swissair acquired a 49 per cent ownership in the Belgian airline Sabena. In 2001, Swissair was not entirely satisfied with the strategy it had adopted, of growth through global acquisition. Its alliance with Sabena has proved to be particularly cumbersome. In late 2001, Swissair was considering ways and means by which it could divest itself of Sabena.

The problem confronting Swissair is one of intercultural management. If its alliance with Sabena is considered, there is a clash of cultures along two dimensions, ethnic as well as corporate. Former students of mine at a MSc Programme in Intercultural Management examined the Swissair–Sabena strategic alliance in late 2000. These students interviewed senior managers from both companies, and inferred that insufficient attention was being paid to the issue of meshing the different cultures together. Many Swissair managers who had been deputed to Brussels to work at the Sabena operations were commuting between Switzerland and Belgium on a weekly basis. They would fly down to Brussels on Monday morning and back to Switzerland (and home) on Friday evening. This effectively meant that these managers were not getting integrated into Sabena at a deep-seated level. Of course, most managers, both from Sabena and Swissair, insisted that this did not affect work relations in any way.

It is difficult to envisage cultural integration taking place in an organization when two culturally distinct groups of managers operate as structurally distinct entities. Cultural integration is in many ways a physical process, in the sense that individuals should physically be located in a new culture. This enables them to imbibe tacit aspects of a culture, almost by osmosis. The insights they derive are accumulated piecemeal, over time. Once in a while, understanding may dawn in a sudden flash of inspiration. More usually, however, understanding is achieved in an incrementalist fashion. That was the experience of the international managers interviewed for this book.

Source: interviews with Sabena and Swissair managers.

ADVERTISING AND CORPORATE STRATEGY

As far as advertising by transnational companies is concerned, Jean-Marie Dru (1996) recommends that they should 'think local, act global'. Advertisements have to appeal to consumers of a local culture. To achieve this, advertisements reflect the everyday life of local inhabitants, as well as the values, attitudes, and beliefs of their culture. However, as a matter of corporate strategy, to view advertising solely in terms of local cultural identities is to err. That is why reference is made to Dru because his message is that 'we must constantly move from the local to the global, and back to the local again'.

Global corporations should encourage their branches to generate high-quality local campaigns. The product and services of global corporations are the same worldwide. The features of the products and services being advertised are then the same for the entire global corporation. The branches, however, construct campaigns to suit the local culture. This is best understood by examining Dru's descriptions of advertising in the United States, France, Japan, Britain, Spain, Germany, China and India.

American versus French advertising traditions

Dru's account suggests that US companies advertise directly, in ways described as brazen in other cultures. By contrast, the French do not engage in hard sell in their advertisements, but prefer to put the message across in a veiled, oblique fashion. The difference is cultural and related to the way the two countries view trade and business. Culture also defines how people construct an effective advertising campaign. In the United States, the spoken word makes a greater impact than the accompanying visuals. Hence, an advertising campaign generally begins with the writing effort. The French are more likely to be influenced by visuals and images. Hence, an advertising effort in France commences with the visualization effort.

According to Dru, there is a vital cultural difference between the United States and France which impacts on advertising campaigns. The French fight shy of sharing their emotions in an impersonal public arena. Americans on the other hand are accustomed to exploring emotions in public. US customers expect advertisements to make an emotional appeal. The French view the same type of advertisements as inappropriately sentimental. The best of advertising in both countries reflects cultural realities in terms of both the content and the conceptualization process.

In France, advertisements are presented as works of art, which are appreciated for their inherent creativity. The French like advertising. US people, on the other hand, view advertisements with scorn and disdain. The task of advertising is complex for a global company that must think local but have global aims.

Japan

The Japanese approach to advertising, Dru notes, is also distinctive and reflective of that culture. The Japanese have a need for spirituality to make their lives meaningful. Advertisements try to address this need. Thus a renovated store announces that it has re-opened with an advertisement that carries the punch line, 'Discovering Yourself'. The stunningly beautiful visual portrays a six-month-old baby swimming in water. The message conveyed is that it is beautiful to aspire for something as elevating as self-discovery. There are usually no themes that stress competitiveness.

At the same time, Japanese advertising is imaginative. The message is conveyed in a non-obvious, elegant manner that enables the recipient to feel serene and uplifted. It is also conveyed symbolically and metaphorically. Commercials often show sequences of beautiful images which when taken together communicate an entire sentence or even a theme. An individual totally alien to the Japanese culture may be unable to derive the intended meaning of an advertisement. The images have been combined in a sequence that relates directly to the Japanese experience and therefore has to be understood in context. The highly appreciated advertisements have inherent harmony.

The UK

The British too have a style of their own. The best British advertisements are masterpieces of understatement. This stems from British culture, where detachment even in business is the preferred style of functioning. British advertising persuades its consumers through suggestions and succinct messages.

Spain

Spain's advertising also reflects the strong but strange aspirations of that culture. Unable to shake off its hangover from once having been a colonial power, Spain seeks to retain a semblance of superiority by taking cues from the United States regarding how business should be conducted. At the same time, it insists that its own business practices are superior to those found in Latin American countries. Spanish companies like Telefonica that have tried to establish niches in Latin America have found the going rough, largely due to inadequate intercultural management skills.

Spain is one of the least developed countries in Europe. It is one of the last countries in the first world to start using advertising. Advertising executives generally have to manage on small budgets. Spanish advertisements are quite simple. The author of this book, having lived in both Spain and Argentina, opines that Spanish advertisements are inferior to those emanating from Argentina.

Spanish advertisements revolve around putting a product on display and sometimes demonstrating how it is used. The manner of presentation can be striking.

Germany

German advertising used to mirror the popular view of German culture. Germans see themselves as the people who give the world immaculate machine parts. The machine parts have high quality and do not need to be publicized. At the most, a German customer needs information about the machine parts. German advertisements are therefore strictly informative, nothing more or less. German customers traditionally appreciate rational and factual advertisements, which above all inform. Advertisements are not supposed to be works of art with a creative value apart from that of the mere data provided. Many advertisements are starkly austere. Germans expect products to speak for themselves. Advertisements that seek to seduce rather than convince are regarded as superficial and lacking in substance. Times are purported to be changing and advertisements are now informing in a creative manner.

China

Chinese advertisements are constructed around themes that are quintessentially Chinese. An example is the theme of filial devotion and responsibility. Most themes are humane and not ones that celebrate attitudes of competitiveness.

India

In India, advertisements are targeted at the very large class of consumers (several million people) who are upwardly mobile. This group is breaking away from the traditional culture that espouses spirituality and downplays materialism. Advertisement themes thus emphasize how desirable it is to possess various products and how much they will contribute to the consumer's sense of having arrived.

A commercial for Pepsi was shown in India with great success in early 2002. It depicts a group of five Japanese-looking sumo players challenging European football players to a match. The European team includes the likes of David Beckham. The prize for the winner is a crate of Pepsi. The football players are no matches for the sumo players who physically block the passage of the ball into the goal with their girth. They also deflect the ball by slapping it away with their chests. Their movements are funny and the manner in which they are able to defeat the ace football players is appealing. Although the advertisement is aimed at cosmopolitan Indians who are familiar with sumo wrestling and Manchester United, it is well appreciated by peasants as well, who can relate to the humour inherent in the commercial.

The Pepsi advertisement is an example of a transnational advertisement with universal appeal. It can be released for consumption in any culture. Some advertisements work because they have a universal theme. Others work simply because a culture's uniqueness is saluted. Wisdom consists in knowing what will work where. Designing and executing advertisements that reflect a global brand equity but have local acceptance is one of the challenges of corporate strategy.

COUNTRY MANAGER AND CORPORATE STRATEGY

In the BMW case profiled at the beginning of this chapter, the global company had decided as a matter of corporate strategy that it would instate a Thai CEO for its Thai subsidiary as soon as an appropriate individual had been groomed for that position. Another example of a global company that subscribes to the perspective of employing country managers from the local culture is P & G. Quelch (1998) has documented the career of Susana Elespuru at P & G, where during the course of an 18-year period she became a country manager.

Susana Elespuru was an ideal country manager from P & G's point of view. She was Peruvian and had worked for P & G Peru for 16 years. She understood the Peruvian environment well, and had managed P & G's business efficiently. In addition, she had the necessary international exposure and experience to fit into a global corporation. She had studied at a US college, and during her course had also studied for a semester in France. While with P & G Peru, she had been sent for a two-year assignment at the P & G headquarters in the United States.

The challenges she faced at P & G Peru were characteristic of that culture. One of the first challenges she faced was hyperinflation of up to 100 per cent per month. Prices of all commodities soared. P & G under Elespuru responded by increasing the salaries of their employees by 100 per cent. As a Peruvian, Elespuru was not thrown out of gear by the hyperinflation that could reach almost 7000 per cent in the worst years. Meanwhile, her managerial abilities enabled her to deal with the situation. And five years after becoming country manager, she succeeded in doubling P & G's sales volume.

Alternative paradigm to that of country manager

An alternative to having country managers is using a transnational model, such as that advanced by Bartlett and Ghoshal (1989). Instead of country managers who direct entire business operations for a branch, this model advocates centralizing strategic decision making at corporate headquarters. It holds that in the wake of globalization, customer preferences are becoming more similar, and hence companies need not engage in product development separately and independently for every branch. Instead global companies are advised to leverage their capabilities across borders, and transplant best practices from one country to another. Additionally, the transnational model recommends that:

1. Senior intercultural managers should think in terms of three dimensions: product, geography and function.

2. Costs should be rationalized and control over all branches, near and far, increased.

3. Well-entrenched country managers should be uprooted, especially if they behave like king-emperors with considerable authority over their branch.

4. Headquarters should try to encourage standardization to the extent possible.

This model is an alternative to the country manager model, and is therefore not inherently better or worse. IBM is an example of a transnational corporation that has followed the transnational model to a large extent.

Quelch and Bloom (1996) have advanced a few reasons why, in their view, the country manager model is the superior one. The first is that for success in local business, it is necessary to have good relations with local governments. Country managers will build up an extensive network of useful government contacts over the years they work for a particular global company. In Quelch's case study about Susana Elespuru, the advantage of opting for a local country manager was that she was Peruvian and understood how things worked within the Peruvian culture. Further, local customers want personal attention in the form of product adaptation to local cultures. Susana Elespuru succeeded in selling Pert Plus, Pantene and Head & Shoulders, the three leading brands of shampoo marketed by P & G, in the form of individual sachets. This was a reflection of the reality in Peru at that time: people could afford sachets but not bottles of shampoo.

Country managers are also well suited to taking on local competition, which consists of other global companies as well as local companies. While in Barcelona in 2001, the author of this book noticed that the Spanish fast food company Pans was giving the US fast food multinational McDonald's a run for its money. Local companies are often well placed to notice and take advantage of local trends. Pans did this when they introduced Spanish specialities like the long sandwich and other forms of tapas as part of their fast food offering with success. Naturally Pans had the necessary market knowledge and experience of Spanish culture to supplement standard fast food fare with typical Spanish items. If a multinational is to compete successfully against local heavyweights, country managers who have the required knowledge of the market and local culture serve them best.

There are other reasons the country manager model has its advocates. Global brands gain local appeal because of their brand image as qualitatively superior products with a worldwide following. By the same token, they lose ground when local brands are upgraded and are sold at lower prices. Culturally sensitive country managers can take stock of the situation. They know how to adapt global brands to local conditions, so that the best of both worlds is made available to consumers. This is borne out in Quelch's case study of Susana Elespuru. When Peru experienced a phase of relative economic stability two years after Elespuru became country manager, Elespuru had this to say, 'Peru's 23 million consumers represent an increasingly attractive target. We anticipate more multi-national brands trying to enter this market. But we intend to capitalize on the fact that P & G has been here all along, through thick and thin, relentlessly building our brand equities.'

A multicultural corporation likes to churn out innovations and best practices. It likes to encourage new ideas to emanate from all their branches, irrespective of whether those ideas can be replicated elsewhere. Quelch and Bloom go so far as to opine that 'new product ideas and marketing best practices – the competitive lifeblood of any multi-national – are usually generated in the field by people who observe and listen attentively to customers, not by company-culture-bound executives at global HQ'. Quelch's case study notes that while Susana Elespuru was country manager, P & G Peru's 400 employees were all local nationals. The expertise for responding to the market was entirely nurtured from the local culture. When Elespuru wanted to penetrate the market for Pepto-Bismol, she hired a Hispanic company to publicize the product, with telling effect. According to Quelch and Bloom, country managers succeed when they operate under conditions of organizational efficiency provided by local stalwarts.

Country manager model versus transnational model

The country manager model as a component of intercultural corporate strategy has much to offer. So does the transnational model. Hence, the issue is not of pitting the country model against the transnational model, but of finding a suitable middle ground. The middle ground is extensive enough to be enacted in a manner that suits an individual global company's requirements. The part of the middle ground that is selected for one culture need not be the part that is applied to another culture. The right balance between globalization and localization has to be worked out for each branch, depending on exigencies.

The country manager model suggests that good ideas and best practices can originate in emerging economies and be replicated in advanced economies. Quelch and Bloom (1996) have cited the example of the construction materials manufacturer Lafarge, which felt that cement plants could be built in the West using the stripped-down lines approach they incorporated in Turkey. They also quote the example of KFC, the food chain that operates primarily as a take-away in the United States and Europe. In Malaysia, KFC adopted the local practice of also operating as a restaurant. It is now considering introducing restaurants to its chains in the United States and Europe. However, this advantage of the country manager model, like so many of its other advantages, is not incompatible with the transnational model. The transnational model in fact advocates the replicating of best practices. Most of the companies profiled as chapter-opening case studies in this book employ a judicious mix of the transnational model and the country manager model.

ADVERTISEMENT FOR HSBC, THE WORLD'S LOCAL BANK

SUMMARY

Corporate strategy assumes a new dimension when formulated and implemented in the context of varied cultures. This new dimension centres on developing corporate strategy that is global in coverage and vision, but capable of local adaptation and interpretation. The corporate strategy thus determined can incorporate local management perspectives, conditioned by the local cultural ethos, without distorting the overall grand design and global objectives. The challenge lies in the integration of local relevance into the transnational corporation's global configuration.

The top management echelon of a transnational organization determines the overall corporate strategy. This echelon must have an understanding of the local context of the countries where the transnational organization has operations. There are many ways in which this understanding can be achieved. One approach is for the members of the top management echelon to actually visit a country and study how its culture interfaces with management practices. Such visits should be conducted at periodic intervals. Local culture can be harnessed to accelerate the execution of strategy if it is properly understood. By the same token, local culture can create barriers if it is not explicitly taken cognizance of and empathized with.

5

Knowledge management and intercultural management

CASE STUDY: IBM

International Business Machines (IBM) was once known almost exclusively as a manufacturer of computer hardware. It now plays an influential role in the design of cutting-edge computer components, as well as in the design of software solutions. The IBM Training Laboratory in Zurich, Switzerland, is one such think-tank wing of IBM. In the 1980s, this laboratory came up with two Nobel prize winning breakthroughs. Gerd K Binnig and Heinrich Rohrer were awarded a prize in 1986 for their invention of the scanning tunnelling microscope, and Georg Bednorz's and K Alex Müller's discovery of high-temperature superconductivity in ceramic materials won them another in 1987. Brilliant thinkers at this Zurich facility pursue their creative endeavours in a relatively sheltered world.

And yet, remarks Dr Philippe Jensson of the IBM Training Laboratory, 'IBM, in spite of the fact that it is multinational, still largely behaves like an American company.' By this, Jensson means that knowledge creation and knowledge transfer are accomplished in the English language. This is a characteristic feature of transnational knowledge management companies. In IBM, and at its Zurich Research Laboratory, the research scientists think in English. The entire knowledge creation and management chain is linked by the common denominator of English. The assumption that implicit knowledge transfer can occur is an important consideration at IBM. That its scientists are English thinking and English speaking promotes this occurrence.

A growing body of research shows that knowledge generation and transfer are successfully facilitated when they are managed. They are not random activities. An organization where knowledge management is successfully achieved is 'skilled at creating, acquiring, and transferring knowledge, and at modifying its behaviour to reflect new knowledge and insights' (Gavin, 1993). Effective knowledge management is particularly germane in such organizations because today, dedicated teams of scientists and not lone rangers achieve technological breakthroughs. The composition of these teams is heterogeneous in more ways than one. In the first place, team members hail from different technical areas of specialization and work disciplines. Additionally, they come from diverse cultures.

This is the case with the IBM Training Laboratory, Zurich, where there are researchers from 27 different countries. Jensson is currently a member of a team constructing a database about the collaborative relations the laboratory has with universities in Europe and the Middle East. The team has engaged in a staggering amount of travelling and use of modern telecommunications facilities to interact professionally.

This constant interacting is characteristic of how the laboratory engages in knowledge generation. The knowledge generated during the course of a year is shared at the annual conference organized by the IBM Academy of Technology. Only the 300 top brains of IBM attend the annual conferences.

One reference point connects most of the top brains of IBM Worldwide, and almost all the foremost researchers at the IBM Training Laboratory, Zurich. These researchers have at some time in their lives gone to the United States and obtained either doctoral or postdoctoral qualifications there. They therefore share common academic training and a common knowledge base. Philippe Jensson, for example, studied at the Massachusetts Institute of Technology (MIT) from 1972 to 1976, and obtained a PhD in computer science. He also worked for two years in Austin, Texas, from 1986–87. At the IBM Training Laboratory, a knowledge tool all researchers understand and use is Lotus Notes collaboration software.

The University–IBM Relations Database was developed for use by IBM researchers worldwide. Its team comprises a scientist/researcher from each of Switzerland, Germany, Italy, France, Spain, and the United Kingdom. The team has been in existence since April 2000. Its members are members of IBM's University Relations Team Worldwide. This team coordinates the variegated associations IBM has with premier universities around the world. The team has also had a few transient members. These were IBM employees who were deployed to it to learn a line of operation different from their own. It is the IBM philosophy that people be temporarily assigned to jobs different from their own so that they are exposed to different lines of work. Employees with technical expertise are sent to business units to become familiar with management practices. Likewise, managers are sent to divisions manned entirely by technical experts.

The University–IBM Relations Database contains exhaustive information about the universities in Europe and the Middle East with which IBM has an association. The association could be of any of four types. The first pertains to sales-related matters. IBM sells a considerable amount of hardware to universities. The second type of association is concerned with recruitment. IBM recruits quite a few PhD holders from universities. The third association refers to collaborative research work. The IBM Training Laboratory, Zurich undertakes joint research work with scientists from universities. The fourth association concerns the various endowments IBM bestows on universities for the hiring of experts, or the purchase of computer hardware and software. The database is classified by country, by university, by department, by professor, and by the partner in IBM. If an employee at IBM is interested in a particular research endeavour at a European university, he or she can use the database to ascertain if that university has an existing association with IBM. The database developed for Europe and the Middle East has proved so successful that it has been replicated in the United States for IBM's Research Laboratory in New York.

An interesting aspect of the University–IBM Relations Database Team (for Europe and the Middle East) is that much of the interaction between team members is dyadic. For instance, in February 2001 Jensson met with team members from Germany at the IBM Training Laboratory, Zurich. They spent an entire day planning and strategizing about the database team, and another entire day developing the database. In April 2001 Jensson went to Italy and Spain and met separately with the database team members from those countries. Both were all-day meetings, devoted exclusively to taking the University–IBM Relations Database forward. The team members have found that by discussing their work in pairs, they benefit and gain several insights about the data building process. Members believe that conducting meetings in pairs is more fruitful than having all six database team members convene. Any breakthroughs achieved through dyadic work are immediately communicated to other team members.

Building the University–IBM Relations Database to the level of sophistication it has today has required the database team members to liaise extensively with IBM employees. Jensson comments:

> Working on the Database has made me take the initiative in networking with people I did not know before. Earlier, I had been accustomed to having my work associates take the initiative in approaching me. . . But I have a greater appreciation now for the process of knowledge transfer. Networking and binding with people is necessary for the accumulation of knowledge. Knowledge that we must have for our work and which we must share with others, that they can use for their work.

Networking with people on a one-to-one basis is an important aspect of the work culture at the IBM Training Laboratory, Zurich. In many instances, the resulting synergy has led to a sharing of knowledge bases, and joint research work. This joint research work has in turn led to the generation of new knowledge. An example is an invention by Nobel laureate Gerd Binnig and Peter Vettiger working in tandem, in early 2001. The two used to play soccer together. After playing soccer, they would discuss their research interests and ongoing work. They found they were both interested in developing commercial applications for micromechanical devices. By pooling their know-how, they complemented each other's thought processes, and accelerated the pace at which they designed a new, efficient tiny semiconductor. Binning brought his action-oriented, 'let's make it work now' knowledge generation approach to complement Vettiger's preference for rigorous and meticulous long-term planning.

Inferences

There are three aspects to knowledge management in an intercultural context, suggested by the experience of the IBM Training Laboratory, Zurich.

Close personal contact amongst researchers facilitates the juxtaposing of knowledge bases

At the IBM Training Laboratory, Zurich, the researchers who work together on a project work closely together. All the researchers learn from their associates on a project, imbibe some of their thought formulation processes, and in turn influence their modes of thinking. This is important for creative problem solving. Otherwise, researchers working on their own can get into ruts in their way of thinking. There can be multiple ways of thinking and approaching a problem. Suppose the following simplified research situation is considered: researchers are attempting to contain a disease. One researcher tries to make human beings immune to the viruses causing the disease. His contemporary focuses on destroying all carriers of the disease. Another researcher seeks to engineer the environment so that the disease-causing germs are annihilated in the atmosphere, before they reach people. The eventual means of combating the disease discovered by the researchers may be inspired by all three approaches.

This has been the experience of the IBM Training Laboratory, Zurich. Like the example given earlier of the Binnig and Vettiger joint research, mention must be made of the contributions of Ute Drechsler and Urs Dürig. These two researchers challenged Binnig and Vettiger's approaches by bringing their own knowledge bases and thought processes to the research effort. Drechsler's preferred way of thinking and working was to plough ahead and overcome obstacles whenever they presented themselves. Dürig was accustomed to thinking deeply, and perfecting his mental models. This diversity in thought processes fostered a cross-fertilization of ideas, and ultimately, the creation of new knowledge.

Such cross-fertilization of ideas through the collision of diverse thought patterns has also occurred in the University–IBM Relations Database Team. Here, diversity was discernible not only because of varying thought processes, but also because members came from different ethnic origins. The member from Germany had a robust technical background. This background manifested itself in his aspiring for more perfection than other people would insist on. When Jensson worked with this German, he found himself paying greater attention to detail than would otherwise be the case. Jensson himself preferred not to get too bogged down by details. He liked to focus on the big picture rather than spend too much time ironing out quirks. However, being part of the research team, he appreciated the power of learning from associates. He therefore kept an open mind when working with his German counterpart on the team and learnt from the latter. He also tried to impress on his German counterpart the importance of not losing the forest for the trees.

The work association has proved to be a mutually beneficial one. Both feel that they were able to devise solutions to problems more quickly by not being preoccupied with the thinking and problem-solving approaches they normally adopt. Jensson opines that his German counterpart's preferred approach to knowledge manage-ment is influenced by his ethnicity. German scientists, managers and technocrats are described as being over-committed to perfection. This generalization may not be an appropriate label for all Germans. It was however true of the German member of the University–IBM Relations Database Team. To achieve perfection in his work, the Ger-man tried to bring reliability and predictability to his work methods. He did this by emphasizing planning and discipline. By working with Jensson, he began accommodating non-continuous and discrete workflows. Jensson, for his part, started maintaining a short-term (weekly) time schedule, to guide his progress. They were able to imbibe to some extent each other's work approaches, because of the basic chemistry between them. These factors acted in concert to enable knowledge generation in a collaborative environment.

The cultural influence was strongest in the case of the German member of the University–IBM Relations Database Team, which is why it has been chronicled here. The cultural conditioning of the other members did not exert such a dramatic influence. What is being stressed is that close personal contact among knowledge builders is a facilitator of the knowledge management effort. Close personal contact can contribute to a juxtaposition of knowledge bases. It can lead to scientists expanding their thought processes by imbibing processes used by their collaborators. This includes imbib-ing a thought process that has been culturally conditioned.

Communication of knowledge throughout the organization
The IBM Training Laboratory, Zurich, like IBM Worldwide, believes that knowledge available in one division of the organization should be accessible to employees in other locations. This prevents the unwarranted duplication of effort that ensues when people set about reinventing the wheel. The need for the speedy commun-ication of knowledge soon after it has been generated is particularly of the essence for a global corporation.

A vital aspect in the communication of knowledge is its articulation. Articulation is the process by which knowledge is described
and made explicit, and transferred through the use of 'writing,
mathematics, graphs, maps, diagrams and pictures. In fact all forms
of symbolic representation which are used as language' (Polanyi,
1962). It is also the process by which elements of knowledge dif-
fused and scattered across an organization are assembled and stored
in one place. The assembled knowledge is then codified, written out
and presented in a logically cogent fashion. Sometimes, 'articulation
pictures the essentials of a situation on a reduced scale, which lends
itself more easily to imaginative manipulation than the ungainly
original' (Polanyi, 1962). Imaginative manipulation leads to knowledge creation. But what is being emphasized here, which IBM
recognizes, is that knowledge creation is dependent on the formulation and execution of knowledge articulation.

The University–IBM Relations Database is the outcome of an
intercultural team's collaborative effort at knowledge articulation.
IBM employees use the database extensively. All users are full of
praise for it, since it offers convenience as well as easily accessible
information. Such databases constitute part of the organizational
capability to create, harness and manage knowledge. The fact that
the University–IBM Relations Database Team is a multicultural one
indicates that knowledge creation in global companies involves
collaborative work between people from diverse backgrounds.

Diversity of knowledge bases is important for creativity. At the same
time, the knowledge organization has to ensure that its researchers
have some common reference points and operates within a shared
paradigm. There are many ways in which common reference points
can be established. Knowledge articulation is one of them.

The following is an illustration of what can happen if there are no
common reference points when the knowledge transfer is made
across cultures. During the Second World War, US shipyards were
provided with British blueprints for the construction of Liberty
freighters. Unfortunately, in the hundred years immediately preced-
ing World War II, the engineering approaches of the two countries
had followed divergent paths. The British emphasized design variety
and innovation. US engineers preferred standardization and replic-
ation. As a result, by the 1940s the ship blueprints used in Great
Britain were so different from those used in the United States that
they could not be applied meaningfully by US engineers (example
from JK Brown).

At the IBM Training Laboratory, Zurich, diversity in knowledge bases is encouraged. There are mechanisms to ensure that the technical and cultural diversity inherent in knowledge bases leads to their juxtaposition. In addition to knowledge articulation, there exists an organizational culture where people are prepared to learn each other's knowledge bases.

The University–IBM Relations Database Team is interesting for two reasons. In the first instance, it was deliberately constituted for knowledge articulation. Second, the members learnt technical knowledge systems and imbibed culturally conditioned problem-solving approaches from each other.

Although this team operates at the cutting-edge, it is facing problems obtaining data from IBM employees for the database. Jensson's experience has been that typical employees are unwilling to take the time to articulate their own knowledge or experience, which can then be input to the database. Of all the countries contributing to the database, it was found that employees with IBM Italy were marginally more cooperative in contributing knowledge to the database than employees of other IBM locations. It is however not known why this is so, and to vouchsafe an explanation on cultural grounds alone would be to err on the side of simplicity.

Simultaneous membership in more than one work group
Jensson believes there are two reasons why he, like other members of the IBM Training Laboratory, Zurich, feels comfortable working in the area of knowledge management with people from diverse backgrounds. First, he has been accustomed to this throughout his work life, and second, he belongs to more than one work team. Jensson's prime activities in 2001 comprised the work he was doing for the IBM Academy of Technology, and the University–IBM Relations Database Team. Both these work groups comprised researchers from different cultures. Thus working with multicultural teams is part of Jensson's ongoing work experience.

Knowledge management in an intercultural setting requires tremendous organizational support. Otherwise, collaborative research efforts might splinter, with only individuals from homogeneous backgrounds working together. Working interculturally also signifies working with people who have different approaches to thinking and subscribe to different intellectual paradigms.

Jensson, of the IBM Training Laboratory, Zurich, designed the University–IBM Relations Database for Europe. It was operationalized by an intercultural team. The database is being accessed and used by IBM employees worldwide. It is regarded as a useful and appropriate contribution to knowledge articulation within IBM. And yet Jensson finds the effort of collecting necessary data for the database from colleagues an uphill task. To quote Jensson in this connection:

> A database has utility, as long as it is up-to-date and current. So this whole thing about database maintenance is a major, major problem. It is more a problem of funding. Ideally, it would be good to have a few people paid full-time to populate the University–IBM Relations Database and then maintain it. But we just cannot afford that within our budget. So we do it as an evening job or a night job. As and when we have the time, we keep pushing it. . . Anyone in the IBM world who knows about the database and wants to contribute to it is free to do so.

Although the Database is widely used, a large number of IBM employees are still ignorant of its existence. These include researchers from Jensson's own laboratory. In the last week of March 2001, a researcher sent Jensson an e-mail about a new idea he wanted to implement: to construct a database with information about all the links the IBM Training Laboratory, Zurich has or had with universities in Europe. Jensson, of course, then took the opportunity of informing the researcher that such a database had been in existence for over a year.

The above example illustrates the complex nature of knowledge management. IBM actively encourages its researchers to collaborate interculturally. It encourages the bringing together of disparate knowledge bases. This has activated knowledge creation. The company has also encouraged knowledge articulation, which is an aid to knowledge creation. And yet, the knowledge that is articulated is not widely communicated across the organization and disseminated extensively. The extent to which knowledge is disseminated and made organization-wide reflects corporate culture. As Hofstede *et al* have pointed out (1990), R & D outfits differ strongly in their orientation towards knowledge dissemination. Some are strongly 'normatively oriented'. Others are more 'pragmatically oriented'. Their work suggests that corporate cultural differences do exist regarding the process of knowledge management.

CASE DISCUSSION QUESTIONS

1. What are the distinguishing features of the IBM Training Laboratory that have enabled it to manage knowledge cross-culturally?

2. Given that Scandinavians have a predilection for working in teams, and the Japanese are primed for group problem solving, what are the synergies and limitations of Scandinavians and Japanese working together to articulate new knowledge?

3. What are the differences between, one, trying to juxtapose knowledge bases originating from different cultures and, two, getting a culturally diverse group of managers to articulate new knowledge?

4. What does the functioning of the IBM Training Laboratory have to say about the process of managing knowledge cross-culturally?

5. What recommendations would you make to the IBM Training Laboratory so that it can increasingly include knowledge bases from ever more diverse cultures in its knowledge generation efforts?

6. Describe the skill-set and mind-set of a proficient knowledge manager who is also operating in an intercultural context.

ACADEMIC DISCUSSION

What knowledge management is

Knowledge management is an emerging area of interest for management practitioners and academicians. The purpose of knowledge management for a global organization is threefold. The first is to understand the process by which knowledge is generated. The second is to document the existing knowledge base so that future global managers can tap it. The third is to facilitate the efficient dissemination of necessary knowledge across branches and cultures.

Knowledge management is thus concerned with the creation and management of intellectual capital. This is an important source of competitive advantage in modern global companies, but is particularly of the essence for companies whose core competence lies in the specialized knowledge of their employees. Examples of such global companies include professional companies such as financial services companies, consultancy companies, and research facilities like IBM's Research Laboratory profiled above. Many knowledge companies retain experts engaging in original knowledge generation primarily for that purpose. The gestation period allowed for the translation of their knowledge into viable products and services is longer than in traditional companies.

The observation made by Arthur (1999) is apposite. No industry can afford to say that it is outside the knowledge management loop, because it is only a matter of time before some player in that industry decides to enhance its competitive position by opting for global connectivity through knowledge systems.

Denning (1999) has described how the World Bank incorporated global knowledge management into its functioning, and became a more responsive and efficient global organization. Prior to using knowledge management systems, the World Bank used to take one month to one year to answer a specialized question. Now, with the aid of knowledge bases and knowledge management systems, it is able to respond to such questions in just one or two minutes. The effective application of knowledge management has also meant that the World Bank is now able to reach a considerably larger client base than was previously possible.

Handy (1989) has observed that knowledge management corporations are cutting-edge corporations that operate in changing environments. These corporations retain knowledge workers and managers as a central core of employees. Core workers have been described by Pollert (1988) as a cadre of permanent employees with a certain amount of job security and retirement benefits. Such employees are multi-skilled and cannot be pigeonholed into a single job category. Knowledge management corporations support the work of their central core with employees who are retained on a contractual basis. Services are also often outsourced. The central core of managers controls the operations and technology. The operations depend on the knowledge and creativity of these managers. These managers need quick access to pertinent information and contemporary developments. They also need to keep their minds constantly challenged and vigorous. Knowledge managers of all cultures are likely to be like this.

Some countries in Asia have recently become rich without having a stockpile of natural resources. They have emerged wealthy by nurturing and tapping the intellectual capital of their populace. Taiwan for instance became the global supplier of microchips for transnational corporations manufacturing computers. Taiwanese multinational Acer captured a significant portion of the market for computers. Likewise, Singapore earned a name for itself as a global supplier of disk drives, and Japanese laptops are sought after all over the world. In fact, it is the Asia-Pacific region that has provided the bulk of the components for computer hardware the world over.

Michael Elliot (2002) has the following comments to make about human capital and prosperity:

1. Recent economists have declared that human capital plays a pivotal role in societal development. Human capital, according to these economists, is a function of the skill-set and entrepreneurial abilities of a populace.

2. Human capital is shaped by education.

3. Human capital depends on a populace's aptitude for using technology.

4. Human capital is strengthened when a populace has exposure to working in multicultural environments.

5. All these conditions are dependent on the quality of education made available from primary school up to advanced university.

The quality of education varies from nation to nation. *The World Competitiveness Yearbook, 2001* notes that eighth-grade students from Singapore, Japan, Korea, Hong Kong and Taiwan register among the highest in the world where science and mathematics abilities are concerned. However, the school systems in these countries are authoritarian. Emphasis is placed on a one-way transmission of knowledge from the teacher to the taught. Students spend most of their after-school hours doing homework. Cramming and rote learning are commonplace.

This type of educational pattern may be an outcome of culture. In these countries, society in general is hierarchically organized. Singapore, though affluent, is not a true democracy, and its citizens seem to have no problem with this. Many schoolchildren in these countries are 'nerds' in much the same way that students of the Massachusetts Institute of Technology are described as nerds.

The output from knowledge management work frequently has an immediate global market. The corporation BEA developed a software package called WebLogic that is now used worldwide in many cultures for online billing and support services. Several transnational corporations sell knowledge management systems along with informational technology services and hardware. The ongoing work of John Daugman and other ophthalmologists in the area of iris recognition, for instance, has resulted in enhanced security at airports from Frankfurt, Germany, to Charlotte in the United States. Heathrow Airport in London, England, is considering allowing passengers to enter the country without passport verification, providing they have registered at an internationally recognized iris database. Thus, the use of knowledge management systems can not only cut across international borders, but also require international cooperation to make applications possible (source: *Time Magazine*, 2000b).

An interesting trend in knowledge creation is that many inventors are thinking in terms of products with applications in many cultures. An example is Dean Kamen, founder of DEKA Research, who is working on a bicycle-like contraption that can transport people more quickly than a conventional bicycle, and with little physical effort. As he was putting together his invention, Kamen envisaged it as a means of transport to be used from Shanghai to Seattle.

The way the vehicle would be used would differ. In China, it is intended as the sole means of transport for millions of people. In America it is visualized as a vehicle to complement the car most people own. For China, Kamen recommends that cities be planned so as to accommodate his new vehicle. Mass-transit systems would have to be built to circumnavigate cities. Meanwhile the central parts of the cities would be free to accommodate pedestrians and people riding Kamen's invention. These central parts are those traditionally used to accommodate cars, buses and so on. In the United States, on the other hand, the roads, highways, tunnels and so on that support travel by automobiles would remain largely intact. Kamen's vehicle would be ridden on existing sidewalks (*Time Magazine*, 2001j).

PROBLEMS WITH IGNORING KNOWLEDGE MANAGEMENT

Denning (1999) has pointed out that clients today desire global knowledge. They want the best expertise they can get from the whole world. If a transnational organization cannot offer world-class service to its clients, it will lose those clients to an organization that can.

Transnational corporations that do not have the capability to engage in global knowledge management are taking a great risk. They are running the risk of losing out to their competitors. Consider the case of Japan's Ministry of International Trade and Industry (MITI). This ministry still uses typewriters and rotary dial telephone systems, and does not have modern knowledge and communication systems like computers and nifty software. By contrast, many of the civil service organs of other countries, especially those that lead the world in economic growth, have become users of expert and knowledge systems. Japan is beginning to lose its former place of pride among world economic powers. *Time Magazine* (2001c) quotes Ryozo Hayashi, a vice-minister in Japan's cabinet at that time, as saying, 'It's been a long time since Japan was seen as a rising sun.'

Colin Coulson-Thomas (1998) notes that global companies that ignored proper knowledge management have experienced problems. For example:

1. Cost cutting and streamlining have led to knowledge bases becoming eroded.

2. Redundancies have resulted in the loss of implicit knowledge that the redundant managers have taken with them.

3. Re-engineering has often caused experts with specialized knowledge to be replaced by generalists who then lack the necessary skills to perform tasks.

4. Outsourcing has resulted in outsiders being provided with capabilities that should have been retained within the corporation to aid its future development.

5. Dependence on high fliers has led to the perpetuation of a class of people who engage in first-class superficial work, but lack the depth for engaging with fundamental issues. Such employees are multi-skilled and cannot be pigeonholed.

Many global corporations fail to take cognizance of knowledge management in a holistic sense. These corporations often concentrate on knowledge bases that yield 'hard' data relating to financial figures. They neglect such issues as the satisfaction levels of managers or their motivational levels. They also overlook the need to keep records of why they have succeeded or failed in particular ventures.

It is desirable for global corporations to record the talents, skills and expertise of their key managers, so that at any point in time, the corporation is able to access the complete range of individual expertise that it possesses. Managers should know where to turn to within their own corporation for specialized knowledge. With modern technology it is not difficult for global corporations to maintain the necessary knowledge databases.

THE INTRANET

Many global companies maintain expert systems that collate, record and transfer knowledge internally. The intranet is an example of a commonly used expert system. The University–IBM Relations Database described in the case study at the beginning of this chapter is an example of such an intranet. Cushway and Lodge (1999) cite a 1997 survey of 259 organiz-ations, which showed that approximately two-thirds of these organizations used some variant of the intranet. Over half the organizations surveyed used the intranet for disseminating internal core values, mission, vision and strategies. Forty per cent of the organizations surveyed used the intranet to obtain immediate data for day to day operations.

All the global corporations studied for this book acknowledged that the intranet had become an indispensable part of their functioning. The Copernicus Project of CSPB maintained several intranet systems. Many of the global managers surveyed reported that thanks to intranet systems, they saved a lot of time by not replicating existing data systems. All of them agreed that they should have intranet systems that document good management practices found successful at their branches. They could then examine whether good management practices found effective in one cultural context could be introduced to other cultural contexts.

BOOZ ALLEN'S INTRANET: KNOWLEDGE ON-LINE (KOL)

In 1994, Booz Allen decided to place its library information services within the purview of its chief knowledge officer. The knowledge about servicing clients more efficiently was to be made available online on the KOL. Knowledge managers worked closely with client service personnel to place relevant knowledge on the KOL. To be effective, knowledge managers had to network extensively within the organization to ferret out vital sources of information. They also had to be good communicators so that they could package the knowledge base in a user-friendly format.

The content for KOL was selected with great care. After selection, it was submitted for review. Knowledge managers who want to follow leads obtained from KOL do so using conference calls and electronic bulletin boards. Client service personnel are frequently challenged to do further research and then make further contributions to KOL.

Source: Bukowitz and Williams (1999).

Much remains to be done by global companies in the area of knowledge management, as can be seen by perusing Mayo's observations (1998) on the required processes for knowledge management in the future:

1. Learning so that new knowledge can be acquired and managed.

2. Capturing, recording and documenting new knowledge created and applied.

3. Sharing new knowledge and disseminating it rapidly.

4. Collaborating to facilitate rapid knowledge creation and application.

5. Organizing knowledge into easily accessible units.

6. Finding new applications for the existing knowledge bases.

7. Expanding and building on the existing knowledge base.

THE INTERNET

Like the intranet, the Internet has enabled global corporations to use their knowledge bases advantageously. These corporations are striving to make possible anytime, anywhere use of the Internet. The newest innovation in the Internet arena is a wireless Internet access system called Wi-Fi, which stands for wireless fidelity (*Time Magazine*, 2002). It is starting to find widespread use in public places like airports, restaurants, railroad stations, hotels, and shopping centres of cosmopolitan cities. It can also be used in houses and offices as part of existing local area networks (LANs). The Wi-Fi allows commuters to download information from the Internet when they are in public places or travelling. Thus, global managers do not have to limit knowledge management usage to specified points in offices.

Even a relatively closed country like China has become hooked on the Internet. Less than 2 per cent of China's population own a computer

(*Time Magazine*, 2001h). Nonetheless, this is 2 per cent of a population of 1 billion. Increasingly, the Chinese are keen to invest in hand-held computers. There is currently an effort on the part of transnational corporations to capitalize on this keenness of a few million Chinese. The research firm BDA China reported in 2001 that China has 21 million Internet users. Its online population is projected as more than doubling every year. The provision of Internet-related services in China has therefore become a matter of interest to transnational corporations. Such global corporations as AOL, Yahoo!, Microsoft MSN Online and Lycos Asia are all seeking to do this. *Time Magazine* (2001d) reports that Lycos Asia spent US~$12.8 million to buy myrice.com, a portal used by Chinese-speaking Internet users.

The use of the Internet as a means of knowledge building and knowledge sharing has become so widespread that lawsuits pertaining to its use have been filed and won/lost, while a legal system to guide its use has emerged. Harvard Law School even offers a course on cyberlaw. There are copyright laws that govern ownership of material put on the Internet.

Business transacted on the Internet has proved profitable for many players worldwide. For example eBay, an online auction company, has 38 million registered users. It has sold items ranging from computer servers to the costumes leading ladies wore in famous movies. It has hewn costs to the barest minimum by dispensing with carrying and holding costs.

Groups with membership spread across the entire world have used the Internet to organize and work towards their objectives. For example, antiglobalization protesters have used it. According to *Time Magazine* (2001g) the Internet has been used by antiglobalization protesters who move from one summit to another, to share knowledge and build knowledge bases in the form of Web sites. The use of the Internet is so cost-effective that a global movement around a social issue can be organized within a 24-hour period, linking together even cash-strapped but committed activists. It is also enabling companies everywhere, from small businesses to transnational corporations, to sell more at less cost.

An innovation put on the market in April 2002 makes it possible for the Internet to link people across cultures more comprehensively. It enables phone calls to be made online for a fraction of the cost of using landline phones. Global managers are seeking systems that offer both communication and computing systems, are portable, and can be used on an anytime, anywhere basis. Computing and communicating capabilities are essential requirements for intercultural knowledge management. Hence, devices with various combinations of computing and communications systems are being fabricated. The mix and match components and properties of such devices include wireless, video, music, computing power, size and broadband.

The creation, dissemination and management of knowledge are all key areas today, but are often not accorded the importance they merit.

PROGROUP'S VARIOUS SOURCES OF KNOWLEDGE

Progroup is a US corporation that focuses on workplace diversity. It not only has its own knowledge specialists who build knowledge bases, but also has arrangements with various corporations from whom it obtains knowledge to supplement its own efforts.

One type of arrangement involves buying specialized knowledge bases from other companies. This involves negotiating formally with the intention of purchasing an intellectual property right. Another arrangement involves the mutual sharing of knowledge by like-minded companies. These less formal arrangements have yielded a synergy that has proved extremely helpful to both the concerned companies over the long run. The arrangement has worked for both partnering companies because each one has been as committed to the success of the other as to itself. Thus the nature of the relationship that exists between both the partners has been important. Investing in a quality relationship takes time and effort but has proved worth this time and effort for Progroup.

Source: Bukowitz and Williams (1999).

Two features about knowledge management from the point of view of intercultural management can be described. First, the process by which knowledge is created by managers from different cultures collaborating together may be complex. Knowledge creation and assimilation may have cultural aspects and an intercultural team should be aware of this Second, the process by which knowledge is transferred from one cultural context to another can also be intricate.

These two points were grappled with by the Legend/AOL Internet partnership. Legend is a Chinese home PC maker, and at the time that it entered into partnership with AOL in June 2001 had 40 per cent of the Chinese market. AOL Time Warner is an American conglomerate that has businesses in the Internet, movies, cable TV and communications areas. In June 2001, AOL Time Warner had Internet operations in 17 countries. The two corporations entered into a partnership to sell Legend home PCs that are Internet-compatible. This was to induce Internet users to subscribe to AOL Internet services. The partnership worked to ensure that the Internet services of AOL, developed in the American culture, were transferred to China, keeping in mind the reality of life in China. In China, the government frequently blacks out Web sites and there is censorship of information that is made available for public perusal.

Legend/AOL took into account that government regulations in China are different from those in America. *Time Magazine* (2001f) reports that AOL's CEO Gerald Levine pointed out at a press conference in Beijing that the company's insistence on autonomy only extended 'to the journalistic enterprises within our company from *Time Magazine* to CNN'. The implication was that the company practice of autonomy and freedom from government interference did not apply to Internet use. Levine went on to say that AOL's Internet services 'respects the cultures and different regulations in each country'. At that conference, a Legend manager observed that AOL had a filtering device that could block out Web sites or portions of Web sites. It was used in the United States by parents to block pornographic material on the Internet from children. It was to be used in China to censor information at the discretion of the government.

Another challenge to the transfer of AOL Internet services to the Chinese cultural context pertains to the habits already formed by Chinese Internet users. Chinese Internet users are accustomed to using Internet services in Internet shops and paying for its use by the minute. Legend/AOL had to try to convert Chinese users to switch to monthly subscriptions.

KNOWLEDGE MANAGEMENT AT IBM GLOBAL SERVICES

In the mid-1990s, the consultancy division of IBM Global Services started a unit for knowledge management. By 1999, the unit comprised 40 knowledge managers worldwide. This unit has focused on getting specialists to both contribute to knowledge bases, and use these bases extensively. Central to the success of this unit are the communities of practice. These communities of practice have been described as 'distributed centres' of knowledge that can contribute in ways that are compatible with knowledge building and sharing through electronic means. A community of practice at IBM Global Service is sponsored by a business unit. Once sponsorship is received, the community of practice institutes a knowledge management team. This team then decides what the knowledge base that it is building should comprise, and what resources the base requires.

Performance criteria are employed to assess the efficacy of each community of practice. Criteria used include the extent of contribution that was elicited and the extent of use of a knowledge base. This is important considering that the knowledge management team spends about 10 per cent of its time managing a designated community's knowledge base. Apart from identifying existing sources of information for a knowledge base, a knowledge management team has to find ways of making that base comprehensive and complete. The knowledge base has also to be kept current.

Source: Bukowitz and Williams (1999).

DIGITAL HOME ENTERTAINMENT PRODUCTS

These are products designed and fabricated by global corporations who do state-of-the-art work in the area of knowledge management. Global corporations ranging from Sony to Sega provide upgrades for existing offerings on an ongoing basis.

Computer games are a product line that can become obsolete within months of being brought into the market. This is aggravated by the fierce competition among knowledge management global corporations. In October 2000 Sony released its PlayStation 2, a technological improvement over its original PlayStation. By this time, computer games had become a US~$20 billion a year global business. Sony had sold 75 million original PlayStations. PlayStation 2 was not only a new offering in computer games, but had a 128-bit processor. The original PlayStation had only a 32-bit processor. The high-powered processor of PlayStation 2 enables it to play CDs and DVDs and can be used with components that permit Internet access and the use of digital cameras and digital music players. With this, computer games fabrication moved to an era where the units could become part of a composite home entertainment unit. PlayStation 2 was put on the market even though it did not have a modem. In other words, it was put on the market even though Sony had not taken PlayStation 2's innovative features to their logical conclusion.

Meanwhile Sega introduced its computer game Dreamcast, which was compatible with Internet usage. However, Dreamcast was less powerful than PlayStation 2.

The worldwide market preferred Sony's PlayStation 2 to Sega's Dreamcast. *Time Magazine* (2001a) reported that while Sony was the market leader with a 66 per cent share, Sega had only 14 per cent of the market.

Various consequences for Sega arose out of this preference and the fact that for four consecutive years it had been making huge losses. The chief consequence was that its image as a loss-making entity made independent game-developing companies steer clear of it. This meant that although Sega had state-of-the-art game consoles for sale, it had no takers because not many customers were interested in the games that were sold with the game consoles.

This was an ironic turn of events for Sega, given that it is one of the pioneers who developed the game console. It is continuing to do pioneering work in the area of hardware development. It is working on making its game console platform compatible with mobile phones and personal digital assistants.

What the experience of Sega suggests is that knowledge management cannot be divorced from general management principles. It may be tempting for knowledge workers to work on technological innovations that are marvels, and developing them can afford them tremendous satisfaction. However, the realities in the market and the preferences of consumers may be entirely different. And if consumers are not prepared to buy technological marvels, the company that has developed them cannot generate profits. As far as consumer games are concerned, consumers want the game to have appeal. The other features merely serve as supplements.

Computer games global corporations are competing to make games aligned with digital home entertainment systems. They are also competing in another arena: that of the actual computer games. These games must have a certain durability of appeal to make them worth playing. The issues facing intercultural management here are:

▌ Expertise in knowledge management is more difficult to acquire than expertise in intercultural management. Companies engage in a war for talent when it comes to attracting and retaining skilled knowledge management personnel. Such personnel are sought out from the whole world.

▮ Global corporations can impart intercultural skills to their knowledge management personnel after they have been recruited.

▮ The training that knowledge management personnel receive is often obtained from higher education institutes that cater to an international student body (*Time Magazine*, 2000a).

An interesting offshoot of the intercultural usage of computer games is intercultural access to music via platforms like Playstation. There are composers today who write cross-cultural music for computer games, and in the process acquire fans from all over the world. The Playstation presents music in a format comparable to CD sound quality, which makes it an attractive medium for popularizing modern music.

Time Magazine (2001e) has described a successful composer of this modern genre, the Japanese Nobuo Uematsu. Uematsu's compositions have won international acclaim and have been appreciated by people from diverse cultures. Some of his pieces of music have been so popular that they have been released as singles all over the world. Part of the reason for his cross-cultural appeal lies in Uematsu's ability to imbue his music with 'grandeur and depth', an ability that seems to have universal appeal. His tunes are robust and emotive with a strong melody that is catchy. They also have complex layers that appeal to a more discerning audience.

MEDIA

The media play a role in making knowledge bases available to the average citizen. Transferring the success formula for the dissemination of information from one cultural context to another is often easier said than done. This is the case even if the difference in culture is not as stark as that between the United States and China. Problems arise even if the knowledge transfer is being effected from Hong Kong to Taiwan. That was what Jimmy Lai, a successful media baron from Hong Kong, found out when he went to Taiwan to introduce his publications there.

Lai's observation about transferring his Hong Kong knowledge base to Taiwan, as quoted in *Time Magazine* (2001b), is, 'You go to a strange place, you have to have humility, not just ability.' Putting this maxim into practice, Lai took the position of only deputy chairman of his media group in Taiwan. The post of chairman was given to the CEO of his Taiwan business house partner. This post was acceded to the Taiwanese even though he had invested only 30 per cent of the venture's capital. Meanwhile, Lai found it difficult to participate directly in the media's knowledge generation effort since he was not conversant with Mandarin Chinese, the language spoken in Taiwan.

As far as the media are concerned, language plays a role in the transplanting of knowledge from one culture to another. The experience of STAR, the cable TV global corporation owned by the Australian media tycoon Rupert Murdoch, is testimony to this.

STAR provides cable TV services in eight languages to 53 countries. Its programmes have 300 million viewers. The network has knowledge regarding programmes that have proven successful to a Western viewership. What it does in Asia is to offer these programmes in the local language, with local stars and representing the local ambience. For instance, the television programme *Who wants to be a millionaire?* has been very popular with Western audiences. This is essentially a quiz programme where contestants have the opportunity to double the prize money they earn for every successive question they answer correctly. In order to make the process more interesting, the contestant can take help thrice. One help option is to telephone and consult a friend. The second is to take a studio audience poll about the right answer. The third help option is to get the suggested four answers reduced to two. A Hindi version of *Who wants to be a millionaire?* has been shown in India by STAR and received well. Questions were posed about the Indian milieu. The quizmaster was a popular Indian film star, and many contestants did win big prize money. The programme had been adapted to suit the local culture.

James Murdoch, CEO of STAR, is quoted in *Time Magazine* (2001k) as saying, 'To assume that you can force-feed American culture is crazy.' He believes that there is more than one mass market. He also realizes that Hindi or Mandarin-speaking people can be global as well. The objective of STAR is to understand the diverse tastes of the burgeoning middle classes in each of its markets, and to adapt its knowledge base appropriately. This includes not swinging in the opposite direction and assuming that popular programmes developed for a Western viewership will have no appeal at all in the Asia region.

Meanwhile, the merger of AOL with Time Warner in late December 2000 makes their wide-ranging wares available worldwide on an anytime, anywhere, anyhow basis. The merger also makes AOL-Time Warner the biggest media transnational corporation in the world. At the time of its merger it was worth US~$202 billion. Its wares included broadcasting, publishing, music and movies. These wares could be made available to consumers via either the Internet or a cable television network. The following points of interest in the context of a world connected by the transmission of knowledge have been noted in *Time Magazine* (2000b):

▮ Broadband technology will enable all AOL-Time Warner wares, from publications such as books and magazines, to movies and music, to the browsing for and placement of shopping orders, to be accessed through cable television lines.

▮ Broadband technology is currently the most versatile medium for making available the entire range of wares to customers. It is much faster than any other medium available for the transmission of such services.

▮ The Internet connectivity offered by AOL-Time Warner allows for the fastest instant messaging possible. One million new users are registered every six weeks.

LEVERAGING KNOWLEDGE MANAGEMENT IN TRANSNATIONAL CORPORATIONS

Transnational corporations often find that they encounter complex problems which, if not appropriately tackled, have serious consequences. Quinn, Anderson and Finkelstein (1998) have described a transient configuration of knowledge management specialists that they call a spider's web. A spider's web can work well for transnational corporations searching for high-quality solutions to complex problems. A spider's web allows specialists located in different cultures to contribute to the solution of complex problems. It also allows a complex problem to be broken down into facets, and each facet assigned to a particular specialist for his or her consideration. This is efficacious for problems which are so multidimensional no single specialist could have all the expertise necessary for solving them.

The spider's web has several interesting features. First, it is a virtual configuration. Second, the configuration assumes some of the features of a networked structure, since lateral communication may be necessary to put together a final, integrated solution. Third, it is used to solve a problem quickly, after which that particular spider's web ceases to exist. Fourth, the spider's web comprises specialists from different disciplines. Fifth, it involves bringing together specialists from different cultures.

Knowledge sharing may or may not happen among a disparate group of specialists. There are some policies that a transnational corporation can pursue in order to facilitate knowledge sharing. One is to link promotion and compensation to the extent to which specialists are perceived by their peers as collaborative. Each specialist is evaluated by every other specialist in the spider's web in the form of a confidential report. If a particular specialist is consistently assessed as being uncooperative by his or her peers on a spider's web, it is concluded that he or she is not a team player, and he/she is penalized accordingly.

An important factor that contributes to the success of spider webs is technology. Electronic, voice and video data banks enable multicultural, multidisciplinary workforces to come together for specific purposes in a highly focused way. Various types of software enable specialists to build knowledge bases and then quickly and efficiently analyse those bases. There is software that enable specialists in a spider's web to engage in knowledge building and sharing in an interactive fashion. There is software that enable specialists to identify and locate sources of knowledge. Often the existence of advanced technology results in the retention of knowledge managers by a transnational corporation. They get used to the technology and are unwilling to move to corporations that cannot offer the same technology.

Quinn, Anderson and Finkelstein (1998) cite Andersen Worldwide as a corporation that has connected 82,000 personnel in 76 countries. It has done this with the help of a system called ANet. The ANet centres on getting specialists to contribute to electronic bulletin boards. These electronic board transactions are supplemented by voice and data exchanges.

Knowledge specialists who work in one particular discipline or in one particular location may develop a sense of elitism which makes them unwilling to form collaborations outside their narrow field. This problem is exacerbated by the fact that it is often difficult to assign credit for individual intellectual contributions when the final output has been pieced together from various contributions. Another factor that acts as a deterrent to knowledge sharing across disciplines and cultures is lack of respect for specialists from other domains. If such feelings are widespread and deeply entrenched, efforts to constitute knowledge groups may cause resentment and eventually prove to be counterproductive.

Technology is being updated at such a rapid rate that an innovation millionaires buy at the time of its invention falls within the reach of the middle-classes in just one decade. Thurow (1999) notes that the reporting system Peter Arnett used to cover the Gulf War in 1991, comprising solar cells and satellites, cost US~$500,000. In 1999, the same system cost just US~$4,999. Without the solar cells, the system cost only US~$1,999.

According to Davis and Meyer (1999), software should be upgraded constantly until it is able to perform all kinds of diagnostic and analytical tasks. They cite the example of the work Mercedes Benz is doing in this regard. Mercedes Benz was developing a system that can be installed in a Mercedes Benz car to diagnose and record the state of health of that car. The moment it detects a flaw, it automatically connects with a Mercedes dealership. The dealer then contacts the owner by telephone, and suggests that he or she call in to have the defect corrected.

GE Medical has a similar system in place. This transnational corporation not only sells a particular type of medical equipment called the MRI machine, but also keeps track of the functioning of the MRI machine's hardware over the Internet. GE Medical also creates patient records digitally for the convenience of its consumers, as part of the service it offers with the sale of an MRI machine. *Time Magazine* (2001i) reports that it is the objective of the CEO of GE, Jeffrey Immelt, to ensure that 20 to 30 per cent of GE's revenue comes from knowledge-based competencies.

REWARDS AND COMPENSATION AT IBM

In the last decade, IBM has introduced a few changes in its approach to rewarding its managers, reflecting the fact that it is now a knowledge-based company, and knowledge management is an activity that merits being treated differently. IBM managers now receive what are termed 'competency-based rewards'. Meanwhile, the managers are accorded membership of one of four levels within their organization, depending on their competence. Each level comprises a wide range of possible jobs. An IBM manager could thus perform a wide variety of tasks and move laterally very substantially. The objective at IBM is to create a culture centred on 'human growth'. In such a culture, individual competence and development is encouraged and rewarded. There is pressure on IBM managers to constantly enhance their skills and acquire new knowledge. This is what is expected of knowledge managers. If they become 'obsolete', this would be reflected in the compensation they receive. Ultimately what this means is that managers at IBM are compensated on a performance-cum-competence basis.

Source: North (1994).

LEADERSHIP IN A KNOWLEDGE MANAGEMENT GLOBAL CORPORATION

Many global corporations have cells or divisions that are knowledge management entities. Usually, knowledge management entities are R & D units that function as organizations within organizations. An example is the Change Management Team (CMT) of the Diageo Corporation, the world's largest alcoholic drinks corporation. Duncan Newsome heads the CMT. It is the opinion of Paddy Miller (2001), who studied the team, that Newsome's refreshing management style is responsible for the success of the CMT. Newsome is a past master at metaphor management, a style that goes down well with the academically inclined, research-oriented personnel typically found in knowledge management entities. He uses analogies found in the writings of the science fiction writer Isaac Asimov to convey how he expects the members of his entity to function.

The metaphors that appropriately describe the CMT revolve around religious or mystical cults: for example, describing the managers of the CMT as missionaries trying to get their clientele to accept a new paradigm or perspective. The perspective can be so fundamentally new that uninitiated clients can form a hostile coalition against the missionary managers of the CMT. This is the challenge with which knowledge management entities worldwide grapple. Knowledge management personnel and managers have to believe so strongly in their innovation or newly formulated perspective that they are able to withstand the pressure of opposition from their clients. And generally, the clients are managers from other divisions of the global corporation. Once the clients are convinced of the proposed innovation's utility, they become converts.

A second characteristic defines the head of a knowledge management entity in a global corporation: he or she often heads a virtual team. There is a limit to the extent to which personnel can get to know each other. Communication by e-mail and videophones has to substitute for face-to-face interactions. The team may be globally dispersed, so that even when conferences are arranged, it may not be possible to assemble all members together. Newsome led his virtual team by ensuring that considerable trust and rapport existed among members. He evolved a flat structure, making it easy for members to relate to each other as equals. He made it clear that being a trustworthy team member was a requirement of the job and not optional. He used peer evaluation to assess whether members were working in ways that won the trust of all others.

However, CMT members needed the trust and professional camaraderie that existed. They were comforted by the thought that there was always somebody they could e-mail or telephone for professional support. Newsome himself was like a father figure who made himself available to his team wherever they happened to be in the world. On one occasion, he flew to Copenhagen from London to help a CMT manager prepare a presentation she had to make to a sponsor. He was viewed as a team coach rather than a traditional leader. People could receive as much coaching as they wanted, but only if they asked for it. They could adopt the position of understudy if they so desired, and learn by doing while an experienced guide provided feedback. There were few rules in existence apart from the fact that trust should exist between all CMT members.

Some more information about the CMT is being given here to throw light on Newsome's leadership style. The CMT's members lived in any place they wished and then commuted to work on projects, even if the commute entailed travelling to another country for the week. For instance Alan McFarlane, one of the CMT's managers, lived in Barcelona but worked mostly in London. He commuted every week to London at company expense. Candy Mackay lived in London but worked in Seoul and had earlier worked in London, Frankfurt, Amsterdam, Bangkok, Glasgow and Edinburgh. Each project a manager from the CMT worked on typically lasted for four months. To enable the managers to spend time at their home base, while working at another location they usually had four-day weeks. This meant that managers could fly in to work on a Monday morning, and fly back home on Thursday evening. The company paid for them to stay in a hotel or flat. Partners could fly down for the weekend at company cost, if a manager did not want to fly home. This meant that the CMT's knowledge managers could live in an 'ex-patriate bubble'. Personnel who work in the knowledge management area tend to be 'close' as people, and may not be oriented towards displaying intercultural skills.

According to Newsome, given the geographically dispersed nature of the team, e-mail was the powerful glue that held the members together. For managers working in the area of knowledge management, being able to 'converse' with each other on a routine basis frequently is important, because they find it difficult to interact with people outside their sphere of expertise. To quote Newsome, 'e-mail can be used as a cry for help when you need help. It is a kind of an anchor keeping you in the team when you are away on assignment.'

A CMT manager observed, 'The team is brought close together by one-liners about a certain topic. It gives a great feeling of together-ness. . . Even though we could be thousands of miles apart we are never alone.' Another manager said, 'I have e-mailed from hotel lounges and airports. I have shocked people with my ability to collect e-mail within 15 minutes of arriving at a place.'

There are problems with increasing camaraderie in a geographically dispersed, intercultural team. In June 2001, the entire CMT congregated in Amsterdam for a conference, and engaged in a group exercise called 'Lost at sea', where they had to pretend they were in a lifeboat. They had to collectively decide what life or death decisions to take. The group exercise proved to be a fiasco, with the CMT unable to function as a team, let alone a cohesive team. A CMT manager remarked, 'Some people were ignored. People talked over each other. There were lots of egos involved.' Another member concluded, 'We provide mutual support, but that does not make us a team.'

What has been reported in the previous paragraph appears para-doxical. However, that is not really the case. Managers of knowledge management entities are often lone rangers who can work with others only up to a certain point. They often prefer to work alone, to the extent that is possible. At the same time, they need affirmation from peers or guides when times get rough professionally. They want like-minded people with whom they can banter. In other words, they prefer to work alone, while being able to draw on the support and professional resources of trusted others whenever necessary. Newsome has striven to cater to this in his CMT.

The CMT emerged as a knowledge management entity whose mem-bers were highly motivated. This is commendable given that managers may be working by themselves thousands of miles from their nearest team member.

Those with the responsibility of managing knowledge-based organ-izations in an intercultural context will benefit from designing and developing new and relevant leadership systems. Knowledge manage-ment is a new and emergent area of research, as is testified by the paucity of literature on the subject. The interface of knowledge manage-ment with intercultural management is an area that is so new it has yet to be studied extensively. In this book, based on the interviews we have conducted and a perusal of whatever literature exists, we suggest that transnational corporations adopt an experimental approach to leadership. This would allow appropriate and effective modes of leadership to evolve. What we recommend is that the leadership of a knowledge-based transnational corporation be permeable, by which we mean that it be capable of accepting inputs from employees lower down. There is a two-way flow of inputs. This becomes more of the essence when the composition of knowledge managers is multicultural. Permeability allows knowledge systems to be open to different paradigms of thinking.

Ultimately what will count in terms of leadership is the extent to which a leader displays the capacity to learn and unlearn. A leader of a knowledge-based, transnational corporation must keep learning and unlearning not only about knowledge and its management, but also about leadership.

SUMMARY

Knowledge management is an emerging but important field of enquiry. It relates to the process of creation, management, storage and dissemination of knowledge, and the timely acquisition of pertinent knowledge bases. Formal or informal groups currently undertake the accretion of knowledge bases, especially if this accretion is being attempted by a transnational organization.

Knowledge management interfaces with intercultural management when the teams of managers working with knowledge bases comprise individuals from differing cultural backgrounds. Culture is one of the variables that influence systems and patterns of thought, and even the manner in which individuals plan knowledge-building endeavours. Managers/researchers from eclectic cultural traditions can complement each other advantageously if the collaborative effort is administered well. Knowledge managers, especially in a cross-cultural context, require singular leadership and management practices. They usually fabricate and devise products and services that are at the cutting edge.

6

Conflict resolution and intercultural management

CASE STUDY: INTERNATIONAL COMMITTEE OF THE RED CROSS

In early 2001, there was only one international organization operating in Afghanistan. This was the International Committee of the Red Cross (ICRC). The ICRC has been operating in Afghanistan ever since 1980, when armed conflict first broke out in that country. Initially the ICRC's delegation in Pakistan extended its activities to cover Afghanistan, but since 1987 the ICRC has maintained a full-fledged base in Afghanistan, with its Afghani delegation headquartered in Kabul.

The mission of the ICRC everywhere in the world is to do humanitarian work in regions where there is armed conflict. This humanitarian work is accomplished by delegations physically present in those areas of armed conflict. In 2001, there were ICRC delegations working in 60 countries. In all these locations, the staff is multicultural and drawn from myriad nationalities. The largest representation is from the country in which the ICRC delegation is working. In 2001, for the ICRC around the world, the expatriate staff numbered 1137, while locally hired staff numbered 8337. Jakob Kellenberger, President of the ICRC from January 2000, describes the enterprise as 'an impartial, neutral and independent organization whose exclusively humanitarian mission is to protect the lives and dignity of victims of war and internal violence and to provide them with assistance'.

In early 2001, the greatest challenge facing the ICRC was the management of its multicultural delegation in conflict-ridden Afghanistan. According to the Swiss head of ICRC operations in Afghanistan, one of the delegation's prime concerns was to obtain access to the victims of Afghanistan's civil war. This was a problem related to the culture prevalent in Afghanistan. The staff deployed to the ICRC mission in Afghanistan had therefore been selected with care. They were selected because they were culturally sensitive. These individuals also had patience and perseverance, and were prepared to work tirelessly to win the confidence of the Afghani militia on both sides of the civil strife. They were prepared to play the waiting game and work for months cultivating relationships with Afghanis. They were prepared to listen and be educated by the Afghanis about their conflict, and why it was important for them to wage war. Frequently, when ICRC staff attempted to cross battle lines to succour war victims, the victorious army's soldiers prevented them from doing so. Then the ICRC staff would talk to the soldiers. This entailed having endless cups of tea with the soldiers and chatting with them for hours just to build rapport. Such an approach flies in the face of modern management paradigms that stress the need for demonstrating performance within time schedules. Jean-Michel Monod, Delegate General for Asia, comments: 'A typical Swiss manager with UBS or Roche would find the pace at which we build relationships in Afghanistan almost unbearable.'

Before expatriates were assigned to the ICRC delegation in Afghanistan, they were educated about the Afghani world-view. They also had empathy for the Afghani people. In Afghanistan, they adopted the Afghani approach to negotiations, discussions and business meetings. Sometimes when members of the ICRC negotiated with Taliban leaders for permission to provide medical treatment to the victims of war, the actual issue was broached only at the third or fourth meeting. When ICRC staff interacted with Taliban leaders, it was understood that the interactions were intended to be part of a long-term relationship. This is the Afghani way of doing business. The ICRC also believed that this was the appropriate way of relating to people engaged in armed conflict. Such people are not living normal lives. They are prepared to listen to others only after their hearts have been warmed by the human touch. Warriors who have been brutalized by war experiences need to connect at the human level. Monod has observed international negotiators trying to work with the Taliban leaders. These international negotiators fly into Afghanistan, have just a one-hour or two-hour meeting with the leaders, then fly out of Afghanistan again. Monod's comment about this modus operandi is that 'It is impossible that they will succeed in their negotiations. This is not the way Afghanis conduct business. For the Afghans, time is not of the essence.'

This case study is concerned with how the ICRC delegation in Afghanistan elicited cooperation from feuding parties. One approach was to use the Afghanis' own styles of working. One reason why the ICRC succeeded in this is that they had been physically present in Afghanistan with a large delegation since 1987. This delegation comprised 64 expatriates and 1033 locally hired staff. By contrast, the United Nations (UN) in 2001 maintained an international staff of 10 inside Afghanistan. The UN's strategy was to manage its operations in Afghanistan from its mission in the neighbouring country of Pakistan. The UN had a staff of hundreds in Pakistan's capital, Islamabad, and these staff would brief their negotiators.

By being physically present in Afghanistan, the ICRC was able to assess the cultural imperatives of the local situation. When they first started their operations in Afghanistan, ICRC delegates had not understood or appreciated the Afghani view of time, so initially they were sometimes denied permission to work with casualties near battlefronts. This forced the ICRC to rethink its approach to working and negotiating with the Afghans. After reflection, it decided that it would have to establish and maintain long-term relationships with all factions. It also decided that staff would spend hours conversing and building rapport at every meeting they held with faction members, in the Afghani tradition.

With effort, the ICRC gained the confidence of the Taliban government. This is exemplified by the following incident. In 1999 the United States attacked with cruise missiles the training bases of the alleged Saudi Arabian terrorist residing in Afghanistan, Osama Bin Laden. UN embassy staff and other personnel decided to pull out of Afghanistan because they feared retaliatory action by the Taliban against foreigners. Unfortunately a UN staffer was killed the day after the shelling, but nothing happened to the ICRC delegation. In fact, the ICRC delegation received a note from the Taliban assuring them that they did not have to leave Afghanistan like other foreigners. They could stay and continue their work, and no harm would come to them. And in fact, no harm came to them as acts of retribution.

There is another reason that all the warring factions in Afghanistan accepted the ICRC. There was a preponderance of Afghanis in the

ICRC delegation (as already mentioned, 1033 Afghanis as opposed to 64 expatriates). The Afghani members of the ICRC constituted a link between the ICRC organization and the Afghani people. They educated expatriates about the nuances of Afghanistan's culture.

The Afghani staffers of the ICRC delegation in Afghanistan were developed, promoted and encouraged to distinguish themselves professionally. Outstanding Afghani staffers were deployed to other countries as expatriates. An Afghani woman doctor was sent to Sierra Leone, to be part of the ICRC delegation there.

The senior Afghani members of the ICRC delegation in Afghanistan have a standing, and are respected for their competence and the fact that they are employed by an international organization. When they present themselves to warring chieftains they are listened to.

There is another reason that the ICRC could successfully conduct its operations in conflict-ridden Afghanistan. Since 1987, the delegation has been with the Afghani people through the thick of wars. Other agencies wound down operations and temporarily left Afghanistan, fearing for the lives of their staff, whenever the embattled situation became fierce. Even in 1992, when the feuding factions of Afghanistan brought their war to Kabul and bombarded the city with heavy artillery, the ICRC delegation persisted with its work of tending the victims of war. At that time it was the only non-Afghani organization still operational, with its entire staff in place.

The first international representative that the Talibans met after consolidating their control over Kabul was the head of the ICRC delegation. The Taliban emissary said, 'We know that you at the ICRC had an excellent working relationship with the Hawani Massoud group, and we sincerely hope that we will be able to establish the same excellent working relationship with you.'

There is a reason for the success of the ICRC with the Taliban. Many of the Taliban members were at one time the Mujahideens who successfully waged a guerrilla war against Russia and managed to drive the Russians out of Afghanistan. These Mujahideens, when wounded, were treated and nursed at ICRC hospitals. The ICRC was allowed to start operations only in 1987, but for a decade before that the ICRC cared for Afghani Mujahideens at its hospitals in Peshawar and Quetta in Pakistan.

Even Mullah Omar, the spiritual leader of the Taliban, successfully underwent surgery at the ICRC hospital in Quetta. From the outset of the ICRC's operations in Afghanistan, the Afghanis experienced, first-hand, its humanitarian work. By the year 2001, one out of every

100 Afghanis had directly benefited from the ICRC in one way or another. That is why, according to Monod, the ICRC was able to successfully pursue its mission in Afghanistan. That is why the Afghanis extended privileges to the ICRC that were not offered to other international agencies. To quote Monod, 'We were allowed to visit prisons. We were allowed to undertake all possible humanitarian activities in the country.'

The ICRC did not transact with Afghanis from the standpoint of 'throwing the book at them'. In other words, the ICRC did not insist that the world order as constructed by the United States or NATO countries or the EU was what the Afghanis should adopt. Afghanis do not respond well when told, 'This is the way we do things, and this is the way you should do things as well.' Their reaction would be, 'Maybe our way of doing things is the right way and you should follow suit.' The ICRC did not assume a judgmental position, and instead established a relationship of mutual trust with all factions. This trust is illustrated by the following anecdote. At one time the Taliban banned the use of the Christian cross, but they allowed the ICRC to use their cross emblem as an exception. The ICRC succeeded in working jointly with the Afghans by presenting their objectives as the joint objectives of the ICRC and the Afghanis. It even worked with a sister organization called the Red Crescent, modelled along the lines of the Red Cross.

The ICRC also persuaded the Taliban leadership to accept that medical care had to be provided to women in need, as much as to men. After the Taliban accepted this, they followed the ICRC's lead and started separate women's wings in their own hospitals. Medical treatment was provided to female patients in these wings by female medical staff. The ICRC for its part incorporated Taliban practices in its operations. The Taliban view was that women should be at home with their families. Women working in jobs were 'unIslamic', except when they provided health care to other women. The ICRC did not employ Afghani women to work in its offices in Afghanistan. It only hired women as medical care providers to other women. Even the Taliban saw this activity as essential, given that one woman in Afghanistan dies every 30 minutes. The ICRC tried to persuade the Taliban leadership that it is not dishonourable for a woman to pursue a career. Its efforts were rebuffed, however. This was perhaps the only occasion when the ICRC attempted to influence the Taliban way of thinking. It can be said that the ICRC never engaged the warring factions in discussions to try and understand the conflict from the actual participants' standpoint. Monod's explanation for this is that 'We are not Muslims.'

This stance suggests that the ICRC cannot understand the conflict situation in Afghanistan from the perception of the parties to the conflict: that is, from the insiders' frame of reference. The organization maintains that it is nonetheless viewed by all Afghanis as nonpolitical, nonpartisan and neutral, which is how it views itself.

Inferences

After the experience of the ICRC in Afghanistan is examined, the following features about intercultural management in a conflict-ridden, turbulent environment can be inferred.

Continuous physical presence in the situation through bad times and worse times

Successful integration into a turbulent and difficult cultural environment requires a long-standing physical presence in that environment. Acceptance by a culture is a complex and special activity that is best achieved through continuous physical interactions. Integration into a friendly culture in a stable environment is itself facilitated by the physical presence of an organization's members. When the environment is conflict-ridden and turbulent, the requirement for the continuous physical presence of an organization's members is heightened.

The ICRC established its Afghani delegation's main branch in Kabul in 1987, and was physically present continuously since then throughout the ceaseless armed conflict. It was given permission by the Afghans to base itself in that country only in 1987. Before that, from 1979, it provided its services to the Afghanis from Pakistan. Links with the Afghanis were forged even before 1979 through the ICRC mission in New Delhi, India. Most important of all, the ICRC remained in Afghanistan even after all other international agencies closed operations and pulled out.

Assimilate by adopting patterns of behaviour from the local culture

Conflict-ridden situations do not lend themselves to influence by extraneous cultures. Such circumstances require that the maximum effort at cultural integration is made by the organization operating there. Research indicates that turbulent environments are to be prepared for, rather than treated as complex externalities. Yet inter-national agencies operating in conflict situations often ignore the need to connect with the environment. The content of what is to be negotiated among feuding factions is well detailed, but the actual sensitive aspect of the process of negotiation is ignored.

The ICRC responded to the situation in Afghanistan by accepting the Afghani notion of time, as already discussed. The importance of achieving things over a long time-frame is an Afghani cultural orient-ation. The ICRC also respected the requests made by the Afghanis. Its observations about how prisons are run in Afghanistan have not been disclosed to the outside world, since keeping assessments confidential is necessary to foster trust with the Afghans. Non-Afghani organizations have no bargaining power that they can leverage with the Taliban. The ICRC employed its approach after fathoming the Afghani mind. And this approach was one of gaining acceptance and credibility with the Taliban, and then working within the parameters prescribed by the Taliban. Monod comments, 'We are not judgmental about the Taliban. We understand where they are coming from. We know about the history of Afghanistan; about the inequitable land ownership systems of the last century that had resulted in suffering for many people. And from that suffering has come a desire to usher in another way of life.' What Monod has observed is in keeping with the views of experts on international negotiation. If there is a single theme running through the literature on international negotiations, it is that the most important consider-ation is the building of relationships over the long run (see for example Ferraro, 2001). The focus has to be on how the views of both sides can be accommodated. This requires a deep understanding of where the other party is coming from, and what that party's cultural imper-atives are. The emphasis has to be on finding common ground based on a relationship of trust and mutual respect.

The ICRC has followed the dictum that it can work with the Taliban without agreeing on everything. What it has not done is lay down conditions. It would go against its cardinal principles if it said to the Taliban, 'We will only tend to your wounded if you change your outlook on how women should be treated.' The credo of the ICRC is to take care of the victims of armed conflict irrespective of the cultural ethos of that place.

This focus on humanitarian work is what contributed to the trust and understanding that existed between the ICRC and the Taliban. The ICRC delegation in Afghanistan has a genuine fondness for the

Afghan people at the person-to-person level. A Swiss member of the ICRC married an Afghani woman in 1999. This event was well received by the entire community. Such intercultural marriages are almost unheard of in Afghanistan. Arguably, only an intercultural marriage with a member of the ICRC delegation could have found acceptance in Afghanistan. At a less striking level, all expatriate members of the ICRC have forged friendships with at least one Afghani. At the human level, the ICRC is not perceived as an alien organization.

CASE DISCUSSION QUESTIONS

1. Why has the ICRC been successful in the conflict-ridden environment of Afghanistan?

2. In gaining acceptance in Afghanistan, what has the ICRC done to take cognizance of Afghani cultural mores?

3. In what ways would an international organization behave differently in a conflict-ridden environment, as opposed to a stable environment?

4. Do international managers operating in conflict-ridden environments have to be imbued with a specific set of attributes?

5. Would the ICRC have to function differently in the Afghanistan of today?

6. Are there any cultural issues associated with conflict situations?

ACADEMIC DISCUSSION

Internal conflict resolution

From perusing the foregoing case discussion, it is clear that cross-cultural management faces enormous challenges when an organization has to operate in a turbulent environment. Quite often, the need for conflict resolution arises because managers from habitually opposed cultural groups have to work together. Nienke Boersma, a former MBA student (2001), narrated her first-hand experience regarding internal conflict while working for an international consultancy company.

Boersma is Dutch, but opines that in her experience, the cultural differences between the Dutch and Belgians are greater than those between the Dutch and any other country. According to her, this resulted in a conflict situation when a Belgian came to head a four-member Dutch team of which she was a member. Belgians feel comfortable in an authoritarian structure, where managers enjoy stature and position depending on their place in the hierarchy. The Dutch on the other hand are expected to demonstrate their competence on the job. Managers do not automatically occupy a position of importance by virtue of their job title.

The first day the Belgian manager assumed his position as the head of his team, the Dutch started experiencing problems getting along with him. They had to develop a business plan for a client, and wanted to start working on it straightaway. The Belgian instead insisted that the team first develop advance plans, and that Boersma, as the most junior member of the team, learn a particular computer programme. Boersma perceived this as an attempt on the part of the Belgian to demonstrate his authority.

The Belgian also proceeded to have a telephone line put in the room where the team met with its client. This enabled him to check his e-mail in that room, instead of in his office that was just next-door. The Dutch viewed this also as an attempt on the part of the Belgian to demonstrate that as the team leader, he was entitled to certain perks. Meanwhile, the Dutch managers felt that he was not showing any performance, and found it difficult to respect him as a professional. Very quickly, the group had polarized into two camps: the Dutch managers versus the Belgian team leader.

Matters came to a head when the Belgian complained to the managing director of the consultancy's Dutch office. This was in keeping with the Belgian way of resolving conflicts; however, it went against Dutch norms. Dutch managers first try to resolve a conflict at their own level, before taking the matter to a higher authority for arbitration. The managing director saw the situation from a perspective different from the Belgian's. He 'resolved' the conflict by summoning the entire team, and informing them of the complaint the Belgian had made. He made it apparent that the Belgian's lodging a complaint with him was tantamount to an admission that he could not handle the situation. He then assigned Boersma the responsibility of providing guidance to the Belgian. It was also suggested to the Belgian that the team should start working on the project assigned to them, instead of spending so much time planning their work procedures.

The Belgian did not make any headway, and seemed to spend his time going around in circles. His Dutch team members soon realized that the hapless Belgian was unable to work on his own. Since he was accustomed to working in a hierarchical system, where seniors did not ask their subordinates for help, he tried to muddle on by himself. In any case, asking for assistance now would have led to considerable loss of face for him. Since no progress was achieved on the project, and the Belgian was viewed as the bottleneck, he was removed from the project and sent back to Belgium.

The project then had to be completed by three people, instead of the original four, and the Belgian fell sick on his return and was not available for work for two months.

We can draw specific inferences from this example:

▌ Boersma suggests that employees adopt the culture of the dominant group of managers when functioning in a cross-cultural context. According to her, adopting the culture of the dominant group means adopting the work culture of the country from which the majority of the employees hail. It also means adopting the work culture of the country a manager is working in. In the above instance, this suggestion may be valid, as in another situation when Boersma was deputed to work in the consultancy company's Singapore office. Being the only Dutch manager in a Singapore branch dominated by Singaporean managers, she adapted to a work culture dictated by Singaporean traditions. She accepted the hierarchical structure that was in place, and the more bureaucratic style of functioning. She did this even though, as a Dutch manager who had until then worked in the Netherlands, she was not comfortable with a hierarchical environment.

▌ Boersma's suggestion has validity in limited situations. However, life is not always that simple. Before we turn to more complex situations, we will examine a few other issues related to the straightforward situation described by Boersma.

▌ Before managers are despatched by an international company to assume a leadership position in another country, the organization should make them aware of the prevailing work culture at their new place of work. They should be mentally prepared to adapt to the prevailing work culture. In the case cited above, the Belgian was not only unaware of how to adapt to the prevailing work culture, but was not very professionally competent. Generally, managers despatched to another culture should have a good level of professional competence. This will facilitate their being accepted more readily.

▍ Sometimes the cultural differences between neighbouring countries can be quite considerable. Managers going to a neighbouring country should do as much prior preparation, to understand both the local culture and the work culture of the company, as they would if they were going to a country on the other side of the globe. Very often, there are very strongly held beliefs about a neighbouring country. Thus, for instance, Dutch people who hear that a Belgian is going to become their neighbour will already have some beliefs about this Belgian. These beliefs may be based partly on their interactions with other Belgians, and partly on their friends' and associates' experiences with Belgians. Because Belgium and Holland are small neighbouring countries, and it is easy to go from one to the other, there is much exchange of visitors. The resulting knowledge about each other's countries has also heightened awareness of differences. Many Dutch people aver that there are many differences between them and Belgians, and vice versa. This is the case with people from many neighbouring countries, such as Switzerland and Germany, Malaysia and Singapore, India and Pakistan, England and Ireland, Argentina and Brazil, Mozambique and Botswana, and Canada and the United States. Consider the case of Switzerland and Germany. Despite the presence of many Germans in Switzerland, the Swiss perceive them as being culturally different. The German language spoken by Germans, called by them Hoch Deutsch (or high German), is very different from the various dialect forms of German spoken by the Swiss.

The author of this book, when working in Switzerland, had a German colleague. She remarked to me that she found the Swiss very different from the Germans, although this was not apparent to people from other parts of the world. Describing the Swiss-German language, she said, 'The Swiss write a language they do not speak, and speak a language that is not written.' Many Swiss view the Germans as the people who started the Second World War.

Differences in recent history, in stage of economic growth, in form of government, in language spoken, in the religion practised by the majority of the people and so on can all contribute to cultural differences between the people of neighbouring countries.

Conflict between managers from different cultures working for a global company can surface, and global corporations are interested in knowing how to deal with this. According to Tjosvold and Deemer (1980), conflict by itself can improve rather than impede organizational functioning. (It may be noted that Tjosvold and Deemer were discussing conflict in a general sense and not with specific reference to intercultural situations. There is no academic work yet that deals comprehensively with the issue of conflict in an intercultural context.) Tjosvold and Deemer believe that when people with opposing ideas try to arrive at an amicable settlement by bringing their differences to the forefront, they become better able to understand the opposing party's point of view.

Let us examine the Tjosvold and Deemer proposition with reference to the caselet described on pages 188–89. The international consultancy should have made the Belgian and the Dutch aware of their different working styles before they were thrown together. If they had been prepared for differences they might have been more tolerant of each other's lapses. In this case, however, the lack of competence of the Belgian was a stumbling block, quite apart from his lack of cultural sensitivity.

International companies could consider having a department at head-quarters for managing diversity. Such a department would prepare expatriates for life in a new culture. It would also prepare local nationals for accepting expatriates from other cultures. Additionally, it would monitor processes when people from different cultures start working together for the first time. When conflicts arise due to cultural differences, the department would work at bringing the differences into the open so that managers could come to terms with them. In fact, a skilled department would anticipate likely conflict areas. In the case of the misfit Belgian manager, the department should have realized that a manager accustomed to operating in a hierarchical structure was being sent to work in a culture were there was not much hierarchy. A conflict should have been anticipated, and methods of working through the conflict thought out. Removing one of the parties from the scene of the conflict is not the best remedy. At some point in the future the company will have to contend with Belgian and Dutch managers working together.

Weiss (1994) has argued that in the context of managing diversity, there is a need to focus on flexible, multi-option avenues for resolving conflicts before they escalate into costly win–lose or lose–lose battles. In a classic article about conflict resolution techniques, Thomas (1997) identified and described five conflict-resolution approaches. These approaches he termed competition, collaboration, avoidance, accommodation and compromise. He also developed a matrix in which the approaches could be positioned. The matrix comprises two dimensions: one, how assertive or unassertive each party is in pursuing its own concerns, and two, how cooperative or uncooperative each is in satisfying the concerns of the other. If people are unassertive about their concerns, and uncooperative with other people in conflict situations, they are said to employ the avoidance approach. People who are unassertive about their concerns, but are cooperative in trying to satisfy other people's concerns, are using the accommodation approach. If people are moderately assertive in satisfying their concerns, and moderately cooperative in satisfying the concerns of other people in conflict situations, they are assuming the compromise approach. People who are both assertive in satisfying their concerns, and cooperative in satisfying the concerns of others in conflict situations, are said to use the collaboration approach. And finally, people who are assertive in satisfying their concerns, but uncooperative in satisfying the concerns of others in conflict situations, are using the competition approach of conflict resolution.

Let us examine Thomas's options for conflict resolution with reference to the misfit Belgian. The Dutch managers initially used the avoidance approach for conflict resolution. As a result the situation grew worse, with resentment from both sides mounting, resulting in complete loss of face to one side in the conflict, and the team project having to be completed by four people instead of three. According to Thomas, avoidance is a worthwhile approach:

1. when an issue is trivial or more important issues are pressing;

2. when you perceive no chance of satisfying your concern;

3. when potential disruption outweigh the benefits of resolution;

4. to let people cool down and regain perspective;

5. when gathering information supersedes immediate decision;

6. when others can resolve the conflict more effectively;

7. when issues seem tangential or symptomatic of other issues.

(Thomas, 1997)

If any of these factors apply to the Belgian/Dutch situation and justify use of the avoidance approach, it could only be number 7, 'when issues seem symptomatic of other issues'. The situation of the Dutch not being able to accept the Belgian as their leader was symptomatic of the main issue: that both sides had not been prepared to deal with cultural differences. The company had not communicated to the Belgian the style of working that would find acceptance among the Dutch, while the Belgian had not done his homework about the leadership style prevalent among the Dutch.

It is interesting that it was never conveyed to the hapless Belgian that the underlying reason for the conflict was that his leadership style was not congruent with what the Dutch managers expected. The Dutch managers themselves did not do this, even though Boersma had correctly diagnosed the root cause of the conflict. The Dutch CEO did not communicate this point to the Belgian when the matter was brought to him for adjudication. This flies in the face of contemporary academic work on conflict resolution, which advocates that the root cause of the conflict should be brought to the surface, and both sides should understand their role in the conflict. It is possible that managers from certain cultures, Thailand for instance, may not feel comfortable when conflicts are discussed openly. Even then, it is preferable if they are enabled to confront conflict situations in a positive fashion, rather than that the situation be avoided and allowed to fester.

By taking up the matter with the Dutch CEO, the Belgian adopted the forcing approach. As a person comfortable with a bureaucratic style of working, he wanted to impose his authority on his Dutch team members. And what better way to achieve this than by having the highest authority in the Dutch subsidiary back him? Obtaining the stamp of approval from the highest authority is standard practice in a bureaucracy.

According to Thomas (1997), the forcing approach is recommended:

1. When quick decisive action is vital (such as in emergencies).

2. On important issues where unpopular actions need implementing (such as in cost-cutting, enforcing unpopular rules, discipline).

3. On issues vital to an organization's welfare when you know you are right.

4. Against people who take advantage of non-competitive behaviour.

If the Belgian's choice of forcing as a conflict resolution approach can be justified, it is on grounds of recommendation 3, where enforcing unpopular rules is necessary. He did not succeed in what he had intended because the CEO reacted in a manner he had not anticipated.

The Dutch CEO also opted for the forcing approach. He proposed a solution that reflected the concerns of the Dutch managers, and ignored those of the Belgian. As a result of his 'conflict resolution' approach, the CEO may have succeeded in taking quick decisive action. But in the process, the Dutch managers seemed to have gained the upper hand, while the Belgian felt humiliated. After he was sent back to Belgium, he was unwell for two months. The conflict arising out of differences in culturally determined working styles was not resolved in a win–win sense.

In this situation, the conflict resolution approach that was most suitable was the collaboration approach. Thomas (1997) recommends this approach when it is important:

1.   To find an integrative solution when both sets of concerns are too important to be compromised.

2.   To learn.

3.   To merge insights from people with different perspectives.

4.   To gain commitment by incorporating concerns into a consensus.

5.   To work through feelings that have interfered with a relationship.

The international consultancy organization should have used the collaboration approach. The operationalization of this approach requires skilled practitioners. The organization would have benefited if it had an internal cell for managing intercultural relations, as recommended earlier.

CREATION BY INTERNATIONAL ORGANIZATIONS OF CONFLICT SITUATIONS IN HOST COUNTRIES: A FAILURE CASE

Mary Cusick, a former MBA student (in 2001), submitted an assignment in which she described conflict situations that arose when an international development organization from the first world made an intervention in a third world country. Cusick had worked for this organization as an evaluation analyst. She had not, however, worked on a development project in a third world country herself. The report in her assignment was based on informal discussions she had with various colleagues.

The project she described was responsible for empowering women in the rural areas of certain third world countries. The project's main purpose was to lift poor rural women out of poverty. The women targeted were living in villages bereft of adult men, who had migrated to urban centres, lured by the hope of obtaining jobs and making it big. Some failed to return; others were absent for extended periods of time. Meanwhile, the women had to contend with poverty. They were also little educated and suffered from malnutrition-related ailments. They were therefore not able to manage their meagre resources or cultivate crops in a manner that would yield profit.

The international development organization project gave the women small loans to be used for specified purposes, as well as training in crop management and farming, and personal finance management. Gradually the women started managing matters in their village. Their conditions of living began to improve. They began to buy modern farm equipment which they learnt to operate to optimal benefit. Their health also began to improve. The project was termed a success by the international development organization. Its main purpose had been met.

What the project had not recorded or taken into account was the social dislocation these women experienced, paradoxically because they had become more independent. When their menfolk returned to the villages, they were displeased to find that their wives no longer depended on or were subservient to them. The traditional norm of male dominance, emanating from the men's role as breadwinners, no longer applied. Some men could not accept this and took recourse to domestic violence.

In this case study, an intervention by an international development agency resulted in its beneficiaries being placed in conflict situations. This arose because the development agency had not understood the culture of the villages where it had introduced its project. Consequently its project was poorly designed and implemented. It should have kept in mind that development is not one-dimensional, and a model of development that works in one country need not apply in another culture. A few of the points the agency was ignorant about were:

▌ Development has to occur in a holistic fashion to be without unintended negative consequences. Efforts to improve the economic conditions of living have to be undertaken along with efforts to enhance socioeducational levels. Development is also an outcome of an enlightened mind-set.

▌ Development is a long-duration effort. Providing support to poor, rural women so that they can become economically independent, without helping them become socially independent, is not enough.

Once the development agency had disturbed the cultural traditions regarding man–woman relationships, it should have continued its developmental efforts. It should have operationalized an additional project to resolve the conflict situations that had been unleashed in the village households.

▌ This second project, since it impinged directly upon the cultural traditions of the village people, would not have met with success if it had been executed by people from a different culture. As far as cultural values regarding marriage and man–woman relationships are concerned, it is not possible for any culture to claim that its view on the subject is the definitive one. In the villages referred to, the cultural tradition was that a marriage was sacred and forever. To ensure that the marriage worked, the wives made more compromises than their husbands. The international development agency was located in a country where one out of every two marriages ended in divorce. Managers from that development agency would not be able to execute the second project by themselves, especially as they had already demonstrated a lack of cultural sensitivity. The project would have had to be designed and implemented by enlightened development agencies and experts from the local culture. The international development organization, together with local experts, would have had to devise ways of thwarting domestic violence without breaking up families.

▌ Development has cultural components. A development project that worked in one cultural context might be wholly inappropriate elsewhere. Development projects that are based on economic criteria can lead to cultural backlashes. An international development organization that unleashes a conflict situation as a result of a development intervention has failed in its objectives. Poverty impacts the culture of a place, and an international development organization should realize this when designing poverty eradication programmes.

ENVIRONMENTAL TURBULENCE FOR HOST ORGANIZATIONS CREATED BY GLOBALIZATION

An important facet of conflict management is response to turbulence. An example is the turbulence generated in the environment of a national company because of competition from global companies. Gill, McCalman and Pitt (1996) discussed how British Telecom faced disturbances when the advent of global cable television networks in Great Britain threatened its telecommunications hegemony. Another example they gave is the competition faced by the shipbuilding industry of Clydeside, Scotland. Until the mid-1990s the industry had an international market, but then it began to lose customers to international shipbuilding companies in Korea and Japan. New production technologies developed by those companies helped them become leading providers of ships at the global level.

Global managers interviewed for this book advise national companies facing global competition to revitalize themselves to meet the challenge of international competition. British Telecom is believed to have risen successfully to the challenge of turbulence in its external environment by discarding its earlier management philosophy of being an innovation-spurning, risk-averse public company. It became a moderately risk-taking private enterprise. It improved its working after effectively adjusting to external competition. Turbulence in the external environment, generated by the advent of global companies, can thus exert a beneficial effect.

CONFLICT ARISING OUT OF DIFFERENT ATTITUDES TO ETHICS

Culture is a factor that influences managerial ethics. When managers are required to take an ethical stand, that stand may be difficult to explain to a person who does not subscribe to the same ethical viewpoint. When managers are placed in a situation where they have to act, but are divided on what action should be taken because of ethical differences, the result can well be a conflict. If the opposing ethical views stem from differences in culture, the resulting conflict can lead to divides along cultural lines.

This example is used in some business school courses on intercultural management. You are a passenger in a car being driven by your close friend. The friend hits a pedestrian by driving at 35 kilometres per hour in a zone with a speed limit of 20 kilometres per hour. There are no witnesses. A lawyer tells you that if you state that your friend had not exceeded the speed limit, he can escape serious consequences. Would you (a) testify that your friend was driving at 20 kilometres per hour, or (b) testify that your friend was driving at 35 kilometres per hour?

It is often found that the responses to this question are culturally influenced. Students from the same culture tend to react from the same ethical position. They do not find common ground with students from other cultures. Including the following add-on conditions can intensify the conflict that has been artificially generated in class:

▮ You must answer positively either (a) or (b), and cannot say (a), but. . ., or (b), but. . .

▮ Your friend was not driving at 35 kilometres per hour, but at 40 kilometres per hour: that is, at twice the speed limit.

▮ The pedestrian was also your friend.

▮ The pedestrian will make a complete recovery.

▮ The accident was the pedestrian's fault.

▮ You have also driven above the speed limit.

▮ Your friend has a tendency to drive above the speed limit.

▮ Your friend was driving at 60 kilometres per hour in the 20 kilometres per hour zone.

▮ The pedestrian was disabled for life.

▮ The pedestrian was young, attractive, successful and disabled for life.

Ethical bases and perspectives on management

According to one perspective on management, the purpose of an organization is to achieve goals and objectives, using resources efficiently. Employees receive a reward for their contribution to the organization. The diametrically opposite perspective is that organizations are above all a collection of people. The needs and concerns of these people have to be taken into account. Otherwise, organizational life becomes meaningless. The first perspective avers that the system is paramount. The latter perspective emphasizes the importance of relationships.

Given the car example, managers who would have testified for their friend were supporting the management perspective that emphasizes the importance of relationships. On the other hand, those managers in favour of telling the truth supported the management perspective that systems should be paramount. In a simple, preliminary survey conducted by a business school in 2001, it was found that:

▮ In the United States, 93 per cent claimed that they would tell the truth.

▮ In Canada 93 per cent claimed that they would tell the truth.

▮ In Australia, 91 per cent would have told the truth.

▮ In the UK 91 per cent would have told the truth.

▮ In Venezuela, 67 per cent claimed that they would testify in favour of their friend.

The business school that conducted the survey notes that the United States, Canada, Australia and the United Kingdom are cultures that uphold the management paradigm that systems are paramount. By contrast, Venezuela is a culture that emphasizes the importance of relationships. When a Venezuelan manager and a US manager have to work together on a matter that has ethical ramifications, they may assume opposite positions, resulting in a conflict between them.

CONFLICT RESOLUTION STRATEGY

Intercultural managers effective in resolving conflicts created by opposing ethical viewpoints are not wedded to discharging the letter of the law. They are of the opinion that a verdict that reflects the law but seems harsh to many is not justice at all. When people assume inflexible positions, are not prepared to examine the underpinnings of their ethical stance, and engage in situational ethics, they are unlikely to be in a position to resolve disputes. Thus in the example above, some individuals will categorically choose either (a) or (b), taking the ethical position that they will always tell the truth or always defend a friend, then refuse to unbend when the facts of a situation are brought to their attention. Such managers will not be suitable for intercultural management.

In every culture there are managers who assume unbending ethical positions, and others who reconsider their position when relevant information is brought to them. All the global managers interviewed for this book were united in their opinion that it is managers who are capable of situational thinking on ethical matters who are adept at intercultural management. Those who have inflexible attitudes to ethical dilemmas are likely to become embroiled in conflict situations when operating in foreign cultures.

The ultimate ethical dilemma that global managers grapple with is whether a good life is compatible with good management. If the two are perceived as incompatible, then conflicts will arise. Managers from cultures where people have no scruples will rule the roost. Fortunately that is not the case, and good management is also ethical management. Global managers need to be clear what a realistic but ethical position is, in business and in life, and make decisions accordingly. It is therefore advisable for global corporations to have a clear stance regarding their ethics, and communicate that code of ethics to their managers.

CONFLICT ARISING OUT OF DIFFERENT ATTITUDES TO CORPORATE CULTURE

When Japanese corporations first started operations in the United States, they faced conflict situations because of their US employees' ethical positions. For instance, in Japan, employees believe in lifetime employment. In the United States, employees (especially managers) frequently engage in job-hopping. The Japanese perceived US employees as lacking in company loyalty. In a *Newsweek* article Asa Jonishi, then senior director of Kyocera Corporation, said, 'Most Americans are very, very individualistic – you could almost say egoist; they are quite different from the way we would like our people to be' (Powell, 1987).

Initially, Japanese corporations had cultural conflicts not only because of the individualism of US employees, but also because of their lack of experience with 'egoistical women'. By the time Japanese corporations came to the United States, the corporate culture in US companies was sympathetic to assertive women. In the 1980s the US female employees of Sumitomo Corporation of America, for instance, complained of discrimination on gender grounds. They went as far as to file a suit against Sumitomo, claiming that they were expected to restrict their career ambitions to clerical positions. They clamoured for opportunities in management positions. Sumitomo settled the suit by offering to increase the number of women in management positions.

Since their early years in the United States, Japanese corporations have learnt to deal with potential cultural conflicts arising out of different perceptions of how corporate culture should be shaped. If managers are open to diversity and different modes of thinking, differences do not have to lead to conflict.

Many US employees who had worked for companies where authoritarian systems were prevalent in the 1980s took to group decision making when they started working for Japanese corporations. Powell (1987) reports that the then assistant general manager of Haseko, Pat Park, commented about his experiences of working for a Japanese corporation: 'There are many times when I'm the janitor here picking rubbish. But there are also times the major decisions are made because I say so. There's more equity in Japanese companies.'

What can we learn about conflict resolution from the experience of Japanese global corporations who came to the United States? First, global corporations have to be prepared for a period of learning when they locate themselves in a new culture and recruit large numbers of employees locally. Second, they have to invest in imparting culture awareness training to the local employees.

The key to the resolution of cultural conflicts is to present the beneficial aspects of the new corporate culture to newly joined local employees. Why did the American Pat Park adapt to a consensual decision-making corporate culture, which is the hallmark of a Japanese corporation? Because he felt that he was not just a cog in the wheel, but somebody who could make a difference to what was happening around him. If Haseko was locating itself in a culture where people experienced difficulty in working in a group situation, its employees would have needed appropriate training before being 'unleashed' within group decision-making situations. Further, the global corporation should make it clear that it is assessing newly joined employees to see if they fit its corporate culture. If the employees are lacking in intercultural skills, they probably are not suitable for a global corporation.

CULTURAL CONFLICT AND MANAGEMENT STYLE

The management style that managers must use in order to be successful will vary from culture to culture. Otherwise conflict situations could arise.

Intercultural managers can avoid conflict situations if they have flexibility in their styles. Colback and Maconochie (1989) profiled what they described as the 'Euromanager'. A suitably expanded version could be used to describe a global manager. 'He, and presumably she, will be a graduate with a second degree in European studies, and will speak fluently at least one European language as well as English, and possibly Japanese. Experienced in working for multinationals, they will understand senior management operations in American, Japanese and European settings. . . Needs to be cosmopolitan in the truest sense of the word, at ease socially, linguistically and culturally in all countries.' Devine (1988) provided her version of the 'Euromanager': 'They understand the languages, the customs and the business and political systems of the countries where their countries operate.' The skills of such Euromanagers could be fostered, according to Devine, by creating multinational boards of directors.

Global managers should not spread themselves thin by learning the languages and mores of more than four countries. A key requirement is comfort with constant adaptation. This should be coupled with the ability to diagnose the context and ascertain what management style is appropriate. Additionally, global managers should be able to learn quickly aspects of management style that are locally appropriate. As they assumed senior positions, the ability to motivate managers in all cultures will stand them in good stead.

Finney and von Glinow (1990) argue that transnational corporations require 'cognitively complex self-monitoring managers who have global perspectives and boundary spanning capabilities, with a geocentric and not an ethnocentric orientation'. They also recommend that intercultural managers have contextual competence to complement their technical competence. Contextual competence refers to the following: capacity to understand the value orientations of different cultures, linguistic skills, capacity to recognize the importance of local customs, religion, history, climate, politics, and social norms, capacity to introduce change in a manner and at a pace suitable for local conditions, capacity to focus on the global performance of the corporation and not on local results, capacity to balance the need for control with the need for autonomy, and finally, capacity to act as a 'boundary-spanning interpreter' connecting home and host country decision makers. Finney and von Glinow also identified a set of attributes for inclusion in a global executive's management style. These are cognitive complexity, self-monitoring ability, boundary-spanning ability, global orientation and geocentricism. The technical term they devised to describe these attributes is 'superordinate value orientation'. They defined these superordinate value orientations as follows:

▊ Cognitive complexity is the ability to use 'multiple solution models', rather than 'one best way' approaches as a management style.

▌ Self-monitoring managers possess the ability to perceive the behaviour and thinking patterns associated with differing value orientations, and match their behaviour to the demands of that orientation.

▌ The boundary-spanning role is one of acting as interpreter between home and host countries about technical and sociocultural issues.

▌ Global community is the ability to gauge the role of home and host countries in the global economy.

▌ The geocentric manager is one who internalizes multiple worldviews and value orientations.

All these attributes enable a global manager to tackle conflict situations. They also enable a global manager to formulate conflict resolution strategies that lead to win–win situations.

CULTURAL CONFLICT AND LEADERSHIP

In the case presented on pages 188–89, the Dutch were unable to accept the hapless Belgian's leadership. This led to a conflict situation. It was 'resolved' by the Belgian being sent back to Belgium.

There has been little effort on the part of transnational corporations to develop intercultural managers whose leadership can be accepted in different cultures. Finney and von Glinow surveyed a small but representative sample of transnational corporations in the United States to ascertain what these corporations are doing in this regard. They were unable to find anything substantive. The corporations placed a lot of importance on 'international experience', on the job experience, and knowledge of a foreign language. They did not address whether the managers were oriented to being geocentric rather than ethnocentric. An ethnocentric manager may have 'international experience' and still not know how to lead a workforce from a different culture.

Sadler and Hofstede (1976) undertook a cross-cultural study of IBM managers to ascertain the extent to which the Tannenbaum and Schmidt leadership schema had acceptance. This study is now dated, and there is a need for definitive work by both academicians and practitioners in this area. We briefly present their main findings:

▌ Managers in Japan registered an above average preference for the authoritative 'sells' style and a somewhat below average preference for the consultative style.

■ Managers in Australia, the United Kingdom and Germany displayed a high preference for the consultative style.

■ Managers in Brazil and France revealed an above average preference for the 'joins' style, and a below average preference for the consultative style.

As well as the fact that the study is dated, one can question whether results obtained from IBM managers are universally applicable. However, the pertinent question still is, how can an intercultural manager lead a culturally diverse group of people without ensuing conflict?

Before we examine this question we will look briefly at a more recent study about cultural differences and leadership by Wills (1996). Wills interviewed in a structured fashion 25 managers from 14 European countries. He found differences in what they expected from managers holding leadership positions. These differences were cultural. However, what these managers from varying cultures agreed on regarding effective leadership is what is of interest here.

The Wills model

Wills arranged the key success factors that culturally diverse managers identified as vital for leadership into three clusters:

■ individual-level issues;

■ bridging issues;

■ social issues.

Individual-level issues are qualities a leader of culturally diverse managers should possess, such as empathy. Wills saw empathy as a leader's instinctive ability to understand what a manager from another culture would want done. The other two individual-level issues are empowerment and emotional intelligence. Wills accepted the view that empowerment is 'the act of strengthening an individual's beliefs in his or her sense of effectiveness'. Managers from different cultures may need to be empowered in different ways. Meanwhile, emotionally intelligent leaders allow their managers to express their emotions instead of suppressing them. Culturally sensitive leaders allow their subordinates to emote in ways consonant with their national or ethnic culture.

Bridging issues connect individual-level issues with social issues. An example is communication. Effective intercultural leaders issue instructions, advice and suggestions in a manner that is clearly understood by their subordinates. They may need to give careful consideration to culture when communicating. In other words, a Swiss leader communicating to a Spanish subordinate needs to make allowances for the fact that a Spaniard might interpret messages differently from a Swiss. The other bridging issues are visioning and charisma. Intercultural leaders with a capacity for visioning are able to get acceptance for their visions by subordinates at all levels and from all cultures. Leaders with charisma are able to get their followers and subordinates to accept their beliefs and align themselves with those beliefs. Needless to say, an intercultural leader will acquire the acceptance of subordinates from various cultural backgrounds.

Social issues are those that reflect the characteristics of the society in which the branch of a transnational corporation functions. The extent of globalization prevalent in a society is an example given by Wills of a social issue. Increased globalization calls for greater skill on the part of a leader to successfully interface with managers from different national and ethnic cultures. The cluster of social issues also includes competitiveness and change. Competitiveness demands that leaders get all their subordinates, irrespective of culture, to be high performers. Additionally, leaders should be able to take change in their stride and inspire their subordinates to do so.

Wills developed his model to ascertain whether a European style of leadership existed. His description of a leader suitable for contemporary Europe could be extended for an intercultural manager required to lead an intercultural team and avoid conflict situations. That is our opinion and that of most of the international managers interviewed for this book.

If the Wills model is applied to the Belgian/Dutch team example, the following can be inferred:

▌ The Belgian leader lacked intercultural empathy. As a result, he was unable to understand what his Dutch managers wanted from him.

▌ The Belgian leader was incapable of empowerment. He erred in not recognizing that the Dutch members of his team worked best when empowered.

▌ He was also bereft of any sense of vision for the team and its projects. On the contrary, he gave the impression to the team that he was motivated by personal goals.

▌ Further, he was unable to communicate effectively with his Dutch team. The Dutch felt he had nothing of value to communicate or contribute.

▌ The transnational corporation that had deputed the Belgian manager
   to lead a Dutch team in Holland had not given due attention to the
   social issue of globalization. Otherwise, it would have selected a
   manager with intercultural competencies.

Wills' model recognizes that the leader of an intercultural group of
managers must possess certain capabilities. The Belgian leader lacked
these capabilities, and was not aware that they were required of him.
This caused the conflict between him and the Dutch members of his
team. Whatever other attributes the Belgian might have had, they could
not offset his deficiencies as an intercultural leader. Conflict in an
intercultural setting can be created by a lack of intercultural competencies on the part of the leader.

SUMMARY

International organizations often have to operate in environments that
are turbulent and conflict-ridden. Local residents may have their own
interpretations of conflict and its resolution. International organizations are advised to assume a neutral and non-judgmental stance
towards the external conflict. They should focus on performing the
tasks they are mandated to do. This implies that they earn the respect
of all the important constituents of their external environment through
the quality of the work they do and the services they offer. It also
requires international organizations to be extremely circumspect and
not make cultural gaffes.

International organizations may face culturally induced conflict
situations from within. This is an issue separate from operating in
conflict-ridden external environments. Where internal conflict situations are concerned, international organizations should play a proactive
role in preventing them as well as resolving them when they surface.

7

Expatriate management and intercultural management

CASE STUDY: ICAS

Independent and Counselling Services Ltd (ICAS) had over 200 client organizations in June 2001. Established in 1982, it is primarily an international provider of behavioural risk management services, operating worldwide through its own network of overseas offices and strategic partnerships. A service it offers that is of interest to us is the Employee Assistance Programme (EAP). EAP facilities are available to all companies who have paid fees (comparable to insurance fees) to ICAS. One component of the EAP is expatriate management.

A prime aspect of expatriate management dealt with by the EAP is culture shock, a term first popularized by the anthropologist Oberg (1960). It refers to 'the psychological disorientation experienced by people who suddenly find themselves living and working in radically different cultural environments'. ICAS believes that the psychological wellbeing of expatriates should be taken care of, as well as other issues that relocating to a new culture entails.

Expatriates can avail themselves of the following services offered by ICAS's EAP: 24-hour free phone, telephone counselling and face-to-face counselling. These services are used by employees having problems in two areas: life management (information about: legal matters, money, family care, consumer rights, general matters) and work. The 24-hour free phone service exists so that employees of ICAS's client organization can phone in and request services around the clock. Suzanne Boèthius, Clinical Services Director of ICAS Switzerland, comments, 'We want expatriates to feel that they have somebody reliable to turn to, who will attend to them at any time, and help them to find solutions to their problems. We do not want them to feel lost and unable to cope.' Suzanne's husband Stephan Boèthius, CEO of ICAS Switzerland, adds, 'If an expatriate is experiencing difficulty adjusting to a new culture, he will be unable to put his best foot forward at his place of work.'

When expatriates avail themselves of the 24-hour free phone service, they can request information about issues ranging from local legislation to how a house can be bought, where a hairstylist or a specialist doctor can be located, or how a suitable school for their children can be identified. Sometimes the questions are standard and the answer can be given straightaway: for example, supplying a list of local gynaecologists. Sometimes, the question requires research from ICAS staffers. For instance, an Italian working in Switzerland might call to say that he had bought a house in Switzerland but his work permit had expired, and he wanted to know whether his family could continue living there.

In July 2001 ICAS introduced a new product called Expatriate Connections, which is basically an assessment of potential transferees' cultural awareness. Based on this assessment, customized training and resource packs are assembled for transferees, to prepare them for life in another country. Along with Expatriate Connections, ICAS launched a second new product called Integrate, which helps integrate transferees and their families into their new surroundings. Each family receives a personal consultant who calls on them regularly to discuss key issues. In addition, they have six-month telephone access to specialist advice and information.

The day-to-day problems expatriates grapple with may seem mundane. However, the reality is that coping continuously with such problems in a new culture can prove stressful, and the time spent on resolving them and defusing the attendant stress can add up. One expatriate interviewed for this case study commented that in his first month in Switzerland, he spent an average of 12 hours a week solving day-to-day problems. On the first day, he found that the dishwasher in his apartment was not working, and needed to locate a repair service. This seems simple enough, but since he did not know his neighbours he found it quite distasteful to knock on their doors, introduce himself, and ask for the address of a nearby service. On the second day he had to drive his wife to a nearby village for a job interview. She felt that if she travelled alone by train and bus she might get lost and be late for her interview. She also did not know how to buy a bus ticket in Switzerland, and felt that this was not the occasion to find out. On the third day he had to ask colleagues where he could find a child-minder to take care of his eight-year-old while he and his wife attended an office party that had been arranged partly to welcome them.

Some expatriates find the process of adapting to the new realities of life stressful. When this becomes apparent to ICAS staffers handling calls on the 24-hour free phone, they may recommend telephone counselling. Sometimes the number and complexity of issues facing callers have overwhelmed them to the point where they seek face-to-face counselling from trained ICAS specialists. For instance, a Norwegian expatriate married to an Indian woman and living in Switzerland might want a divorce. He would not know the relevant Swiss legislation, and could well be under unusual stress. ICAS would be able to provide information and counselling in his own language, since its typical European phone service is offered in nine languages. The EAP services are available not only to an employee of a client organization, but to their partners, dependent children and parents as well.

It is important to ICAS that it involves the entire family in its expatriate management efforts. Hence it uses an instrument called the Cross-Cultural Adaptability Assessment (CCAA), which is administered to prospective expatriates and their families. ICAS does not place its CCAA in the public domain, but Table 7.1 reproduces a comparable tool called the Cross-Cultural Adaptability Inventory (CCAI), to give the reader an insight into the kind of information that is collected.

The CCAA measures the extent to which prospective expatriates and their families possess intercultural competencies. The scores obtained by ICAS are communicated to the client organization. It decides, based inter alia on ICAS feedback, whether expatriates should be despatched or not. Before expatriates are despatched to a country, they and their family are briefed about the norms of behaviour there. The briefing is detailed, and has practical utility. Information is provided on such matters as how much to tip at a restaurant, and how to pay a utilities bill. If a wife accompanying her husband is anxious about how to spend her time, ICAS ascertains

Table 7.1 *Cross-Cultural Adaptability Inventory*

The purpose of this inventory is to help you assess your ability to adapt to living in another culture and to interact effectively with people of other cultures. Read each statement carefully and choose the response that best describes you right now.

Indicate your response by circling the appropriate abbreviation to the right of the statement. For example, if you think that a statement 'tends to be true' about you circle TT next to that statement.

Some items may sound similar. Don't worry about being consistent in your answers. Just choose the answer that best describes you right now.

Use a ballpoint pen or a pencil to place a tick in the appropriate column (DT, T, TT, TNT, NT, DNT). Press firmly when making your choice. If you decide to change your answer, draw an X through your original answer and then tick your new answer.

Key:
DT: Definitely true
T: True
TT: Tends to be true
TNT: Tends to be not true
NT: Not true
DNT: Definitely not true

	DT	T	TT	TNT	NT	DNT
1. I have ways to deal with the stresses of new situations.						
2. I believe that I could live a fulfilling life in another culture.						
3. I try to understand people's thoughts and feelings when I talk to them.						
4. I feel confident in my ability to cope with life, no matter where I am.						
5. I can enjoy relating to all kinds of people.						
6. I feel that I can accomplish what I set out to do, even in unfamiliar settings.						
7. I can laugh at myself when I make a cultural faux pas.						
8. I like being with all kinds of people.						
9. I have a realistic perception of how others see me.						
10. When I am working with people of a different cultural background, it is important to me to receive their approval.						
11. I like a number of people who don't share my particular interests.						
12. I believe that all people, of whatever race, are equally valuable.						

	DT	T	TT	TNT	NT	DNT
13. I like to try new things.						
14. If I had to adapt a slower pace of life, I would become impatient.						
15. I am the kind of person who gives people who are different from me the benefit of the doubt.						
16. If I had to hire several job candidates from a background different from my own, I feel confident that I could make a good judgement.						
17. If my ideas conflicted with those of others who are different from me, I would follow my ideas rather than theirs.						
18. I could live anywhere and enjoy life.						
19. Impressing people different from me is more important than being myself with them.						
20. I can perceive how people are feeling, even if they are different from me.						
21. I make friends easily.						
22. When I am around people who are different from me, I feel lonely.						
23. I don't enjoy trying new foods.						
24. I believe that all cultures have something worthwhile to offer.						
25. I feel free to maintain my personal values, even among those who do not share them.						
26. Even if I failed in a new living situation, I could still like myself.						
27. I am not good at understanding people when they are different from me.						
28. I pay attention to how people's cultural differences affect their perceptions of me.						
29. I like new experiences.						
30. I enjoy spending time alone, even in unfamiliar surroundings.						
31. I rarely get discouraged, even when I work with people who are very different from me.						
32. People who know me would describe me as a person who is intolerant of others' differences.						
33. I consider the impact my actions have on others.						

	DT	T	TT	TNT	NT	DNT
34. It is difficult for me to approach unfamiliar situations with a positive attitude.						
35. I prefer to decide from my own values, even when those around me have different values.						
36. I can cope well with whatever difficult feelings I might experience in a new culture.						
37. When I meet people who are different from me, I tend to feel judgmental about their differences.						
38. When I am with people who are different from me, I interpret their behaviour in the context of their culture.						
39. I can function in situations where things are not clear.						
40. When I meet people who are different from me, I am interested in learning more about them.						
41. My personal value system is based on my own beliefs, not on conformity to other people's standards.						
42. I trust my ability to communicate accurately in new situations.						
43. I enjoy talking with people who think differently than I think.						
44. When I am in a new or strange environment, I keep an open mind.						
45. I can accept my imperfections, regardless of how others view them.						
46. I am the kind of person who gives people who are different from me the benefit of the doubt.						
47. I expect others will respect me, regardless of their cultural background.						
48. I can live with the stress of encountering new circumstances or people.						
49. When I meet people who are different from me, I expect to like them.						
50. In talking with people from other cultures, I pay attention to body language.						

her hobbies. If she were an amateur golfer, for example, ICAS would supply her with a list of golf courses and golf clubs at her prospective place of residence.

Some expatriates contact ICAS to obtain information, while others are in stressful situations. In the six-month period January–June 2001, 57 per cent of the expatriate management cases handled by ICAS pertained to relationship issues, and the remaining 43 per cent to life management issues (consumer, housing, insurance, divorce legislation, Swiss law). Of the cases that pertained to relationship issues, 75 per cent advanced to the stage of face-to-face counselling. The remaining 25 per cent reached the stage of telephone counselling.

We cite here three examples supplied by ICAS of the work it does. The cases have been fabricated but are based on actual situations.

Illustrative case 1: life management

The wife of an employee – let us call her Angela – called at about 9.00 am. Her voice was calm to begin with, but as she started to tell what was on her mind, she became more emotional and distressed. The counsellor could hear small children in the background, and sometimes Angela had to stop talking because the baby was making its way up the staircase. After making sure that the service was confidential, she began to talk.

Her husband had been transferred from the United States to Switzerland 13 months ago. Just recently, they had bought a beautiful home and ordered a new fitted kitchen. When the kitchen arrived after three and a half weeks of delay, it was obvious that the measuring had not been done properly. The kitchen company took the responsibility, after trying to blame a man who had ceased to work for it. Four weeks previously almost the entire kitchen had had to be taken out again. Since then, the kitchen company had not reacted to her phone calls. She had problems speaking in German, although she was starting to learn the language, and the people she rang pretended they couldn't understand English. Her husband was constantly on business trips, and when he came home, too tired to bother with such matters. This made Angela feel even more alone with the problem.

When the counsellor asked if she had any friends who could help, she answered that she felt quite isolated in Switzerland, because of the language, and because she had to be at home to look after her children, who were too young to take to a nursery where she might meet other mothers. She mentioned that she couldn't understand the mentality of the Swiss people. She could feel the cultural shock. In the United States, before she had had the children, she had worked as a freelance real estate agent and been financially independent of her husband. She had had friends, family around her, and her mother-in-law who happily babysat when she needed to do shopping, go to the dentist or whatever. Now she was locked up in her home with her young children, dependent on a husband she hardly ever saw. In addition, the family now had no kitchen and nothing was moving. Her question was simply, what could she do to get her kitchen?

The counsellor understood that there were many issues involved, including emotional ones, but first of all the practical problems had to be solved. She helped Angela write a letter to the kitchen company. Angela wrote her claims in English and faxed the document to ICAS, who translated it into German.

Second, the counsellor talked to Angela about the possibility of help in the house, and gave her a list of agencies where she could find an au-pair or a cleaning lady who could take over the hardest work. This would give her some freedom to move about again. The financial part of this was not a problem, as the husband had a good position and earned well. Angela just had not thought of this option herself.

ICAS also found an English-speaking nursery not far from their home, which took children from two and a half years of age. Angela was delighted.

Angela went on to get a babysitter and a cleaning lady once a week. This gave her the opportunity to take some German lessons, and the contact to other mothers at the nursery made it possible to start making new friends. She also received the address of the American Women's Club. She had not known it existed, and this too was very welcome to her. After a while the kitchen was installed, and she didn't have to wash the dishes in the bathroom sink or buy fast food any more.

All this had of course been a nuisance to the couple, who had been afraid that their relationship, which had been very good before they moved to Switzerland, would suffer. Now that the practical problems were solved, they both felt much more at ease.

ICAS let Angela know that she could call anytime, day or night, as many times as she wanted.

Illustrative case 2: counselling

Rita (names are made up) called ICAS in the afternoon, talking in a determined manner. She must have been upset, but did not want to let anyone know. The problem was rolled out very quickly: her husband had cheated on her with a woman at work. She had just found out and she was not mistaken. There was proof and John had finally admitted it. This was not the first time he had been with other women, but Rita had decided it was going to be the last time. She wanted a divorce and she wanted to know her rights. She had been married to John for 29 years, had travelled along with him all over the world, raised two children, put up with his affairs for so long, and now she had had enough.

Rita was Iranian and John Canadian, and both had lived in Switzerland for nine years. Rita knew nothing about the Swiss divorce law, so ICAS did some research, called her back and gave her the information the following day. What was remarkable was that Rita didn't take any notice of the answers she received. Instead she seemed very quiet, quite the opposite of her attitude the previous day. The counsellor asked what was distracting her. Was she not happy with the answer? Yes, she said, very happy. Then the counsellor heard her voice start to tremble, and soon she broke into tears.

The anger had disappeared and only her total despair remained. For a while Rita just cried, but then her whole story started to develop. She said afterwards that it was so nice that someone who was not judgmental had had the time to listen to her. The counsellor spent about half an hour in assessment and counselling, talking about how Rita felt, asking her questions such as did she have a doctor she could see, did she have friends who could support her, did she take any drugs, alcohol or medication to calm her down, did she ever think of suicide, where were the children now, and whether there was any other practical help she needed. The counsellor asked if Rita would consider marital counselling to clear things between herself and John. Rita said that in spite of her love for him, she was now so hurt that she was not willing to get her hope back only in order to lose it the next time he cheated on her. In addition she had suggested therapy to him before, but he had always refused.

Then the counsellor told Rita about the opportunity to see somebody face to face, a psychotherapist close to where she lived, who would assess her situation and discuss with her how to proceed. Rita said she would think about it and call back the next day.

The following day Rita rang back and agreed to see a psycho-therapist in Geneva. She thought it was a good idea although she was a little nervous because she had never had therapy before. The counsellor assured her that ICAS therapists were very experienced and the service confidential.

ICAS always tries to get in touch with affiliate psychotherapists as soon as possible, but with Rita the counsellor thought it was urgent, because she seemed quite alone and depressed, although she had not expressed any suicidal thoughts and was not taking any drugs. The case manager called Mrs P, a skilled psychologist, who immediately made an appointment with Rita for two days later. Mrs P later called the case manager and confirmed that Rita had attended.

After two sessions of assessment, Mrs P suggested that Rita should receive long-term therapy to support her during the inevitable divorce. The ICAS Employee Assistance Programme only guarantees two professional face-to-face assessment sessions. If the case can be categorized as short term and the focus is on pure problem solving the therapy can go on for up to five to eight sessions, otherwise the client has to be referred to another therapist and be paid for by health insurance or privately.

So Rita was sent on to another psychotherapist. She went there for six months, during her divorce. The ICAS case manager called her back after three months, and Rita told her that she finally was able to take her life into her own hands. She had moved away from John, taken a small apartment in Geneva, and was slowly getting back on her feet. Communication with John was easier now, and she still missed him, but she didn't regret the divorce.

Illustrative case 3: general

Mr W called ICAS in the afternoon. He was Irish and had worked for a big company in Switzerland for the previous five years. His question was about Swiss law on the acquisition of real estate. He wanted to buy a house for himself. He was about to get his 'C' work permit but was not sure whether he could buy a house; if he could keep it if he were transferred abroad for three years; and if he could keep it if he left Switzerland for ever. He also wanted to know if he would be able to rent it out to third parties when he was abroad, and whether there was a limit to the size of the house he could buy.

ICAS could give him a relatively immediate answer, because it had dealt with these issues many times. Basically, the answers to his first four questions were yes, if the acquisition took place after 1997. The answer to the final question was that the size of the living area or the surrounding land is not limited as long as it is not in any way used for speculations.

ICAS also gave him the address of the home page of the Swiss Federal Office of Justice, where he could link in to the English translation of this particular legislation. To make things easier for him, it also faxed him a German printout with arrows that indicated the way through the German pages to the English version.

ICAS did not only assist Mr W in finding information, but helped his company too, because Mr W did not need to take time during office hours to do this time-consuming research himself. In this way Mr W could go ahead with his job assignments and leave his questions to ICAS.

Inferences

As the three examples suggest, expatriates often find that moving to another location can create problems in family life. According to ICAS, this is the prime adjustment problem that expatriates face. Global managers may enjoy working in different cultures, but their families may not be primed for accepting change in their lives.

The experience of ICAS affirms the findings of several studies which emphasize the importance of the expatriate's family adjusting effectively to a new culture. One study by Tung (1981) has designated ineffective spouse adjustment as the predominant factor leading to expatriate failure. Usually the burden of dealing with the practical aspects of a new environment falls on the hapless spouse. These practical aspects relate to non-professional matters, varying from locating suitable food outlets to enrolling children in school. Ferraro (2001) notes in his book, 'Whereas the expatriate employee may see the international transfer as a positive career move, the accompanying spouse may see the move as little more than the disruption of his or her own career.'

ICAS's experience suggests the following requirements for successful expatriate management:

▌ Institutional support for managing the practical problems of setting up hearth and home in a new culture is essential for enabling an expatriate to settle in.

■ The provision of timely psychological counselling for expatriates encountering problems of adjustment can contribute to their mental health and performance.

■ The families of employees should also be assisted in their efforts to find their feet in a new culture.

ICAS provides all the services that expatriates and their families require for assimilating into a new cultural context. Many multinationals are retaining ICAS (or comparable organizations) to oversee their expatriates' assimilation process. Other multinationals are developing the expertise to provide support in-house. It is assumed that these multinationals have selected their expatriates with great care, and that support is being extended to people who are culturally sensitive. The caveat suggested by the ICAS experience is that the selection process should be extended to the expatriates' families as well. Many companies, like Du Pont and Conoco, are following this approach.

Suzanne Boèthius says of the assistance ICAS provides with practical problems, 'We always give information to our clients about the place they are going to, so that they know about simple but everyday matters such as how to fill out pay bills, how much tip to leave at a restaurant, and so on. This is just so that they can feel at home a little earlier than if they had to find out all these things after arrival.' She says of the provision of psychological counselling, 'It really is astonishing how the provision of psychological counselling can make the wife of an expatriate more willing to adapt to a new culture. Once in a while, wives of expatriates suffer from depression when relocated. That is where psychological counselling helps.' Regarding the extension of assistance to family members of expatriates, she notes, 'If the family is not happy, then the expatriate will not be happy. He will therefore be unable to work properly. So for us, we cannot just look after an expatriate, without looking after his family as well.'

CASE DISCUSSION QUESTIONS

1. Why have the services provided by ICAS been well received by transnational corporations engaged in expatriate management?

2. What sort of competencies should an effective expatriate manager possess?

3. What are the differences between a European adjusting to life as an expatriate manager in Asia, and an Asian adjusting to life as an expatriate manager in Europe?

4. Why does ICAS provide such a wide array of services?

5. What recommendations would you give to ICAS so that it can enhance its services?

6. What role does training play in aligning expatriate management with intercultural management?

ACADEMIC DISCUSSION

The services offered by ICAS cannot compensate for lack of cultural awareness on the part of expatriates. Given culturally sensitive expatriates who are eager to learn, institutional support such as that provided by ICAS, coupled with cross-cultural training, is the key to expatriate management. It has been estimated by Brewster (1995) that about a third of US expatriates receive pre-departure cross-cultural training, about 69 per cent of European firms engage in cross-cultural training, and 57 per cent of Japanese firms resort to cross-cultural training. Quite often such training tends to be short term, and lacking in depth. What is necessary is ongoing support and provision of information. That is what ICAS does, and it believes it contributes to positive and purposeful expatriate management.

Nothing can damage the image of a company more acutely than the despatch of expatriates who have received no brief about what to expect from their new environment, and therefore make cultural gaffes. A former MBA student (in 2000) who had worked for the English shipping company Graig Ship Management had a regrettable experience when he was sent to China. This student had been sent to Shanghai, along with some of Graig's most qualified and competent engineers. The engineers were received in China by a sizeable delegation of Chinese managers from the Chinese company that had requested their services. Each member of the Chinese delegation in turn asked the engineers a question. The engineers found that a few of the questions were beyond their capacity to answer. They had not been briefed that it is customary in

China to welcome business partners with a question and answer session, so each Chinese manager comes to these sessions prepared with a question.

Most transnational corporations possess systems and practices designed explicitly for expatriates. In some corporations these practices have evolved incrementally, and have not been formally institutionalized. A few have standardized procedures for taking care of expatriates. Quite a substantial number of corporations prefer to take specialized assistance from organizations such as ICAS. The bulk of the effort embedded in expatriate management centres around, first of all, the careful selection of managers who are going to be expatriates. Once selected, they have to be prepared for and educated about the foreign culture they are going to. And finally, the expatriates have to be given a helping hand when they start operating in the new culture. Transnational corporations are united in their opinion that all three aspects of expatriate management mentioned here are equally important and should be integrated into a comprehensive expatriate management programme. Research by Mendenhall and Oddou (1985) indicates that in practice, not many companies systematically develop such programmes. Of the companies that have offered formal pre-departure training to their expatriates, less than 25 per cent included cross-cultural considerations.

WHO EXPATRIATES ARE

Expatriates are managers who live and work in a country that is not their own. They are often referred to as home-country nationals: that is, individuals who belong to the country in which the company has its headquarters. Not all expatriates are necessarily home-country nationals. There are many reasons why a global company may choose to deploy expatriates rather than employ host-country nationals. These reasons include:

▌ Expatriates are well-thought-of managers with a successful track record. The company therefore trusts them to advance its interests in a new locale.

▌ The expatriates possess the necessary mind and skills-sets to make a significant professional contribution. Their skill-sets include their technical background and expertise. Their mind-sets reflect their personal orientation that is in synchrony with the company's core values and culture.

■ The company is interested in developing a pool of global managers with intercultural competencies. Expatriates from this pool can be rotated constantly among its various international operations.

■ The company may espouse the notion that it uses the best talent in the world and is therefore not limited by ethnicity or any other cultural determinant.

ELEMENTS OF EXPATRIATE MANAGEMENT

This section details the different constituent elements of expatriate management. Companies place varying degrees of emphasis on these elements.

Expatriate selection

Stone (1991) enumerates the following criteria used by companies for expatriate selection: ability to adapt; technical competence; spouse and family adaptability; human relations skill; desire to serve overseas; previous overseas experience; understanding of host country culture; academic qualifications; knowledge of language of country; and understanding of company culture. Additionally, most companies prefer managers who have good interpersonal skills, and are able to establish rapport with different types of people.

Black and Mendenhall (1990) have arranged the adaptive characteristics of expatriates in three clusters:

1. Those associated with resilience, such as high self-esteem and a high threshold for stress.

2. Those associated with the ability to form relationships with people from other cultures, such as tolerance and flexibility.

3. Those associated with the ability to assess, perceive and understand behaviour in new cultures.

An expatriate who possesses technical expertise, but lacks adaptive characteristics from the above three clusters, will be unable to perform satisfactorily. In that event the expatriate may have to leave, either by personal choice or by company request.

The existing literature indicates that although cross-cultural adaptability should play a role in the recruitment of expatriates, in practice insufficient attention is given to this capability. A study of 50 major US firms by Solomon (1994) revealed that 90 per cent of expatriates were selected on the basis of their ability to demonstrate technically superior performance.

All the companies in the case studies in this book have engaged in some form of assessment of the cross-cultural skills of their expatriates. Nestlé carefully grooms potential expatriates, so that by the time they are sent on an international assignment, they have already been exposed to more than one culture.

Multinational corporations are still trying to develop reliable means for predicting 'ability of an expatriate candidate to adapt to a foreign culture'. Multiple sources of information are used to elicit information on this, including in-depth interviews, special instruments, past actual behaviour of the candidate, and behaviour of the candidate in simulations. BMW involves prospective expatriates in problem-solving exercises that require them to sift and analyse actual case studies from other cultures. The problem-solving efforts also involve making a two-week visit to the country where the case study has been set.

Most of the expatriates surveyed for this book reveal a preference for being posted to cosmopolitan cities and towns. Their rationale is that small towns tend to be parochial and provincial, even ethnocentric. Even if expatriates are willing to savour a new culture, they may not be received into the mainstream of that culture. Although an expatriate is expected to make the lion's share of the effort in achieving assimilation, the process is two-way. The give and take of assimilation is most likely to be evidenced in a cosmopolitan, pluralistic city, with a population that is international in orientation. The choice of Singapore as the location for Credit Suisse's Project Copernicus has enabled the company to attract best-of-breed expatriates.

Pre-assignment orientation

Many global corporations believe that certain types of academic training predispose managers for international assignments. The world's top-rated business schools generally provide inputs in international management. Examples in Europe are the London Business School in the UK, INSEAD in France, IMD in Switzerland, the Instituto de Empressa in Spain, and SDA Bocconi in Italy. Top-rated US business schools include Wharton, Harvard Business School, Sloan School of Business, MIT and

Carnegie-Mellon University's Business School. Well-known business schools in other parts of the world include the Asian Institute of Management, Philippines; Australian Graduate School of Management; University of Cape Town Graduate School of Business; the Chinese University of Hong Kong; and the National University of Singapore Graduate School of Business. These business schools attract an international community of students and faculty. By the time they graduate, the students have already experienced life in a culturally diverse enclave.

Companies often formally assess a potential expatriate's strengths and weaknesses for cultural adaptability. A favoured method is to use instruments such as the CCAI mentioned in the ICAS case study. These instruments identify areas in an expatriate's cross-cultural competencies that require bolstering. Accordingly, appropriate training is provided. Such training should be custom made, keeping in mind an individual expatriate's special needs. Ultimately, an expatriate's fit into a new culture depends on that individual's effort to assimilate with an entire society.

Customized individual training is usually complemented by general awareness training programmes. These programmes educate expatriates heading towards a particular country about the customs and behaviour patterns of that country. Expatriates come to know how people in the country they are going to relate to each other socially.

Pre-assignment orientation is essential. Aeppel (1996) has observed that European companies such as British Petroleum, ABB Unilever, Volkswagen and Bayer AG operate regional assessment centres comprising both host-country representatives and specialists, to select and orient expatriates. Swank (1995) has recorded that Ford uses international human resources teams with local representatives, to conduct assessments and prepare expatriates for their overseas assignments.

Organizational support at the new locale

Organizational assistance in adjusting to work life at the new branch is a source of succour for an expatriate. It is important that expatriates integrate themselves into the culture of the new branch and establish congenial work relations with their colleagues and associates. If they experience difficulty getting socialized into the new branch, they will be unable to perform effectively on the job. This then reduces their motivation to cope with the new culture.

Mentoring enables expatriates to assimilate into their new places of work and new countries of residence. Cultural anthropologist Marie

Andersen, in her book *Around the World in Thirty Years*, used the term 'informer' to describe the mentor who continuously informs a newcomer on aspects of culture. According to Andersen, having an informer is the key to gaining acceptance speedily in a new culture. An expatriate's mentor informs him or her of the nuances of corporate culture, as well as ethnic culture. Expatriates may prefer to be mentored by two people, one for providing information about corporate feedback, and another for serving as a link with ethnic culture.

Many Japanese companies connect expatriate families with host families at destination countries. Kumaga (1991) records that Mitsui assigns mentors for their international employees both at home and in the destination country.

A study of 1,100 Swedish expatriates by Torbiorn (1982) reports that all of them were at least fairly satisfied with their experiences abroad, while some were very satisfied. Part of the satisfaction stems from the fact that the expatriates were motivated to venture overseas and experience a new culture. They were recruited appropriately. Their companies gave them organizational support. Torbiorn suggested that the expatriates were likely to be satisfied in countries where the overall standard of living was similar to their own. Similarity of language and religion also contributed to the expatriates' overall sense of satisfaction. The companies and expatriates surveyed in this book postulate that when expatriate motivation and organizational support are at optimal levels, expatriates can experience satisfaction even in cultures dissimilar from their own.

One method by which companies provide the necessary organizational support to their employees is through the dissemination of uniform core values at all their branches. Expatriates can then feel they are in a familiar environment at least professionally. Nestlé has adopted this strategy.

Hall (1995) has described how Unilever, by contrast, has branches across the globe, each with its own corporate culture. The expatriates surveyed for this book opine that they would prefer to work for an organization that disseminates uniform core values across all its branches. This is parallel to the philosophy propagated by Kets de Vries and Mead (1992) for expatriates to conduct themselves: 'Truly global leaders need a set of core values that will guide them in whatever environment they may find themselves.' In other words, expatriates should have strong values that they can draw on in order to have a sense of self.

Shell Corporation uses the expression 'the road to Hell is paved with good intentions' in its expatriate training programmes, to illustrate that despite good intentions, problems can still arise when expatriates interact with host country nationals. According to Shell expatriate trainer Gareth Evans, problems can arise because of a lack of trust on both sides. The issue of trust then has to be addressed specifically.

Expatriates should ascertain, a month after they have arrived in a new culture, whether local managers trust them. If trust has not been established they should take remedial action, before the lack of trust degenerates into distrust. Quite often expatriates may not recognize that trust does not exist between themselves and the local managers because the latter do not make known their reservations until the relationship is beyond salvage. Expatriates who have not earned the trust of local managers often note that they encounter a glass barrier when they try to reach out to local managers. A mistake expatriates might make at this stage is to try to break through that barrier. The more they try to break through that barrier, the more they alienate themselves, and the more local managers recoil from them. The situation is exacerbated when both sides are evaluative of each other, instead of being objective. Being judgmental in circumstances where there is no trust is tantamount to adding insult to injury. In cross-cultural situations, the process of being evaluative will be coloured by cultural biases.

While many transnational corporations invest time, effort and resources in easing expatriates into a new culture, very few prepare local managers for the adjustments they have to make when accepting colleagues and bosses from another culture into their fold. Local managers have to be educated about the culturally determined behavioural patterns of expatriates, to obviate avoidable misunderstandings. They should never be made to feel that 'rule by expatriates' is being imposed on them.

In some countries, expatriates live and work under residence permits granted because they hold specialized expertise not found locally. Bahrain is an example. After getting independence from the United Kingdom in 1971, it has established a diversified range of industries including aluminum processing, shipbuilding, iron and steel processing, furniture and door making, and offshore banking. Wherever it was noticed that Bahrainis did not possess the requisite specialized knowledge for managing any aspect of these industries, expatriates were brought in from overseas (Ellement, Maznevski and Lane, 1990). Expatriate managers are treated deferentially in Bahrain and occupy senior positions in the firms that employ them. However, the residency permits can be revoked whenever the Bahraini employing company decides that the expatriates' services are not required. Expatriate managers of skill and competence prefer to work for the Bahraini branches of global companies.

A US woman who worked in Bahrain for some time found that lack of trust between US expatriates and Bahraini colleagues arose due to differences in the perception of 'truth'. It seemed to her that ' "truth" to a Bahraini employee was subject to an Arab interpretation, formed over hundreds of years of cultural evolution' (Ellement, Maznevski and Lane, 1990). When a Bahraini manager did not see something as the truth, it was not believed, and therefore not accepted. A US manager convinced by facts might see the same matter as an obvious 'truth'. Bahraini managers have quickly rejected US managers who have gone to Bahrain inadequately prepared for such eventualities.

Expatriates from first-world countries need to understand the implications of life in an Islamic country like Bahrain before they set foot there, if they are to be accepted. 'To function successfully [in an Islamic country like Bahrain], the expatriate must understand and learn to accept a very differently structured society' (*Gulf Daily News*, 1987). Islam requires that Muslims pray five times a day. Since the prayer timings are distributed across the day, they need to pray at their place of work three times a day. A devout Muslim could spend 10 minutes at a time in prayer, thus using half an hour a day of company time in prayer. During the Muslim fasting month of Ramadan, it is illegal for a Muslim in an Islamic country to work after 2 pm.

Differences of religion are not a bar to good professional relationships or intercultural friendships. However, ignorance about religious practices that impinge on workplace behaviour can lead to the irrevocable breakdown of trust. An uninformed expatriate who comments to a Muslim subordinate in an Islamic country, 'You could be so much more productive if you were to pray in your off-office hours', is inviting trouble. An expatriate manager is well advised never to comment on a local national's religion and religious practices.

Female expatriate managers in countries like Bahrain have to be prepared not only for overall cultural differences, but also for culturally conditioned attitudes regarding women's role in society. Expatriate women managers in Bahrain sometimes have to fight the opposition of Bahraini males to having women in managerial positions.

WOMEN EXPATRIATES

Women expatriates have to be resilient and resourceful if they wish to be successful in foreign cultures. Men in all cultures are expected to seek gainful employment. Women in all cultures face resistance by some men when they try to advance their careers. This is often the case with management careers. The fact that senior women managers are few in number and complain of glass ceilings has been much discussed by researchers. It is stressed here that women expatriates have to be more skilled at adjusting to a foreign culture than their male counterparts.

A US woman working in Bahrain will find many Bahrainis looking askance at her, since home making is not her first priority. Ellen Moore was often greeted with sympathy when she revealed that she had no children (Ellement, Maznevski and Lane, 1990). Most married Bahrainis like to have children, and at least one son. Hence most Bahraini women regard their careers as subordinate to their roles as mothers. A woman like Ellen Moore trying to befriend local Bahrainis finds that she is often asked questions about her life choices, and even treated as a woman who has made inappropriate life choices. A man in Ellen Moore's position might invite the admiration of local nationals. Ellen Moore, on the other hand, is received with mixed reactions. Some Bahrainis might advise her that she is in some way 'incomplete' because she has no children. Women expatriates have to respond to such situations in ways that reflect their own individuality.

One response is to maintain strictly formal relations with local nationals. Then a woman does not have to justify her life decisions. This can be onerous when done on a continuous basis. Women who opt for such a response can end up feeling lonely. Another response is to challenge the interlocutor's views on a woman's role in society. Such a stance may convey the impression that the woman expatriate is discourteous. A third response is for the woman expatriate to take people's curiosity, even disapproval, in her stride. Assuming a liberal position regarding the way people react to her would reflect maturity on the woman expatriate's part.

AN EXAMPLE OF AN EXPATRIATE WHO FAILED

There are many cases of expatriates who succeeded in one foreign location, but then proceeded to fail in another. In a piece entitled 'The case of the floundering expatriate' (Adler, 1995), the novelist Gordon Adler, who lives in Switzerland, describes the unfortunate experience of a US manager who failed as an expatriate in Switzerland. This man, called Bert Donaldson in Adler's piece, had been deputed to Argos Europe from the United States headquarters because among other things he was viewed as a seasoned expatriate, having been Professor of American Studies in Cairo for five years.

In Cairo, Donaldson had behaved as the quintessential US academician. That was what had been expected of him as a Professor of American Studies. His students wanted to learn about US culture from him and through him. At Argos Europe, his mandate was to mesh together a cohesive team from managers of all the disparate European companies Argos had recently acquired.

What Donaldson failed to do in this assignment was to view the situation from a European perspective. Instead, he behaved as though being completely American (the way he had been in Cairo) was the way to go. For his Cairo assignment, Donaldson had been found to be charismatic. When he was trying to execute his European assignment, his charisma was viewed as abrasive. Though he was working in the German-speaking part of Switzerland, he made no effort to learn German. On the whole he conveyed the impression that he was not trying to fit in by making cultural adjustments. The European managers were thus not won over, so they were less than willing to accept him as a person who could bring them together as a cohesive team.

Much of the content of Donaldson's assignment in Europe was comparable with his earlier assignment in Cairo. Both required him to conduct educational sessions. However, in Europe, his 'students', who were practising managers comparable to him in status and work experience, complained that Donaldson tended to provide too much information and 'over-explain'. He gave the impression of condescension. This also signified that he did not know how to teach Europeans, by addressing them in class at the appropriate level of difficulty.

As the boxed case study illustrates, many problems can arise on account of the inappropriate attitudes, behaviour and skills of expatriates. An erroneous position expatriates can adopt is to assume that they are always right, and that problems arise because the local culture is not sufficiently enlightened. In other words, using the parlance of transactional analysts, they think, 'I am OK, you are not OK.' Other problems expatriates can create include:

▮ using management practices developed in one culture in another culture, without ascertaining whether those practices would find acceptance;

▮ being overly friendly or overly distant;

▮ not adapting to the social patterns of the company in the new culture.

If it is customary for managers to congregate together over a leisurely lunch, expatriates might indicate their desire to be part of the group by adopting that custom. An expatriate interviewed for this book recounted the mistake he made when he joined a subsidiary in Spain. He found Spanish managers taking an hour's lunch at 1 pm. An American, he was accustomed to having a sandwich at his desk for lunch, and continued to do so. He was proud of using even his lunchtime for company work. He was subsequently astonished to find that whenever he went to a Spanish colleague's office to discuss professional matters, the colleague would politely convey that he was busy at that moment. Fortunately he was advised that the Spaniards used their lunchtime to network with colleagues and establish rapport, so subsequent professional interactions are facilitated. Since the US manager did not have the time to establish congenial work relations at lunchtime, the Spaniards did not have time for him when he went to see them in their offices. It was not a straightforward case of tit-for-tat. The Spaniards genuinely did not have time for the small talk that the expatriate wanted to engage in before getting down to business.

A problem that expatriates often face is readjustment to their own culture once they are repatriated. Expatriates can feel that they are looking at their culture through new eyes when they return home. They may see how certain things in their own country could be done in a different way, since they have actually seen those things being done differently in another culture.

Several organizational implications arise from expatriates returning home to work. First, they will be able to identify areas that can be improved in their home branch. They should make recommendations in a way that is acceptable in their culture. Second, they should have acquired the ability to step out of a situation and view it from many angles. An expatriate interviewed for this book, a Spaniard who returned to Spain after spending some time in the United States, described himself as having become more reflective on his return.

AN EXPATRIATE RETURNS HOME

Clemence Lovie (2001), an MBA student at a top-rated European business school in 2001, commented that she felt 'foreign in her own country'. She had returned to her country France a couple of years earlier, after a lapse of 14 years. She found it difficult to adjust to the French way of doing things because although she was French, she had changed. She was flabbergasted to find that the French kept whining and complaining about everything; as flabbergasted as a foreigner would have felt. Most of her compatriots were not only ignorant about other cultures, but also inclined to think that the French culture was the only one worth knowing about. Since she had seen other cultures, she found herself being quite judgmental about France. She found it difficult to be objective and detached about the French as a true foreigner could. At the same time, she was conscious of being French and took pride in being the national of what she patriotically believed to be a great country.

She finally resolved her dilemma in a novel way. She left France to live in Spain. She preferred to live as a foreigner in another country, than be a foreigner in her own country.

GAINING ACCEPTANCE AS AN EXPATRIATE MANAGER

The majority of the intercultural managers interviewed for this book agree that expatriate managers should introduce management practices in a different culture in an incrementalist fashion. We use the following analogy to demonstrate how an expatriate could do this. Consider a frog that has been tossed into a cauldron of boiling hot water. Its reaction will be to leap out immediately. Imagine instead that the frog is taken out of a pond, along with a substantial amount of pond water and bracken, then placed in a cauldron along with the pond water and bracken. The cauldron is made to resemble the pond from which the frog was removed. The temperature of the cauldron is then raised gradually, degree by degree, until it reaches boiling point. It will then be found that the frog has got cooked to death, without realizing what has happened.

An expatriate manager introducing a management practice into a foreign culture should do it so gradually that the local employees imbibe the principles behind that management practice without even realizing it. If an expatriate manager were to introduce the practice in such a fashion that it completely supplanted what the local employees had been accustomed to, they would reject it as too revolutionary, and in the process, reject the expatriate manager as well.

Expatriate managers must have considerable patience when trying to introduce a management practice in a new culture. Since they need to do so incrementally, they may have to wait for quite some time before they can see the results of their efforts. Often, expatriate managers would like to demonstrate that they are performing well on the job, and have successfully transplanted a management practice. However, they cannot artificially hasten the adoption process.

John Kortright is a Canadian expatriate owner of a sandals factory in Mexico who successfully managed to introduce Total Quality Management (TQM) in his company, the Sandalias Finas de Cuernavaca, SA (Ager, Lane and Kamauff, 1995). (Some of the analysis given is by Ager, Lane and Kamauff.) The effort of disseminating TQM throughout his company took five years to achieve. Kortright succeeded because he did not force the pace. He also explicitly took stock of the cultural reality of his company, then designed a TQM initiative that would find acceptance.

TQM is a set of comprehensive management practices that have worked exceptionally well in Japan. Especially after its success in Japan, it has been adopted by companies in various parts of the world, notably in the United States. Notwithstanding this widespread success, Kortright felt that he should first assess the prevailing work culture in Mexico. Dras (1989) has opined that Mexican employees do not challenge the views of their bosses or employees more senior to themselves. Mexican subordinates like to perform tasks in close consultation with their seniors, and are not comfortable with delegated responsibility. Since Mexican employees are not given authority to match their responsibilities, they seldom feel comfortable with enhanced responsibilities.

Mexican managers interviewed for this book aver that times are changing, and that Dras's description of the Mexican workforce is outdated. Dras recommends that expatriate managers desirous of introducing new management practices in Mexico should first invest in developing rapport with their co-workers. This is necessary because Mexican employees like to be reassured that they have the backing and support of their bosses. Additionally, the self-confidence of the Mexican employees has to be bolstered. Then they can derive satisfaction from working independently on enriched jobs. Mexican managers, especially junior managers, have to learn that taking the initiative actually serves to improve their performance.

Keeping in mind Mexico's culture, the first question that an expatriate in Kortright's situation has to ask is whether TQM is too revolutionary a management practice to introduce to the company. When Kortright first bought his company, he found that 'Sandalias Finas resembled an artisan shop rather than a factory'. However, over time, he managed to revamp the organization, and structure the company into a series of departments. A supervisor or coordinator, ultimately responsible to Kortright, oversaw each department. The coordinator could interrupt work processes when a special or rush order had to be attended to.

The efficacy with which Kortright had managed to replace a traditional form of organization with a more professional one would suggest that he could introduce TQM in his company. The workforce had adapted to the change, although the reorganization was effected over a decade and not overnight. It would therefore appear that a TQM initiative could be attempted. And that is what Kortright chose to do.

According to Ager's case study, the employees within each department performed their tasks as individuals and not in teams. In the cutting department, for instance, 'A cutter completed an order individually. Seldom was an order split between two cutters.' But a TQM intervention requires some changes to be introduced at the group level. One can therefore ponder whether Kortright's choice of this management practice was appropriate.

Kortright's main concern was to revitalize his company so it could become internationally competitive. In 1989, 14 years after he had bought an interest in Sandalias Finas de Cuernavaca, he found that as a consequence of economic liberalization, the Mexican footwear industry was being swamped by imports. Suddenly imports amounted to 30 per cent of sales. One reason the imported footwear found a ready market was its lower price. Kortright therefore had a legitimate interest in increasing the productivity of his workforce. He also had to demonstrate to his customers that his company's shoes were comparable in quality to imported shoes.

An expatriate manager in Kortright's position might be tempted to introduce the TQM approach because it is an organization-wide effort that attempts to involve all employees in organizational processes.

Participation is an integral component of TQM. However, the Mexican employees of Kortright's company had not participated in decision making until 1989. So when a TQM effort is initiated in such a context, what ensues is 'imposed participation'. Imposed participation is paradoxical, but it succinctly describes what eventually happened at Sandalias Finas de Cuernavaca.

Imposing participation requires skill and patience. The targeted employees have to first participate in training sessions before attempting TQM on the job. Thus, a TQM effort conducted in Kortright's Mexican company would have to be subdivided into a larger number of sequences than would be the case for a comparable company in Kortright's home country of Canada.

Training employees to be participative would have to be followed by training in empowerment, a more difficult concept to translate into action. When empowerment occurs, the empowered personnel are in a position to accept responsibility and take the initiative. It can be asked whether empowerment is a culture-specific concept. Can Kortright as a Canadian expatriate manager expect his Mexican employees to behave as empowered personnel?

The success of TQM in Japan suggests that it can work even in societies where broad-based participation is not the norm. In Japan, problem-solving TQM teams have been happy to find solutions to problems that affect conditions at their own level. They therefore do not view their behaviour as that of upstarts, or of employees who feel they know more than their seniors.

Quite often, as David Holt (1998) has noted, recommendations made by work groups in Japan are communicated upwards to the senior management echelons for approval and affirmation. When senior management has reservations about a proposed course of action, it is 'referred back' to the group for its reconsideration. This type of an approach could find favour at Sandalias Finas de Cuernavaca. Work groups can be empowered to devise solutions for problems that arise at their level. The problem solving can be conducted in a participatory fashion. Meanwhile, the fact that the final say on whether a recommendation is adopted rests with senior management can provide the safety net that Kortright's Mexican employees need while they adjust to TQM.

We have provided this brief analysis to suggest how expatriate managers can take cognizance of culture when introducing management practices in a new location. Expatriate managers are normally expected to contribute to the overall productivity of the company they work for, so they cannot fight shy of bringing in change where it is called for. However, if they ignore the cultural dimension, bringing in change may prove to be catastrophic.

Eventually Kortright introduced TQM to a single cell of employees, which he selected with great care. It comprised his best employees, those most receptive to being trained and developed. Gradually, TQM practices were disseminated throughout the company. But that was after the first cell had established a visible track record of success that served to motivate the rest of the company.

This method of first introducing TQM to a single cell was devised by Kortright after he had carefully considered how the concept could be effectively introduced to his Mexican employees. As a Canadian expatriate attempting to introduce a new system of management practices to Mexican employees, he also took into account the cultural dimension. Hence he succeeded in his endeavour of bringing TQM to his company, and eventually succeeded also in making his company internationally competitive.

SUMMARY

Expatriate management is central to the discussion about management within an intercultural context, because it is expatriates who have to work in diverse cultures and bear the brunt of cultural adjustment. Cultural sensitivity cannot be told easily. It is a special kind of manager who can become a successful expatriate. And it is a special kind of global organization that can prepare both prospective expatriates and the host organization for an impending crossing of cultures.

8

Conclusion: diagnosis and prognosis

We now examine the discussions we have had till now and see what inferences we can draw about the subject matter of intercultural management. We also consider the developments that are likely to take place.

DIAGNOSIS

A few attributes about intercultural management have implications for both policy makers and administrators.

Implications for policy makers

Several aspects of intercultural management involve the management of paradoxes or the bringing together of opposites. There is the issue of having shared core values to hold the organization together. At the same time, strategies that are responsive to local cultural imperatives have to be evolved. Policy makers have to gauge when to design approaches that are global in orientation and reflect the credo, vision and corporate culture of the organization. They also have to ascertain when to use methods that are local in character and scope. Sometimes the challenge is to reconcile the two orientations. At other times the challenge is to invent approaches that are capable of adaptation despite inherent dualities. This process of invention has to be an ongoing, continuous one, given the dynamic nature of intercultural management. The management of people from different cultures is accompanied by constant change in organizational behaviour, as the constituents influence and are influenced by organizational processes. One force that exerts influence in such situations is the ethnic culture of members. Externally as well, transnational organizations have to take stock of local cultures. These cultures themselves are in a state of flux and evolution.

High-performance corporations have devised approaches and systems explicitly to take cognizance of intercultural management. A few of their efforts have been documented in this book in the form of case studies. These case studies indicate that what is being actually attempted in practice is commendable and deserves to be studied and critiqued.

Implications for administrators

Many local managers of transnational corporations have displayed skill in applying corporate strategy and approaches to local cultures. At the same time, they have been able to put themselves in the mould of global managers capable of thinking in international contexts, and living in diverse cultures. Many of these global managers have had backgrounds compatible with their current roles, but all of them have learnt skills that enabled them to be effective in cross-cultural situations. This underscores the fact that many elements of intercultural management lend themselves to being learnt.

Global managers have to be schizophrenic in a way. They have to be comfortable in the local context. They also have to align themselves with international practices and mind-sets. Further, they have to be capable of continuously adapting to changing work environments as organizations evolve and adjust to the demands of intercultural management. It is in the past decade that corporations have had more diverse workforces. It is also in the past decade that globalization has become more widespread, and an increasing number of corporations have started operations in new locations and in different cultures.

Organizations have learnt to cope with the demands of globalization and enable their managers to be successful and happy in cross-cultural environments. The field of human resources management has expanded to include expatriate management. One approach to looking at culture is in terms of the shared meaning and values upheld by the people of that culture. It is therefore possible to envisage a manager as having membership in both a corporate culture and an ethnic culture. It is one of the objectives of human resources management to ensure that managers are not torn apart by any conflict between the demands of their corporate culture, and those of their ethnic culture.

PROGNOSIS FOR INTERCULTURAL MANAGEMENT

The current interest in intercultural management, on the part of both managers and researchers, has arisen because of recent developments. Many corporations now view the whole world as both the market for their products and services and a source for their personnel. This has led them to become transnational corporations.

Global managers are becoming more homogeneous. Shaped and conditioned by multiple cultures, they are becoming adept at dealing with and managing diversity. Having always lived in a multicultural environment, they feel comfortable laying themselves open to different and even new cultural influences. As global managers increase in number and efficacy, they will constitute an elite cadre. Transnational corporations have to invest in catering to their needs. Competent young men and women everywhere will aspire to join their ranks. Their entry will however be limited by whether they possess an intercultural orientation to begin with.

Since intercultural management is an emerging area, there is scope for both practitioners and researchers to take a proactive stance in shaping it. The shape the field assumes is of significance, given its importance.

This book suggests that a particular configuration of organizational variables should be in place for intercultural management to be successful. These variables include a structure enacted by organizational members, strong core values, core values that place an emphasis on intercultural competencies, a corporate strategy that is global in scope but capable of local adaptation, communication that has a common content but whose processes reflect local culture, relevant expatriate management practices, and empathy for the external environment and culture.

Areas in the field of intercultural management that require more attention are teamwork and leadership.

There are a few managers who argue that the world is becoming so small we will soon reach a stage where we are all 'citizens of the world'. It is not so much that we will be living in a world without borders, as that there will not be many cultural differences to separate countries and regions. It would be as if everybody was part of a global United Nations. This is not going to happen in the short run. In fact, it is unlikely to happen in the twenty-first century. The reality is that there are considerable cultural differences separating not only countries, but regions within countries. The cultural impact of religion also plays a role.

The shared meanings that a cultural group uphold are often very deeply felt at an emotive level. This has enabled those values to survive the test of time. Just as it is difficult to envisage a world subscribing to a single religion, it is unlikely that the world will become a monoculture. Hence the need for skills in intercultural management is going to remain for a long time.

References

Adler, G (1995) The case of the floundering expatriate, *Harvard Business Review* (7 January)

Adler, N J (2001) *International Dimensions of Organizational Behaviour*, South-Western Publishing, New York

Aeppel, T (1996) Westinghouse now is charting an uncertain course, *Wall Street Journal* (13 Nov)

Ager, D, Lane, H and Kamauff, J (1995) *Sandalias Finas de Cuernavaca, S.A. Total Quality Management (A)*, Ivey Management Services, University of Western Ontario, Canada

Alterman, S (2000) In my opinion. . ., *European Business Forum* (Winter) (4)

Anderson, L (2001) Schools learn the value of English, *Financial Times* (12 Dec)

Arthur, W B (1999) New economies for a knowledge economy: the law of increasing returns, in *The Knowledge Advantage*, ed R Ruggles and D Holtshouse, Ernst & Young LLP, Dover, USA

Bartlett, C and Ghoshal, S (1989) *Managing Across Borders: The transnational solution*, Harvard University Press, Boston

Bartlett, C and Ghoshal, S (1999) Transnational management: text, cases, and readings, McGraw-Hill Higher Education, New York

Bedeian, A G and Zammuto, R F (1991) *Organizations: Theory and design*, Dryden Press, London

Bem, D (1970) *Beliefs, Attitudes and Human Affairs*, Wadsworth, New York

Bergstrom, R (1994) Probing the softer side of steelcase: a reflection, *Production*, **196** (11) (Nov)

Black, J S and Mendenhall, M M (1990) Cross-cultural training effectiveness: a review and a theoretical framework for future research, *Academy of Management Review*, **15** (1), pp 113–16

Boersma, N (2001) unpublished MBA student assignment, IESE Business School, Barcelona

Brewster, C (1995) Effective expatriate training, in *Expatriate Management: New ideas for international business*, ed J Selmer, Quorum, New York

Brown, J K, Design plans, working drawings, national styles: engineering practice in Great Britain and the United States, 1775–1945, *Technology and Culture,* (41)

Buchanan, D and Huczynski, A (1997) *Organizational Behaviour*, Prentice-Hall, London

Bukowitz, W R and Williams, R L (1999) *The Knowledge Management Fieldbook*, Prentice Hall, New Jersey

Buoyant, M J (1991) *Comprehensive Multicultural Education*, Allyn and Bacon, Boston

Burgelman, R A (1988) A comparative evolutionary perspective on strategy-making: advantages and limitations of the Japanese approach, in *Innovation and Management: International comparisons*, ed K Urabe, J Child and T Kagono, Walter de Gruyter, Berlin

Burns, M J (1978) *Leadership*, Harper & Row, New York

Cartwright, S and Cooper, G L (2000) *Managing Mergers, Acquisitions, and Strategic Alliances*, Butterworth-Heinemann, Oxford

Chakravarthy, B S and Perlmuter, H V (1985) Strategic planning for a global business, *Columbia Journal of World Business*, **20** (2)

Chen, G-M and Starosta, W J (1998) *Foundations of Intercultural Communication*, Allyn and Bacon, Boston

Colback, S and Maconochie, M (1989) ...And the rise of the executive nomad, *Business World* (December)

Copeland, L (1985) Cross-cultural training: the competitive edge, *Training* (Jul)

Coulson-Thomas, C J (1991) Developing tomorrow's professional today, *Journal of Industrial European Training*, (15)

Coulson-Thomas, C (1998) Knowledge is power, *Chartered Secretary* (Jan)

Craig, J C and Grant, R M (1993) *Strategic Management*, Kogan Page, London

Cray, D, Mallory, R M and Mallory, G (1998) *Making Sense of Managing Culture*, International Thorson Business Press,

Cushway, B and Lodge, D (1999) *Organizational Behaviour and Design*, Kogan Page, London

Cusick, M (2001) unpublished student assignment, IESE Business School, Barcelona

Daniels, J D and Radebaugh, L H (1998) *International Business*, Addison-Wesley, Reading, Mass

Davis, S and Meyer, C (1999) The role of knowledge in the connected economy, in *The Knowledge Advantage,* ed R Ruggles and D Holtshouse, Ernst & Young LLP, Dover, USA

Denning, S (1999) The knowledge perspective: a new strategic vision, in *The Knowledge Advantage*, ed R Ruggles and D Holthouse, Ernst & Young LLP, Dover, USA

Dess, G G et al [please name co authors] (1995) The new corporate architecture, *Academy of Management Executive*, **9** (3)

Devine, M (1988) Time to create Euromanagers, *Sunday Times* (20 Nov)

de Wit, B and Meyer, R (1998) *Strategy: Process, content, context*, International Thomson Business Press, London

Dras, E S (1989) *Management in Two Cultures: Bridging the gap between US and Mexican managers*, Intercultural Press, Yarmouth, USA

Dru, J-M (1996) *Disruption: Overturning conventions and shaking up the market-place,* John Wiley, New York

Durcan, J (1994) *Leadership: A question of culture*, Ashridge Management College, Berkhamsted

Economist (1995) The trouble with teams, *Economist*, p 75

Ellement, G, Maznevski, M and Lane, H W (1990) *Ellen Moore in Bahrain*, Ivey Management Services, University of Western Ontario, Canada

Elliot, M (2002) Test scores don't say it all, *Time Magazine* (15 April)

Evans, G, *The Road to Hell*, Harvard Business School Case Studies, Harvard Business School, Boston, Mass

Ferraro, G P (2001) *The Cultural Dimension of International Business*, Prentice Hall, Englewood Cliffs, NJ

Finney, M and von Glinow, M A (1990) Integrating academic and organizational approaches to developing the international manager, *Journal of Management Development*, **7** (2)

Fombrun, C J (1984) Corporate culture and competitive strategy, in *Strategic Human Resource Management*, ed C J Fombrun, N M Tichy and M A Devanna, John Wiley, New York

Gavin, D (1993) Building a learning organization, *Harvard Business Review* (Jul–Aug)

Ghoshal, S and Nohria, N (1993) Horses for courses: organizational forms for multinational corporations, *Sloan Management Review* (Winter)

Gill, R, McCalman, J and Pitt, D (1996) *Organizational Structure and Behaviour 2*, Strathclyde Graduate Business School, University of Strathclyde, Glasgow

Gulf Daily News (1987) Resident in Bahrain, *Gulf Daily News*, Bahrain

Hall, E T (1960) The silent language in overseas business, *Harvard Business Review* (1 May)

Hall, E T (1987) *Hidden Differences*, Anchor/Doubleday, New York

Hall, W (1995) *Managing Cultures: Making strategic relationships work*, John Wiley, Chichester

Handy, C (1989) *The Age of Unreason*, Business Books, London

Handy, C (1996) The white stone: six choices: part 1, *Financial Times* (17 May)

Haslett, B, Geis, F L and Carter, M R (1992) *The Organizational Woman: Power and paradox (communication and information science)*, Ablex, New York

Hendry, C (1994) The Single European Market and the HRM response, in *Human Resource Management in Europe*, ed P S Kirkbride, Routledge, London

Hofstede, G (1980) *Culture's Consequences: International differences in work-related value*, Sage Publications, Beverly Hills

Hofstede, G (1991) *Cultures and Organizations*, McGraw-Hill, London

Hofstede, G (2001) *Culture's Consequences: Comparing values, behaviours, institutions, and organizations across nations*, Sage, Beverly Hills

Hofstede, G, Neujen, B, Daval Ohayv, D and Sanders, G (1990) Measuring organizational cultures: a qualitative and quantitative study across twenty cases, *Administrative Science Quarterly,* (35)

Holt, D (1998) *International Management: Text and cases*, Dryden Press, New York/ Forth Worth

Humboldt, W von (2000) *On Language: On the diversity of human language construction and its influence on the mental development of the human species*, Cambridge University Press, Cambridge

Janis, I (1982) *Victims of Groupthink: A psychological study of foreign policy decisions and fiascos*, Houghton Mifflin, Boston

Kaplan, R S and Norton, D P (1996) Using the balanced scorecard as a strategic management system, *Harvard Business Review* (Jan–Feb)

Katayama, F H (1989) How to act once you get there, *Fortune*, **120** (3), pp 69–70

Kelley, C and Meyers, J (1995) *CCAI Cross-Cultural Adaptability Inventory*, National Computer Systems, Minneapolis

Kets de Vries, M and Mead, C (1992) Development of the global leader, in *Globalising Management*, ed V Pucik, N Tichy and C Barnett, John Wiley, New York

Krackhardt, D and Hanson, J (1993) Informal networks: the company behind the chart, *Harvard Business Review* (Jul–Aug)

Kumaga, N (1991) Mitsui's commitment to foreign staff responsibilities, *Inside Business Japan* (Nov)

Laurent, A (1989) A cultural view of organizational change, in *Human Resource Management in International Firms*, ed P Evans, Y Doz and A Laurent, Macmillan, Basingstoke

Lawrence, P R and Lorsch, J W (1967) *Organization and Environment*, Addison-Wesley, Boston, Mass

Lerpold, L (2000) Lessons in alliance integration – the case of BP–Statoil, *European Business Forum* (Winter) (4)

Lovie, C (2001) unpublished student assignment, IESE Business School, Barcelona

Lowry Miller, K L (1995) Siemens shapes up, *Business Week* (1 May)

Martin, J (1992) *Cultures in Organizations: Three perspectives*, Oxford University Press, Oxford

Mayo, A (1998) Memory bankers, *People Management* (Jan)

McClelland, D (1985) *The Achieving Society*, Free Press, New York

McHugh, M P and Wheeler III, W A (1995) *Beyond Business Process Re-Engineering: Towards the holonic enterprise*, Wiley, Chichester

Mendenhall, M M and Oddou, G (1985) The dimensions of expatriate acculturation, *Academy of Management Review*, **10** (2), pp 39–47

Miller, P (2001) *The Change Management Team at Diageo: Duncan Newsome and his globally distributed team*, unpublished

Neale, R and Mindel, R (1992) Rigging up multicultural team working, *Personnel Management* (Jan)

Newman, B (1995) Global chatter: the world speaks English but often none too well, *Asian Wall Street Journal* (23 Mar)

Nicholson, M (1996) Language error seen as cause of Indian air disaster, *Financial Times* (14 Nov)

Nonaka, I (1988) Toward middle-up-down management: accelerating information creation, *Sloan Management Review*, **29** (3)

North, S J (1994) IBM hives off its payroll services, *Personnel Today* (31 May)

Oberg, K (1960) Culture shock: adjustments to new cultural environments, *Practical Anthropology* (Jul–Aug), pp 177–82

O'Hara-Devereaux, M and Johansen, R (1994) *Global Work: Bridging distance, culture, and time*, Jossey-Bass, San Francisco

Open University (1985) *International Perspectives: Managing in organizations*, T244, Unit 16, Block V (Wider Perspectives)

Orleman, P, *The Global Corporation: Managing across cultures*, Master's thesis, University of Pennsylvania

Ouchi, W (1981) *Theory Z*, Addison-Wesley, Reading, Mass

Pascale, R T and Athos, G (1981) *The Art of Japanese Management*, Warner Brothers, New York (also (1982) Penguin, Harmondsworth)

Pepper, G L (1995) *Communicating in Organizations: A cultural approach*, McGraw Hill, Boston

Peters, T J and Waterman Jr, R H (1982) *In Search of Excellence*, Harper & Row, New York

Polanyi, M (1962) *Personal Knowledge: Towards a post-critical philosophy*, Harper & Row, New York

Pollert, A (1988) The flexible firm: fixation or fact? *Work, Employment and Society*, (2)

Porter, M (1990) The competitive advantage of nations, *Harvard Business Review* (Mar/Apr)

Porter, M (1998) *Competitive Advantage: Creating and sustaining superior performance*, Free Press, New York

Powell, B (1987) Where the jobs are, *Newsweek* (2 Feb)

Prahalad, C K and Doz, Y L (1987) *The Multinational Mission: Balancing local demands and global vision*, Free Press, New York

Quelch, J A (1998) *International Marketing Managers (A): Susana Elespuru*, Harvard Business School Publishing, Boston

Quelch, J A and Bloom, H (1996) The return of the country manager, *McKinsey Quarterly*, (2)

Quinn, J B, Anderson, P and Finkelstein, S (1998) Managing professional intellect: making the most of the best, *Harvard Business Review on Knowledge Management*

Reihlen, M (2001) Does national culture induce a style of management? *European Business Forum* (Spring) (5)

Robbins, S (1990) *Organization Theory: Structure, design and applications*, Prentice-Hall, Englewood Cliffs, NJ

Sadler, P and Hofstede, G (1976) Leadership styles: preferences and perceptions of employees of an international company in different countries, *International Studies of Management and Organization*, **6** (3)

Schein, E H (1984) Coming to a new awareness of organizational culture, *Sloan Management Review* (Winter)

Schein, E H (1986) What you need to know about organizational culture, *Training and Development Journal*, **40** (1)

Schneider, S C and Barsoux, J-L (1997) *Managing Across Cultures*, Prentice-Hall, London

Schuller, I (2000) In my opinion..., *European Business Review* (Winter) (4)

Scruton, R (1998) *An Intelligent Person's Guide to Modern Culture*, Duckworth, London

Senge, P et al [please name coauthors](1999) *The Dance of Change: The challenges to sustaining momentum in learning organizations*, Doubleday, New York

Shea, C (1994) *Moscow Aerostar*, case study prepared under the supervision of Professor H Lane, Ivey Management Services, University of Western Ontario, Canada

Solomon, C M (1994) Success abroad depends on more than job skills, *Personnel Journal*

Solomon, C M (1998) Building teams across borders, *Global Workforce*, **3** (6)

Stone, R J (1991) Expatriate selection and failure, *Human Resource Planning*, **14** (1)

Swank, R A (1995) Expatriate management: the search for best practices, *Compensation and Benefits Review*

Tagore, R (1997) *The Heart of God: Prayers of Rabindranath Tagore*, ed H F Vettiger, Charles E. Tuttle, New York

Thomas, K (1997) Towards multi-dimensional values in teaching: the example of conflict behaviours, *Academy of Management Review* (July)

Thompson, W E (1983) Hanging tongues: a sociological encounter with the assembly line, *Qualitative Sociology* (Fall) (6)

Thurow, L (1999) Brainpower and the future of capitalism, in *The Knowledge Advantage*, ed R Ruggles and D Holtshouse, Ernst & Young LLP, Dover, USA

Tichy, N M and Devanna, M A (1997) *The Transformational Leader: The key to global competitiveness*, John Wiley, New York

Time Magazine (2000a) 30 Oct 2000

Time Magazine (2000b) 26 Nov 2000

Time Magazine (2000c) 25 Dec 2000–1 Jan 2001

Time Magazine (2001a) 15 Jan 2001

Time Magazine (2001b) 22 Jan 2001

Time Magazine (2001c) 26 Mar 2001

Time Magazine (2001d) 9 Apr 2001

Time Magazine (2001e) 28 May 2001

Time Magazine (2001f) 25 Jun 2001

Time Magazine (2001g) 23 Jul 2001

Time Magazine (2001h) 6 Aug 2001

Time Magazine (2001i) 10 Sep 2001

Time Magazine (2001j) 10 Dec 2001

Time Magazine (2001k) 17 Dec 2001

Time Magazine (2002) 22 Apr 2002

Tjosvold, D and Deemer, D (1980) Effects of controversy within a co-operative or competitive context on organizational decision making, *Journal of Applied Psychology*, **65** (5), pp 590–95

Todd, M (2001) *Cross-Cultural Management*, unpublished MBA student assignment, IESE Business School, Barcelona

Tomlinson, J (1999) *Globalization and Culture*, University of Chicago Press, Chicago

Torbiorn, I (1982) *Living Abroad*, John Wiley, New York

Trompenaars, F (1993) *Riding the Waves of Culture: Understanding cultural diversity in business*, Economist Books, London

Tung, R L (1981) Selection and training of personnel for overseas assignments, *Columbia Journal of World Business*, (16), pp 68–78

Urech, E (1998) *Speaking Globally*, Kogan Page, New Hampshire

Vikhanski, O and Puffer, S (1993) Management education and employee training at Moscow McDonald's, *European Management Journal*, **11** (1)

Walker, W (1980) *Human Resource Planning*, McGraw-Hill, New York

Weick, K E (1995) Organised improvisation: 20 years of organising, *Communication Studies*, **40** (4)

Weiss, S E (1994) Negotiating with Romans, Part 2, *Sloan Management Review* (Spring)

Wills, S (February 1996) European leadership: key issues, *European Management Journal*, **14** (1)

Wilmott, H (1993) Ignorance is strength, freedom is slavery: managing culture in modern organizations, *Journal of Management Studies*, **30** (4), pp 215–52

Yukl, G (2001) *Leadership in Organizations*, Prentice Hall, London

Index